GIANT KILLERS

MICHAEL PERTSCHUK

Giant Killers

W · W · NORTON & COMPANY · NEW YORK · LONDON

First published as a Norton paperback 1987

*The text of this book is composed in Avanta, with display type set in Avanta and
Typositor Fat Face. Composition by the Haddon Craftsmen. Book design by*
Marjorie J. Flock.

Library of Congress Cataloging-in-Publication Data
Pertschuk, Michael, 1933–
  Giant Killers.
  Includes index.
1. Lobbying—United States. 2. Lobbyists—United
States. 3. Public interest—United States. I. Title.
JK1118.P47 1986   328.73′078   86—5419

ISBN 0-393-30435-3

W. W. Norton & Company, Inc., 500 Fifth Avenue, New York, N.Y. 10110
W. W. Norton & Company Ltd., 37 Great Russell Street, London WC1B 3NU

1 2 3 4 5 6 7 8 9 0

To David and Kathleen and all the other good lobbyists

Contents

Preface

I'M NOT EXACTLY NEUTRAL about lobbying. For the last 20 years, I've seen myself as a partisan of public interest causes. Where I wasn't participating—and lobbying myself—I was cheerleading. And though we've blundered from time to time, and can hardly claim a lock either on virtue or wisdom, I do believe that the goals we've sought embody the most generous impulses of the American tradition. And there was much joy in the effort.

This book began simply as a celebration of "great moments in public interest lobbying history"—a chance to tell some good stories for the first time. For the truth is that journalists as a rule have not been much interested in the stuff of lobbying—unless it gives off a foul aroma. Private interest lobbying sometimes does; public interest lobbying, rarely. If there is corruption in public interest lobbying, it's likely to be corruption of the spirit, which is generally less newsworthy than PAC contributions. Political scientists, on the other hand, tend to weigh lobbyists by the gross in divining whether the scales of government are properly balanced, leeching the life-blood out of lobbying in the analytic process.

And for all its high—or low—purpose it is also useful to acknowledge that lobbying is, for all of us at times, a game. Of course we like to win in part because we believe our cause is just, but also because winning is more satisfying than losing. Playing is also satisfying, especially the knowledge of having played skillfully. Then, when the game is worth the candle, when the lobbyist feels in his or her bones that the cause serves the public interest, the pleasures are immeasurably heightened.

What can we learn about public interest lobbyists, and how can we take the measure of their contribution? In getting the answers to these questions, I had two advantages and one liability. First, 25 years mucking about in the legislative process at least left me with some understanding and smell for the dynamics of lobbying —and of legislative myth and reality. Second, I was known and, generally, trusted as a colleague by public interest lobbyists.

I had to get the lobbyists to talk of things which most lobbyists prefer to keep quiet. Most lobbyists believe that their effectiveness shrinks in inverse proportion to their notoriety. They are also reluctant to dispense "trade secrets" indiscriminately. So I had to find lobbyists who shared my belief that the benefits (and the pleasures) of shedding light on their successes outweighed the risks—especially those who believed that a part of the obligation of the public interest advocate is to demystify the process. They also had to trust me.

The liability is the other face of trust, and should be baldly disclosed: at least half of the lobbyists I've chosen to memorialize —on both sides,—are old friends. And those who weren't friends before, are now!

There are obvious risks in this—and losses. As I interviewed them, I urged them to be as open and candid as possible—with the understanding that if, seeing their words in print, they experienced the sinking feeling that they had alienated a potential ally, or turned a casual opponent into an enemy, I would drop or modify the offending words. Their sensitivities varied greatly and often erupted where I least expected them. I didn't end up deleting much that I thought was important, but there were a few keen insights and some colorful characterizations which had to be muted.

On the other hand, I did not rely on the lobbyists to evaluate their own successes. Those judgements come from neutral observers, and, most convincingly, from their opponents.

If friendship exacts an inevitable toll in objectivity, it also has rewards for the reader. I caught several of the lobbyists in the first flush of victory. The first interviews with David Cohen and Kathleen Sheekey on the MX campaign took place a few days after the climactic vote in 1984. The sense and feel of the campaign was fresh. The memories had not yet become old war stories. In many places, what you will read are their true and unrehearsed voices: the natural song of the public interest lobbyist.

These are not legislative case studies, attempts to record exhaustively all the critical events and causes leading to the outcome. For each of these campaigns, that would take a book—a tedious book.

Instead, I've tried to highlight in each case the particular qualities that made that campaign special. That causes problems: the stories are by no means "the whole truth." As I circulated the drafts of each campaign story to the central figures for comment and protest, there was a uniform, predictable response: first, the reader would take honest pleasure at seeing his or her labors generously memorialized; then horror, with the realization that everyone else involved in the campaign would resent the choice of heros and, unfairly, suspect self-promotion when none had taken place.

Of course, no one is likely to be disturbed when a legislative disaster is laid at someone else's door. But these are success stories, and it is the coarsest of clichés that while failure is an orphan, success has a thousand progenitors. There will be dozens, perhaps hundreds, of participants who will read each of these accounts and grouse: "Hell, I played as important a role as these guys, and, besides, the critical moments and decisions took place at a different time and in a different forum"—and they may be right.

As David Cohen is fond of saying, lobbying is additive. Lots of people do lots of things right, and you may win. I myself have toyed with a theory that the "compleat" public interest lobbying campaign resembles a matchstick pentagon (or hexagon; I waver). This theory suggests that, in the absence of extraordinary circumstances, no significant public interest campaign which confronts a substantial adversary can succeed without five sides: (1) a broad "outside" grass-roots movement or its proxy, an organized constituency; (2) "inside" leadership, committed congressional and congressional staff leadership; (3) a network of supportive policy professionals/experts; (4) alert and sympathetic media, and (5) professionally sophisticated lobbyists. An exhaustive analysis of each campaign chosen would reveal the presence of each of these elements. I've tried to touch on each of them, but for the most part, lightly. Which means that there are lots of deserving citizens whose contributions are slighted. From them, I beg forgiveness—especially when they've paid for the book, expecting justice.

So this book, which sprung from the simple urge to tell good stories, ended up freighted with larger ambition.

To the citizen despairing of our democratic institutions, I want to sound a note of hope. Most Americans, polls tell us, believe that the government in Washington is not responsive to the needs and desires of "people like me." That's often a fair assessment, but it isn't always so. Citizen movements—and especially the coupling of those movements with the craft of political advocacy—can make Washington and other legislatures respond and topple giant private interests.

To the leaders and volunteer workers in great and small public interest movements, I hope to convey a sense of the requisite skills, strategies and tactics by which citizen groups with limited resources can prevail. I'd like to overcome lingering aversion to the moral untidiness and ambiguity of politics, and especially of lobbying, to celebrate public interest lobbying as a flowering, not an excrescence of democracy.

To young people tempted to forego the comfort and security of corporate and other private sector careers, I confess to a proselytizing urge: there is a need for public interest lobbyists. There is a career to be made out of the craft of lobbying for the things that you believe in. Though you will lag behind your contemporaries in BMWs, if not Cuisinarts, it's really worth it. It's as if you had a chance to join a sandlot team, which perversely insisted upon taking on the Yankees and then miraculously won—certainly not always, not even often, but often enough to keep hope alive. Also, in a world of institutions that seem hopelessly bureaucratized and impersonal, lobbying is the most personal and individualistic of crafts. Even on the national stage, individuals can make a difference—Nader calls them "sparkplugs."

A skeptical interviewer once challenged the unquenchable Democrat, I. F. Stone: "And you believe people can still turn the defeat we all face into a victory?" Stone responded: "A friend once gave me a word of hope; he said, 'You know Izzy, if you keep on pissing on a boulder for about a thousand years, you'd be surprised what an impression you'd make.' You never can tell; sometimes you win."

Acknowledgments

THIS BOOK WAS WRITTEN with minimum pain—and much pleasure—simply because its principal subjects, the good lobbyists, were such generous and spirited story-tellers. Indeed, the only tension that arose between my estimable editor and friend Don Lamm and myself during the course of the book's gestation grew out of his concern that the voices of the lobbyists threatened to eclipse the voice of the author. We compromised, but I still believe I could have disappeared entirely, serving only to string together the natural voices of the public interest lobbyists, without much loss. That's one reason the book is dedicated to them.

My debt extends to the not-so-good lobbyists who, knowing of the author's reformist proclivities, nonetheless entrusted him with their perspectives (though sometimes taking the precaution of enforced anonymity). I owe much, also, to the insights of those who played major roles in the featured campaigns—leaders in Congress, staff members, coalition partners—who did not fit the scheme of my book, but who deserve more than a footnote. To set the stage for each campaign story, I was able to lean heavily upon the published writings of informed and perceptive journalists, such as Elizabeth Drew and William Grieder.

Most of this book was conceived, researched and written at the top of a seven story Smithsonian tower (67 steps), at the Woodrow Wilson Center. For the ten months I served as a Wilson Fellow, the center nurtured this work. From Michael Lacey, the historian who kept watch over my efforts, challenging me always to reach for more understanding, to Margie DiNenna, who transformed a computer illiterate into a word-processing fanatic, the staff and fellows both stimulated my thoughts and left me in peace to pursue them. To all at the center, much gratitude.

Just as I was chilled with the foreknowledge that the ten months wouldn't be quite enough, the Law Center at Washington and Lee extended an invitation for another fellowship to pursue the writing. So, in October and November 1985, I retreated to the sanctuary of Lexington, Virginia, and the friendship and daily encouragement and help of Lash LaRue, the center's director, and his assistant, Margaret Williams, who smoothed every obstacle that threatened to intervene between me and the word processor, and braced me when computer trauma struck.

At the Wilson Center, I had the good help of research assistants David Mehrle and Louis Grossman, who kept retrieving amazing sources from the Library of Congress's mysterious computers, and uttered encouraging words at the tentative early drafts. While my fingers actually typed most of the words you are about to read, the task of transcribing the extensive interviews (occasionally cacophanous) fell to the patient hands of Suzanne Jones and Frieda King, who also painstakingly shaped the raw, unkempt text into a presentable manuscript.

Lamm was a fierce task-master (but never discouraging). The concept and scheme of the book owe much to his counsel, and you have him to thank for the extended, arguably tedious quotes through which you will not be called upon to persevere. After the first, rough drafts, I sought out the help of Jill Cutler, poet, editor, friend, whose strategic suggestions and "yellow stickies" challenged me to rethink and recast and rewrite.

Friends nurtured this book, checking their harsher critical instincts to fuel the early going ("perhaps a few too many long quotes"): Tom Whiteside and Anna Mary Portz and Barry Rubin and Bill Rothbard and Bill Byler. Byler came within a hair's breadth of being enshrined as a hero in this book for his quiet lobbying for Native Americans, yet insisted to the end that public interest lobbyists were "nerds, not heroes."

My wife Anna and stepson Dan were both participants and occasional victims of the book writing. They reviewed drafts and brought no-nonsense critical insights to the process. Just when I would be convinced that a latest draft of a chapter was close to perfection, Anna and Dan would read it and, with furrowed brows, raise good and maddening questions, which led inescapably to the conclusion that one more round of disciplined rewriting was demanded.

GIANT KILLERS

1

ALL LOBBYISTS MUST EAT

SOME OF MY best friends are lobbyists. And some of the best lobbyists are my friends. Not all represent benign causes, though many among them represent what they believe are public interest causes: nuclear arms control; civil rights; environmental and consumer interests; tax equity; public health; the welfare of Indian tribes, blacks, women, ethnic minorities, and poor children. About them much more later.

But others among them represent cigarette companies; defense contractors; life insurance companies; retailers; big oil and small (but not very) oil; real estate; railroads and airlines; truckers; merchant marine interests; advertising agencies; cable television operators; and, like George W. Koch, big grocery manufacturers—Procter and Gamble, General Foods and Nestle.

George W. Koch is the President of GMA (the Grocery Manufacturers of America). Before that he was chief lobbyist for Sears. George is my friend; he has also been my adversary for nearly twenty years.

In the mid-sixties, I was a staff member of the Senate Commerce Committee, assigned to consumer protection legislation. I saw myself, then, as a latter-day Scarlet Pimpernel—to outward appearances, a mild-mannered clerk; below the surface, a guerilla fighter for truth and light, or, at the moment, truth in packaging and labeling. George led the powers of darkness.

In the late sixties and early seventies, our band of consumer guerillas, emboldened by Ralph Nader's vision, fought for the creation of a Consumer Advocacy Agency. George led the benighted resistance; we were beginning to get used to each other.

By the late seventies, I was at the Federal Trade Commission, determined to rid the country of the blight of television advertising directed to very young children. George led the opposition.

He also refused to let the Grocery Manufacturers of America join in a lawsuit filed by the advertising, broadcasting, and toy industry groups which sought to remove me from the proceeding as biased beyond tolerance. George said he was confident I would be fair and objective in applying the law. I was surprised and moved; I wasn't so sure about myself.

In the first years of the Reagan administration, defrocked as chairman but with three years left in my term as one of the FTC's five commissioners, I lobbied within the commission and in Congress for mandatory salt labeling; preservation of the "Delaney" clause, which bars from food products any trace of substances causing cancer in laboratory animals; and for U. S. support for United Nation's action condemning infant formula promotion in third world countries. George masterminded the opposition to all three.

In many ways, George W. Koch is a remarkable—and good—man. A stubborn rectitude led him to a rare and unsettling challenge to a pillar of the Washington establishment: the Congressional Country Club, of which he was and is a member. At a personal cost of tens of thousands of dollars, George first questioned politely, then confronted, then legally challenged the club's economic exploitation of its mostly black and Hispanic low-income workers. In recounting his lone struggle, the Washington Afro-American said, "If you didn't know that George Koch (pronounced Cook) was a white, middle-class conservative Republican lobbyist for the grocery manufacturing industry, you might think he was Martin Luther King, Jr. Certainly their stories are similar and Koch's courage appears to be as great."

On January 21, 1981, I was still chairman of the Federal Trade Commission, but not for long. This was Ronald Reagan's first day as president. And as a Carter appointee and a demon regulator, I was fated for swift removal as chairman. On my calendar for that day was lunch with George Koch. I hadn't remembered setting the date, and when I arrived at the elegant Four Seasons to join George at his customary table overlooking the garden, he told me that he had set the date with Darlene, my secretary, a month before. He'd figured that the day after the Reagan inaugural, facing my imminent fall from grace and power, feeling displaced and forgotten, I'd need a dose of good cheer—a dash of reassurance and a good meal. George, of course, had been an early and enthusiastic Reagan supporter—but he didn't gloat.

Like ancient veterans of opposing armies, we share an arcane interest in old battle tactics and maneuvers, and we soon lapsed into old war stories and confessions.

"Did you ever wonder," George suddenly asked, "how the Democratic platform in 1972 happened to include an endorsement of the 'amicus amendment'?"

My mind was blank for a moment. "Amicus amendment"? What had that been all about? Then I remembered: the consumer movement was then riding like a juggernaut through Congress. Throughout the late sixties we had gained enactment of a series of major consumer protection measures. By 1972 we were on the threshold of the creation, by Congress, of a powerful new Consumer Advocacy Agency, with broad license to intervene in the proceedings of regulatory agencies which were slow, timid or indifferent to the aggressive pursuit of the consumer interest.

The teeth-gnashing business lobbies had been able only to slow the agency's momentum. Its passage in the next Congress appeared imminent.

As a last line of defense, George and his allies had pressed to limit the consumer advocate to the advisory role of a "friend of court" or "amicus curiae"—a mere kibitzer.

I remembered. I also remembered how stunned I had been when, in the midst of this heated conflict, the Democratic platform emerged from that most liberal of conventions—the McGovern convention—with a ringing endorsement of the "amicus amendment" to the Consumer Agency bill.

"Yes George, I wondered how that happened."

"Mike, you probably don't remember, but as soon as the platform appeared, you called me and asked how it happened, and I didn't tell you. Now I will tell you.

"We had a man on the platform committee. A very distinguished North Carolina lawyer—very proper, very sober, very conservative. You may remember what that convention was like. All sorts of people were delegates—hippies, yippies, old radicals and student radicals, and for the first time, openly, gays.

"The convention was even more of a mad house than usual. The platform committee was the focal point for demands by all that ragtaggle of dissident groups; meetings of the platform committee dragged throughout the day and deep into the night. Our man was sitting next to the representative of the gay caucus on the platform committee. It was well after midnight when the question of the endorsement of the Consumer Advocacy Agency was placed before the committee. Our man had arranged for the amicus language to be proposed to modify the convention's endorsement of the Consumer Agency. His gay neighbor had dozed off and awoke with a start to hear a strange and unfamiliar discussion of the 'amicus amendment.' He turned to our man and asked, 'what is this amicus amendment all about?' And our fellow leaned over, put his hand on his colleague's knee, looked him soulfully in the eye, and said, 'amicus . . . means 'friend'. ' Whereupon the gay delegate spoke briefly but passionately in support of the amicus amendment, then lapsed back into a deep sleep. The amendment carried."

What a rotten trick, George: cynical, manipulative, and exploitive!

Like Henry Higgins contemplating the dreary future fate of the ungrateful Eliza Doolittle who has just walked out on him, I thought: "How frightful!" . . . and, then, "How delightful!"

I was seized with an inspiration, "George, that's a great—though shameful—story. With all your wicked ways, you must have dozens like it and must have heard dozens more from your black hat colleagues. I have a few favorites from our side. Why don't we write a book together: *Great Moments in Lobbying History?*"

George was intrigued, but he noted, wisely, that the best stories could not safely be told until the participants were dead (or out of power). We agreed that it was a great potential joint venture for our mutual retirements—or semi-retirements—still many years away, of course.

I was so delighted by George and the lunch that I relaxed my customary fastidiousness and let George pick up the check for that conspiratorial hiatus in the public interest/private interest war.

Yes, lobbying is a game. It can be petty, tedious, boring, and demeaning. But sometimes it's played out on a great stage full of bold strategies, fatal missteps, shrewd tactical feints, and intricate maneuvers. The fate of the world—or at least a share of its fate—may rest not on grand policy debates or the massive realignment of political forces, but upon the play of greed, ambition, quirky alliances and coalitions, deep loyalties and deeper emnities, corroding envy, and yes, affection, even love.

Nobody tells the good tales of lobbying for the sake of the stories—and the craft. We could do that.

Three years later, in the fall of 1984, I had lunch with another old friend, David Cohen.

Early in 1984 David had agreed to serve as the strategist and chief lobbyist for a new coalition of professional groups drawn together in alliance against the nuclear arms buildup: the Union of Concerned Scientists; the Physicians for Social Responsibility; and the Lawyers' Alliance Against Nuclear Arms. At the same time, Kathleen Sheekey, whom we both admired and respected enormously, had become chief lobbyist for Common Cause. David and Kathleen had both been at the center of the fight to stop production of the MX-missile. In the sharing of tasks among the peace groups, Common Cause had taken primary responsibility for coordinating the national effort to halt production of the MX, an effort which had fallen short the previous year.

In 1984 Reagan had sought authorization for the production of forty MX missiles. As the anti-MX campaign gained momentum, support for the MX eroded. Soon even military sycophants in Congress were willing to fight for only twenty-one missiles. Four weeks before we met, a desperate White House had compromised further, down to fifteen. Yet the House approved even fifteen by only six votes. Then, two weeks later, the House reversed its action. By two votes it denied all funding for the MX—unless Congress affirmatively approved MX construction the next year.

Against the Pentagon, against the ingrained tradition of deference to the president on military affairs, against the client relationship of armed service committees to defense contractors, they had nonetheless triumphed beyond rational expectations. It had to be a glorious tale, and it was.

It was a tale of how congressmen—cool, calculating, venal and cringing; fiercely independent, fearful, partisan, intimidated, or furious; eager to do the right thing, but uncertain; unconvinced; chronically conditioned to seek the safe middle—wiggled, waffled, walked, ran, turned again, held firm, buckled; then at one moment came together and held firm for the critical twenty minutes of a recorded vote.

It was a tale alive with tensions, stress and high drama (and low comedy), grand strategy, artful maneuver—the bridging of mature lobbying skills to a broad and deeply committed citizen movement.

I went back to my office in high glee. I had captured a treasure. David and Kathleen were as artful a team as had ever practiced the lobbying art. Here was the centerpiece of any book on great moments in lobbying history.

But I also knew that what I had learned was more than a good lobbying story.

It was not just a Washington inside story, nor was it a cynical story. It was a story of democratic possibility, of the hitching of a citizen movement to the skills needed to translate the moral force and energy of that movement into effective action. That's the essence of public interest lobbying at its best, and it is why there really is a difference between the role of the private interest lobbyist and the public interest lobbyist.

This book owes much to these two lunches: to lunch with George, for awakening the sense of play and story which are the mostly untold legacy of an uncelebrated craft; to lunch with David, for the reminder that beyond craft and story lies democratic promise.

1981 and 1982 were unrelievedly dreary years in Washington for those of us who viewed the capital as occupied by an alien force. The rambunctious high spirits of those who formerly challenged the government to do good things was displaced by the grimness of those who looked upon government with the enthusiasm of morticians.

Nowhere was this more palpable than in Washington's restaurants, in which the boisterous hubub of unkempt Democrats had been replaced by the sour hum of reaction and the low buzz of yuppies. So we were startled, our family and friends, one night at dinner in the summer of 1982, at a restaurant close by the Senate, to witness the entry of a whooping throng: Ralph Neas and Bill Taylor and a bunch of their cohorts from the Leadership Conference on Civil Rights. And they were actually celebrating. They were celebrating the Senate's passage of amendments to the 1965 Voting Rights Act. They were celebrating not only the extension of protections which were scheduled to expire, but the strengthening of those protections in the teeth of opposition from the chairman of the Senate Judiciary Committee, the chairman of its Constitutional Rights Subcommittee, the assistant attorney general for Civil Rights, the attorney general, and the president of the United States. So infectious was their delight, that we all ended up smiling like idiots.

Just when I was beginning to get used to the idea that public interest causes had been flattened by the Reagan juggernaut and would remain down at the heels of a reactionary or supine Congress until the next millenium, something good had happened.

Though much we had dreaded came to pass, I began to notice other reassuring and remarkable congressional surprises like the voting rights victory: a public health triumph here, an environmental one there; a poverty program saved; a corporate crusade for freedom from safety regulation frustrated; a new weapons system chilled. And I knew, or guessed, that behind each of these legislative upsets was a core of professional public interest lobbyists, like Neas and Taylor.

I made a little list, and, when I set about developing the scheme of this book, I went right to these victories and the stories behind them.

I screened them through a largely idiosyncratic series of screens.

The first was the most arbitrary: I wasn't going to celebrate anybody I didn't like. Nor tell stories that didn't yield at least a modest quota of suspense, villainy, drama, humor, and heroism—though not precisely of the Rambo variety.

I looked for campaigns in which both professional public interest lobbyists and committed grass-roots activists appeared to have played a significant role in affecting the outcome.

I hoped to find exemplary campaigns in several of the policy arenas which are commonly spoken of as public interest causes: arms control, civil rights, environment, public health, economic regulation. And in telling of those campaigns, to be able to illustrate the range and diversity of skills, grand strategies and practical tactics that make up the stuff of citizen group lobbying. ("What do lobbyists do?" is a question that nobody who reads this book should have to ask again.)

The book should suggest the many entry points or fulcrums for legislative advocacy. There should be cases in which bad things were stopped, and cases in which good things were enacted—ordinarily more difficult.

Lobbyists can affect the legislative process both early and late. They can motivate and influence the issue agenda of members and committees, shape bills before they are introduced, structure hearings, influence "mark-ups"— the committee executive sessions in which amendments are considered and the content of bills evolves. They can affect the timing of action on the floor of the House or Senate, lobby the conference committees in which senators and representatives meet to resolve differences between the two Houses, and they can influence the force working on a president who may be contemplating a legislative veto. Our stories at least ought to sample techniques for lobbying at each stage of the process.

But most important, each campaign chosen ought to teach us something we hadn't known before about the peculiar genius of the successful public interest lobby—of the secrets of giant killing.

So we come to the five campaigns celebrated in the next eight chapters:

First, passage of the Cigarette Labeling Act of 1984 requiring a series of four deadly warnings to rotate on cigarette labels and in all cigarette advertising, in which the mythic tobacco lobby was leveled by the parliamentary legerdemain of an adroit, deftly directed health lobby.

Next, the defeat of the American Medical Association's strenuous effort to escape consumer protection and antitrust regulation, in which the doctors' torrent of campaign contributions was transformed into a political albatross through media outrage engendered by a young lawyer in Ralph Nader's Congress Watch.

Third, preservation by Congress of the Tuolumne Wild River in California, snatched from the clutches of the dam builders and real estate developers, by a high-spirited campaign organization which captured the political left, center, and right, and monopolized all the emotive symbols of debate.

Fourth, the overwhelming victory for a Voting Rights Act stronger than any of its advocates dared to hope for, in large part through timely compromises—and resistance to untimely compromises.

Finally, the Thermopylae of citizen lobbying campaigns: the defeat of the MX missile in 1984, in which an all-star network of public interest lobbyists on Capitol Hill linked arms with thousands of organized citizen activists in swing congressional districts throughout the country.

Large forces were, of course, afoot in each of these campaigns. Movements, or at least broad, popular impulses, loom behind each of these triumphs. As the issues were ultimately cast, the outcomes, in each case, truly reflected the will of the majority—as reflected in opinion polls, if not election polls.

There were also, in each case, uncommonly dedicated and effective leaders within the Congress—within the ranks of both its members and its staffs.

There were sympathetic, or at least responsive, media voices.

There were, at least in the tobacco and AMA cases, important supportive advocates within the administration.

There were, "on the outside," broad citizen group and affected interest group coalitions—commonly slow-forming, hesitant; thinly staffed and funded; distracted by other urgent battles—but ultimately a coherent force.

And, at the heart of each of these campaigns was a core of professional lobbyists—veterans of legislative campaigns stretching back over many seasons and often ranging over diverse causes within a broad spectrum of policy arenas.

2

SMOKE SCREEN

REVEREND (addressing congregants): We thank Thee particularly for
those people who till the soil, those folks who grow the crops that
feed us. And then we will thank Thee for those people who work
diligently to preserve a program that has been so much to our tobacco
farmers. Give us a safe journey home and then, before we close, our
Father, we'd ask Thee to give us a good tobacco season.
—"The Golden Leaf," CBS Reports, September 1, 1982

THE TOBACCO LOBBY has been the mythic untouchable of
corporate lobbies, invincible in the pursuit of lethal ends. That is
why a tale of its unraveling, with the spirited assistance of a skillful
and subtle health lobby, merits first place in this volume.

The time is the early eighties, the first Reagan term. The cause,
the pursuit of a new, stronger cigarette labeling law to compel
cigarette labels, ads, and billboards to spell out the dreadful roll
call of smoking's diseases: lung cancer, heart disease, emphysema,
and, in pregnant women, fetal injury. The tobacco lobby fiercely
resisted this effort to highlight these and other unpleasant truths
about smoking. In the words of one of our six anonymous tobacco
industry sources (who, adamantly resisting public celebrity, will
henceforth be identified collectively only as "Deep Cough"), tobacco executives not only resisted this law, but "feared and
loathed" it. Yet they lost.

As in each of our tales, this public interest victory yields up a
choice of heroes (as well as a tasty assortment of foiled villains).
No significant legislative triumph is possible without "inside"

leaders: congressmen, senators, and their staff members. And so it was here.

Most significant was the leadership of the chairman of the House Subcommittee on Health, Representative Henry Waxman of California, and the willingness of a tobacco state congressman, Albert Gore of Tennessee, to take an unselfish risk as an honest broker of a decent compromise—and stick to it. Quite simply, no legislation would have emerged had Waxman not led and masterminded the charge, and had Gore not hung in over months of tedious negotiation. The drama also features such supporting players (not to say, character actors) as the irascible staff director of the House Energy and Commerce Committee, Mike Kitzmiller, whose low tolerance for charlatans proved a formidable obstacle to the last-minute feints and stratagems of the tobacco lobbyists.

But our primary interest is the leadership of the "outside" forces, the citizen lobby. And our central theme is the emergence, for the first time, of a formidable "Coalition on Smoking Or Health," and, at the right moment, of a Talleyrand of public interest lobbyists to lead it.

In addition to being something of a moral fable, this tale of the tobacco industry's comeuppance also illustrates a central principle of public interest lobbying, which, borrowing from Chinese Taoist antiquity, might be called "the *yin* of public interest lobbying." *Yin* is that principle of combat which has always served well the frail combatant who agilely steps aside and sticks his foot out at the precise moment when his 300 pound assailant is charging with unmanageable momentum *(yang)* in the wrong direction.

WHAT TOBACCO WANTED, TOBACCO GOT

Woody Allen, the distinguished mythologist, tells of a great mythical beast with the head of a lion and the body of a lion—but it was the wrong lion. So, in this chapter we have what should be an author's joy: the just and triumphal defeat of the villainous tobacco lobby in a legislative arena in which the author himself has played a not inconsequential role for two decades.

Except I kept losing. And it wasn't until I was (mostly) on the sidelines, that the tobacco lobby stopped having its way.

In the mid-sixties, those otherwise bright years for the consumer movement, I had the woeful assignment, as a Senate Commerce Committee staff member, of shepherding the first cigarette labeling bill through the Congress. It made little difference that I saw my role as that of guerilla warrior against the tobacco scourge, or that I served committed congressional consumer champions such as Commerce Committee Chairman Senator Warren Magnuson and Senator Maurine Neuberger, liberal Northwest Democrats from Washington and Oregon, respectively. Nor was Congress much moved by the heralded Surgeon General's Committee on Smoking and Health, which had delivered its solemn scientific verdict condemning smoking as a proven health scourge. That first labeling bill ended up a sorry piece of tobacco knavery.

It was a bill which emerged from the Congress so distorted and compromised that the *New York Times* condemned it as "a shocking piece of special interest legislation . . . a bill to protect the economic health of the tobacco industry by freeing it of proper regulation."

The *Times* was right. In the guise of mandating a tepid warning label on all cigarette packs ("Caution: Cigarette Smoking May Be Hazardous to Your Health"), the law's true purpose was to subvert action by a steadfast Federal Trade Commission requiring strong warnings both on labels and in advertising. And, more mischief, the law also barred action by any other federal authority or any state or city which might be moved to restrict cigarette advertising out of concern for the health of its citizens.

This is not the place for a labored chronicle of that misbegotten legislation. But it does afford more than a glimpse of the nature and character of the tobacco lobby. More painful, it also provides some insight into the process by which typically inexperienced, if well-meaning, congressional staff can be overwhelmed, and even seduced, by the glittering phalanxes of a corporate lobby.

SENATOR CLEMENTS

It is always easier to perceive pure evil from a distance. And when I first began to work on smoking-control legislation—before I had actually talked to anyone connected with the tobacco industry—evil seemed to me most perfectly embodied in the person of the Honorable Earle Clements: president and chief lobbyist of the Tobacco Institute. Clements, I learned, had been governor, then senator, from Kentucky. In the mid-fifties, he had risen to Democratic Whip, right hand to Senate majority leader Lyndon Johnson. Then, in a curious career twist, he had been defeated for the Senate, but stayed to serve as staff director of the Senate Democratic Campaign Committee, where he engineered—and financed—the great Democratic Senate electoral victory of 1958. A whole generation of Senate Democrats thus owed him the most personal of debts.

His influence was palpable—and he was not reluctant to display it. In 1965, during the hearings on the first labeling bill, I was hardly surprised that Thruston Morton, the shrewd senator from Kentucky, felt obligated to taunt the health society witnesses (and to observe, with some malice, that he had begun smoking heavily during committee hearings—so heavily that, from time to time, he had to lurch for the door to the private antechamber so that he might cough violently—off-camera. "I can't wait," he grumbled, "for these hearings to end, so I can cut down on my smoking!").

And at least one sharp-tongued senator from a northern state also displayed a puzzling, implacable hostility to their earnest testimony. I speculated upon the source of his antipathy, given the absence of a single acre of tobacco in his state. I had my answer on the day when one of the hearings on the labeling bill had just been gaveled to order by Chairman Magnuson. No other committee members were present. I was standing in the Commerce Committee meeting room, its inner sanctum behind the public hearing room. In strode Clements, invoking the tradition which maintains for former senators the "courtesy" of free access to Senate chambers. Ostentatiously, he commandeered the committee phone, and in a stage whisper, summoned the attendance of the northern senator—one of his "class of '58"—to do his bidding.

What about the public health lobby? Where were the organized medical, scientific, and citizen constituencies? Every uncorrupted medical and scientific body in the world that had ever taken a look at the evidence, had concluded that smoking was a major health hazard. But they were represented at the hearings mostly by the part-time, elected heads of the major voluntary health organizations, Cancer, Heart, and Lung—none of them expert in the research itself, and none of them prepared for the hostile, pseudoscientific cross-examination of the industry's friends in Congress. Under fire, the spokesmen for the voluntaries wilted or blustered; they proved less than compelling witnesses. And that testimony was the high point of citizen action on behalf of strong cigarette labeling legislation.

On the other hand, there came forward a procession of thirty-eight doubting scientists; skeptics, if not cranks, they had stepped forward from around the nation, compelled by a shared passion for scientific integrity (and, it later appeared, for not insubstantial consulting fees from the Tobacco Institute). Charter members of the "Flat Earth Society," with brows furrowed they challenged the verdict of proven casuality.

Clements, of course, was by no means the only palpable presence in the legislative process of the tobacco lobby. The appearance of these witnesses was orchestrated by the lawyers for the tobacco companies and, like Abe Fortas—Lyndon Johnson's lawyer—they represented the nobility of Washington's legal hierarchy.

So, shortly after the hearings had concluded, I found myself surrounded and grilled by a dozen or so elegant and captious tobacco lawyers. We were seated at the great mahogany conference table in the elegant old townhouse that then served as the offices for the firm of Arnold, Fortas, and Porter.

In the interest of "fairness and objectivity," I felt compelled to defend every clause of a draft memorandum I had prepared for the members of the Commerce Committee, summarizing the scientific testimony which had been presented to the committee during its hearings.

Those hearings had not exactly proved models of enlightenment. But in that coven of corporate lawyers, I amended my summary of the evidence against smoking, yielding inch by inch under the pressure of powerful and sophisticated arguments: softening findings of casuality; excising critical pieces of scientific evidence which had not formally been presented to the Commerce Committee; and treating with respect pseudoscientific quibbles offered up by the industry's witnesses. The lawyers knew that the rules of evidence which govern court proceedings did not apply to Congress, which was free to review the scientific literature no matter what was formally presented to it in testimony. They knew; but I wasn't sure.

Only one lawyer spoke up to suggest that they had an ethical responsibility not to take advantage of the relative youth and inexperience of the committee's staff lawyer. No one seemed to hear him.

But Clements remained for me the personification of tobacco's evil—up to that moment when he began to pay attention to me—a lot of attention. And it was then that I began to lose the edge of my righteousness. Clements proved in the flesh an intriguing figure, touched with history, not so unambiguously villainous. In our first encounters, he told me of his efforts to bring civil rights to Kentucky, no small virtue for a politician from a southern border state.

Clements laid down a conspiratorial atmosphere like a yellow fog, and I was drawn in, only half aware. I was young. I was twenty-nine. I was flattered by his attention and fascinated by his power. Gradually, I slipped into a bargaining relationship with Clements—a weak bargaining relationship.

The House Commerce Committee seemed totally in the grip

of Clements and his allies. Even before the legislation passed, its chairman and members threatened and intimidated the FTC into suspending its effort to force cigarette advertising to warn of smoking's hazards.

Clements's allies seemed ubiquitous. President Johnson himself called FTC Chairman Paul Rand Dixon and excoriated him for persecuting the tobacco industry. And one morning, Senator Magnuson's secretary told me that Abe Fortas, soon to be appointed by Lyndon Johnson to the Supreme Court, had called to ask Magnuson to ease his support for a stronger labeling bill. Magnuson paid no attention. But I paid attention. Magnuson had few allies, and I felt the helplessness of fighting so powerful an enemy. And Magnuson, who had many other battles to fight, did not pay close attention to the details of the bill.

Opportunism eroded idealism. I knew that the labeling bill would ease through Congress with Clements's blessing—if it also had the preemption against federal agencies and the states taking any further action to regulate advertising. It seemed futile to stand in the way of tobacco's legislative juggernaut. So I thought I might as well go along with it and at least gain the credit for Magnuson as the proud author of the law putting the warning on the package.

On January 12, 1965, I circulated a draft copy of the bill to the staff and members of the Commerce Committee for the first time. No one paid any attention to the fine print about the preemptions—because no one else was privy to its full implications. Then I circulated the draft among a few friends outside the Commerce Committee. One of them was Stanley Cohen, the Washington editor of *Advertising Age*. Cohen, who had been covering regulation of advertising in Washington since 1947, had become a close friend. He also knew right from wrong. I asked him what he thought of the bill, and I can still remember my face flushing when he cried, "Shocking! It's shocking."

It was only then that I faced up to what I had done. Stan knew immediately that it was Clements's bill. I had been both cynical and naive. And I had been found out. I remember going out to dinner that night, with family and friends—it was my birthday— haunted by shame.

I couldn't sleep that night. Magnuson was due to introduce the bill the next morning. I rushed in to see the committee's staff director, Gerald Grinstein. When he had listened to what by then seemed to me a confession of abject corruption, he calmly suggested we simply take the offending preemptions out. And so we did. And Magnuson introduced an honorable bill.

Of course, Clements's legion of allies made certain that the preemptions remained in the version of the labeling bill which passed the House. But Magnuson, in the Senate-House conference, held out until the House conferees agreed to free the federal agencies to resume regulating cigarette advertising after a three-year hiatus. It didn't seem like much at the time (the *New York Times* certainly wasn't impressed), but it did lead to strong action by both the FTC and the FCC in the late sixties, which, in turn, led ultimately to the congressional ban on all broadcast advertising.

Now, there was a defeat for the tobacco lobby, no? No. I was the senior staff member working on that bill, too. Though, as Pete Seeger once remarked while graciously acknowledging an audience's applause for a rousing harmonica solo, "That is not precisely what I would like to be known for."

So in 1969, when the three years were up, the tobacco industry *needed* a new law to prevent the Federal Trade Commission from taking regulatory liberties with cigarette advertising. It needed also to neutralize the uncharacteristically aggressive Federal Communications Commission's requirement that broadcasters air one antismoking commercial for every three cigarette ads.

Pursuing a strategy of calculated withdrawal, the cigarette companies determined that it was in their own best interest to vanish from the airwaves. They were nervous about the image-deflating potential of the antismoking counter-ads. They knew that their competing brands had little to differentiate one from the other beyond imagery—a costly contest in prime time. They anticipated no radical reduction of their market, because smoking remained a deeply entrenched addictive and socially sanctioned habit.

By then, the young children of this country were violating family tranquility—and the rules of grammar—by chanting incessantly, "Winston tastes good like a cigarette should!" Parents indifferent to the ordinary outrages of advertising were becoming increasingly disturbed at the acculturation of their children to the smoking habit. Off the air meant out of mind, and off the political agenda.

So the true author of the broadcast advertising ban was Earle Clements, who took great pride in convincing the truculent cigarette companies that the ban was in their own best interests.

Nor had I seen the last of him. In January 1975, as Earle Clements prepared to retire from the Tobacco Institute to his Kentucky home, he left one parting gift that was to dog efforts to restrain cigarette advertising and promotion for years to come.

The Democrats had just trounced the Republicans in the Watergate-dominated congressional elections. In the process, the tobacco industry's current guardian on the Commerce Committee, Senator Marlow Cook of Kentucky, had been defeated by his Democratic rival, the governor, Wendell Ford.

Earle Clements called me, as ingratiating as ever. The new senator was anxious to gain a seat on the Commerce Committee. "You'll like him, I know," said Clements. "He was a strong consumer advocate as governor."

I was not exactly confident that Clements's image of consumer advocacy and mine coincided, but I was not worried. "I'm sure he's a fine fellow," I responded gingerly, "but committee vacancies are not going to be filled." I knew that both the committee chairman, my boss Warren Magnuson, and the senior committee Republican, Senator Norris Cotton of New Hampshire, were determined to *shrink* the membership of the committee, which now exceeded its normal membership of fifteen.

Clements was utterly unfazed: "He's a very decent fellow; I'm sure you'll enjoy working with him."

Committee assignments are made in the Senate by the Democratic Steering Committee, a creature of the Democratic Caucus, and, at that time, fairly representative of the Democratic majority. Clements went quietly to work on his former colleagues. A few days later, the committee met, expanded the Commerce Committee to 18 seats to accommodate one new Democrat and one new Republican—and added Wendell Ford of Kentucky.

In one of those exquisite ironies which are more pleasurable in the telling than the experiencing, just as President Carter was naming me FTC chairman in the early spring of 1977, Wendell Ford was claiming, through seniority, the chairmanship of the Consumer Subcommittee, and Senator Magnuson was giving up the chair of the parent Commerce Committee to run the Senate Appropriations Committee.

One of our first priorities was to take action against cigarette advertising and promotion practices. The FTC staff had commissioned extensive opinion surveys which revealed that while most people knew generally that cigarette smoking was harmful, very few realized just *how* harmful to *them.* That smoking caused more deaths through heart disease than lung cancer was unknown. That smoking by pregnant women posed a severe health risk to the unborn child was news to substantial percentages of young women. That smoking is truly addictive was substantially underappreciated. And there remained other misperceptions of the risks of this habit which, by 1977, was cutting down prematurely 300,000 of us each year.

The staff's analyses of cigarette advertising and promotion convinced them that the companies' advertising and marketing strategies were designed to allay incipient fears about smoking and to deflect the attention of smokers, and would-be smokers, away from the realities of smoking. Sure, there was a warning on the label, but it had paled with familiarity, its generic message having long since lost whatever modest communicative value it once possessed. And it was drowned out by the seductive and reassuring imagery of the advertising.

With the commission's blessing, the commission staff fell to preparing a bold scheme for action. The commission would issue a rule under its broad general powers to police "unfair" as well as deceptive advertising. Patterned on Sweden's pioneering law, the rule would require not one, but a series of fierce and explicit warnings to rotate periodically on package labels and on all advertising—and not just in fine print but boldly and prominently!

On a parallel track, the commission was also wrestling with concerns about the $600,000,000 of TV advertising, mostly for junk food, beamed at the unresistant brains of three-, four-, and five-year-olds. In 1978 we opened hearings to examine the possibility of banning *all* advertising to young children.

Not surprisingly, this proposal outraged the First Amendment sensibilities of advertising, cereal, toy and candy civil libertarians. Simultaneously, our other aggressive consumer and anti-trust initiatives (actually, mostly our aggressive *threats* of action) grieved the rest of the business lobbies. As citizens, they invoked their constitutional rights to petition Congress for redress of their grievances. As lobbyists, their campaign financing checks preceded their petitions; Congress was sympathetic.

"It's a good thing they passed the antilynching laws before you got appointed," Senator Hollings, a friend and Democrat from South Carolina, told me with avuncular affection. "You're like the cross-eyed javelin thrower: you never hit anything, but you sure keep a lot of folks on the edge of their seats."

Senator Ford was equally expressive, but proved not nearly so avuncular: "You have managed to alienate the leading citizens of every town and city in Kentucky," he marvelled, and then proceeded in stentorian tones to call the roll: "lawyers, doctors, dentists, optometrists, funeral directors, real estate brokers, life insurance companies and salesmen, new and used car dealers, bankers, loan companies, Coca Cola bottlers. . . ." The list was imposing.

The commission's foes launched a campaign to eliminate the commission's statutory authority to issue rules barring "unfair" practices.

But Senator Ford was the chairman of the Senate Consumer Protection Subcommittee, as such the Senate's designated consumer champion. Surely he would defend the integrity of the commission's consumer protection powers against the assault of the special interests. Surely, his best instincts would impel him toward the commission's defense.

Alas, Ford was of mixed loyalties. In his defense of the nation's consumers, he had also to weigh his responsibilities to Kentucky's tobacco farmers. And, he bore the weight of yet another burden: his peers in the Senate had demonstrated their faith in Ford's capacity to milk stones, by reelecting him to an unprecedented second term as chairman of the Democratic Senatorial Campaign Committee. Called upon to raise funds for his colleagues' reelection campaigns, he was sore put to match the coffers of his Republican adversaries, though in this latter chore, it was his good fortune to be ably assisted by an enthusiastic citizen volunteer, Tommy Boggs—loyal Democrat and lobbyist for both Mars Candy and the Tobacco Institute.

It is a tribute to Senator Ford's genius that he conceived a bold plan to resolve all of these competing interests—well, almost all. So it was that, in the commission's darkest hour, Consumer Subcommittee Chairman Ford called the press to unfurl his plan to save the FTC. To stave off the commission's enemies, he declared, he was offering amendments to eliminate the commission's power to issue rules barring unfair practices. Unless this radical surgery was performed by those who had the consumers' interest at heart, as he did, he explained, a far worse fate awaited the commission at the hands of its enemies (though, to be truthful, nobody could imagine a worse fate).

Though Senator Ford did not make much of it at his press conference, his scheme for saving the FTC precisely mirrored the plan offered to curb the FTC by the General Counsel of the Brown & Williamson Tobacco Co., in testimony before Senator Ford's subcommittee.

It was a plan that was stunning in its felicity: though it sharply curtailed the FTC's authority, consumers, Ford insisted, should be grateful that the FTC would, at least, be left standing. The senator's tobacco constituents would no longer face the threat of aggressive FTC rule making, and Senator Ford, deftly doffing the cap of consumer protector and donning his alternate guise as chairman of the campaign committee, could simply open his arms to receive the outpouring of campaign contributions from grateful corporate citizens.

Except that we turned out to be sore losers. We weren't aware that the commission faced any threat worse than the abolition of its unfairness rule-making authority. And we denounced Ford in every forum we could gain access to.

In turn, Wendell Ford was deeply hurt that I could suggest that he had placed the interest of the tobacco industry over the interests of tobacco's victims. He called to tell me that unless we took his medicine (sounding more the executioner than the physician) FTC might very well not survive.

At this moment President Jimmy Carter, who cared more about consumers' rights than any president within recent memory, intervened. He called Senate and House Commerce Committee members to the White House and told them he intended to fight to preserve the FTC's integrity and that he'd veto any bill that gutted the commission's rule-making powers.

As Senator Ford stood on the White House lawn after that meeting, surrounded by the White House Press corps, he airily characterized his legislative designs as minor corrective surgery. Hearing him, Senator Robert Packwood of Oregon, who had supported the FTC's efforts to restrain advertising's excesses, thrust his way through the pack and spoke without the customary senatorial courtesy:

Three principal groups want this bill changed [Senator Ford's way]— advertising, sugar, and tobacco. They're getting their way.

I'll tell you what stopping the commission's unfairness authority means. You're going to have a generation of kids with rotten teeth and cancerous lungs because of this bill; henceforth any ad that is unfair, alluring, any ad directed to our children that you can't prove is false, is going to be allowed.

The end result was a compromise, in which Wendell Ford didn't get to save the commission by quite so brutal surgery as he proposed. But rule making at the FTC had received so severe a political pummeling that once fearless commissioners began to fear to tread. Me, too. The cigarette rule and the children's advertising rule were quietly interred.

BLEAK PROSPECTS

The election of 1980 was now close at hand; the shadow of Ronald Reagan and his crusade against regulation was falling on the FTC. On the southern route of his campaign trail, Candidate Reagan was promising that his administration "will end what has become an increasingly antagonistic relationship between the federal government and the tobacco industry. . . . I can guarantee that my own cabinet members will be far too busy with substantive matters to waste their time proselytizing against the dangers of cigarette smoking."

If the FTC was to do anything about cigarette labeling and advertising, the time was nigh. We devised a new scheme: before Reagan could appoint new commissioners allergic to regulation, we would summon up all the evidence and rhetoric we could muster, issue a report laying out the case for new rotational warnings, and urge Congress to require such warnings by legislation.

By the time the report was ready, Reagan had taken office and designated David Clanton, a sitting Republican commissioner, as acting chairman. Clanton was honorable but prudent. He pressed ahead with issuance of the report, but quietly. The report built a strong case that the single existing warning had failed to bring home to consumers the full measure of smoking's hazards, and that rotating warnings might cure that failure.

But on the day the report was submitted to Congress, the *Washington Star* duly noted, "The commissioners made it clear they did not necessarily endorse the staff findings. 'The commission has reached no conclusion as to the need for action.' So wrote Chairman Clanton in submitting the report to Congress."

But Clanton was a regulatory tiger compared to his successors, the new Reagan crowd of regulatory nihilists at the FTC. Their world view is nowhere better captured than in the words of their chief economist, Robert Tolleson, who patiently explained that an advertising claim by a cigarette company might not justify FTC action to cure the deception since the "natural reaction" of a consumer to the ad would be, "You mean cigarettes can cause cancer?" Thus deceptive ads can generate wholesome debate!

No wonder the *New York Daily News* headlined their story, Cig Makers Say the FTC Will Never Hurt Us. The *News* quoted Walker Merryman, the director of communications for the Tobacco Institute:

It looks as if the FTC has labored mightily and brought forth a mouse. We don't really see that this will have a tremendous adverse effect on us.

There is not too much sentiment in Congress for what the FTC wants to do, so we don't have to wage an all out battle. The general sense one would have based on last November's election is that the Administration and Congress are not interested in further regulating protrusion (sic) into a consumer's business.

We're concerned, but we were not tearing our hair out.

For once, I thought the Tobacco Institute had it about right. Reports to Congress suggesting controversial action, unaccompanied by political momentum, ordinarily move the Congress with all the force of a bulldozer with an empty gas tank. Moreover, when the recommendations propose an elaborate new regulatory scheme to a Congress hell-bent to free the Fortune 500 from the fetters of regulation, how much lower must be the odds for action?

For a while, that gloomy prognosis seemed to be borne out. To be sure, there were a handful of good and true legislators who introduced and cosponsored bills in each House to carry out the FTC's proposed scheme.

But even that handful began to shrink. And it turned out that Clements's successors had been busily about their mischief. Ordinarily, nothing is more shadowy than tracing the paths or the impact of particular lobbying sorties. How can anyone really know what takes place in private encounters between lobbyist and lobbyee? Indeed, there is a substantial body of skeptical opinion which holds: not much. I well remember Senator Magnuson lamenting at the end of a wearying day, "I spent this whole day seeing people who never even tried to persuade me of anything. They just wanted to be able to report to their clients, "I saw Magnuson today.'!"

Lobbyists, of course, have an economic need to overstate their influence. Who can tell, beyond speculation or instinct, whether or not a particular lobbying initiative really made any difference?

But, in this case, a series of chance encounters in the spring of 1982 at least afforded a glimpse of the process. One afternoon, I was visited by a CBS researcher who was doing some background digging for a possible CBS investigative report on tobacco lobbying. She was especially curious about her discovery that four senators who had initially sponsored the cigarette labeling bill had recently withdrawn their names: Republican Lowell Weicker (Conn.); and three Democrats—Bill Bradley (N.J.), Patrick Moynihan (N.Y.), and Max Baucus (Mont.). What was most puzzling is that these four were among the Senate's most respected members, and certainly the least likely to be sympathetic to the tobacco lobby.

I had some clues. By the most felicitous of coincidences I had just enjoyed a convivial lunch that noon with Marlow Cook, who had been the Republican senator from Kentucky until defeated by Wendell Ford. In the grand tradition, he was now a lawyer lobbyist for the Tobacco Institute. We had come together for no purpose other than the pleasure of swapping political gossip.

I confess a weakness for old adversaries. He and I had tangled repeatedly and nastily while I was on the staff of the Commerce Committee. In particular, he had suspected me of planting a story in the Louisville *Courier-Journal* which suggested that Cook's rhetorical commitment to the consumer cause was not matched by his votes behind the committee's closed doors. In revenge, he had vetoed my cherished plan to spend 13 Senate-funded weeks honing my professional staff skills at Harvard Business School. Still, I rather preferred his open warfare to Ford's subterranean subversion. Besides, we tend to share with our old adversaries a common fascination with old battles that no one else gives a damn about. We confessed past sins: I was the source of the leak; he did block my Harvard boondoggle.

Cook can be disarmingly candid, as he was at that lunch. He complained that the fund-raising chores that were the lobbyist's lot were coming to be a dreadful burden. To illustrate, he told of co-hosting a fund-raising dinner for Senator Lowell Weicker only to discover that Weicker had cosponsored the cigarette labeling bill. Cook said he called Weicker to ask him how the hell he expected him to raise money if he did things like that?

Although Cook had said nothing about the confidentiality of his comments, I felt constrained by the social conventions of Washington not to disclose our conversation to the CBS investigator. I did, however, suggest that the investigator look into recent fund-raising ventures for the defecting cosponsors. Of course, I do not know that there was a direct connection between Cook's phone call and Weicker's withdrawal. Weicker is a fierce First Amendment civil libertarian. Perhaps he had second thoughts about First Amendment burdens on cigarette labels.

At first, the defection of the Democrats puzzled me. I knew that campaign contributions past or promised would not have moved them. Then, I remembered Ben Palumbo. Ben is an old and good friend. To this day, he and I, and an informal group of our aging cronies, who once served as key staff members for Democratic Senate committee chairmen, gather for breakfast on Friday mornings to retell old war stories, recirculate bad political jokes, and prescribe brilliant cures for a government we no longer run. Ben is a deeply committed political liberal. He was also, at the time, a lobbyist for Phillip Morris; indeed, he was Phillip Morris's resident liberal Democrat.

Ben did not choose to share with me his activities on behalf of his client. But I could figure. I knew Ben was a good friend and political counselor to Montanan Baucus. He was also deeply involved in New Jersey politics, Bradley's state, and knew Bradley well. Phillip Morris was headquartered in New York, Moynihan's state. So was the Sea-Land shipping company, a subsidiary of another tobacco giant, R. J. Reynolds.

There was the connection. Still, withdrawal of sponsorship, especially *en masse*, was highly unusual. What magic could Ben have worked?

I think I know. Republicans Orrin Hatch and Robert Packwood were the principal Senate sponsors of the labeling bill. Vote for the bill, if you must, Palumbo must have argued, but for God's sake don't help Jesse Helms (the scourge of all that liberal Democrats hold sacred, then in a tight reelection campaign against North Carolina's Democratic governor, Jim Hunt) portray Democrats as the enemy of tobacco!

Bradley's office was across the hall from Ford's; the avuncular Ford had early extended himself as a Senate mentor to Bradley, who had, himself, become a member of the Senate Democratic Campaign Committee. So the persuader must have been Palumbo, the good Democrat, or Ford, former chairman and still conscience of the Democratic Campaign Committee. Not a breath of impropriety would have passed their lips. They would simply have appealed to party responsibility against a common enemy.

When I next saw Palumbo and confronted him with this theory, he smiled, confessing nothing; but as a friend I sensed an air of satisfaction. (I learned later that Republican tobacco lobbyists had pleaded with Republican senators to withhold their support for the labeling bill to save "poor Jesse" from defeat at the hands of the Democrats who were portrayed as poised to stamp the bill as Republican!)

Why was sponsorship important, especially since all four senators would surely vote for the bill? Because cosponsorship is symbolic of intensity. And the withdrawal of cosponsorship had to be seen as a signal of weak support.

So the labeling bill was in deep trouble.

To insiders, it was manifestly dead.

Until two things happened: the tobacco lobby stumbled, and a newborn health lobby skillfully gave it a helping trip.

3

TRIPPING UP THE TOBACCO LOBBY

VERY LARGE ANIMALS have certain advantages in confronting very small or weak prey. But big is not always best. Brain power tends to lag behind muscle power. Agility and flexibility suffer. The momentum of a large animal can be awe-inspiring, but only so long as it is headed in the desired direction.

A very large lobby directed by a diverse assortment of imperfectly synchronized brains, or brains which are capable of converging only upon the one course of conduct which has proved successful in the past, is in trouble. If its behavior is also marked by the habit of duplicity; if its intelligence-gathering apparatus is distorted by grandiose delusions; if it is both overly confident and overly fearful; if it is equally prone to alienate friend and adversary alike, it is in trouble.

And if it is opposed by a lean lobby with a light touch—flexible, resourceful, trustworthy, reasonable, good-humored, and principled—it may very well lose.

Which is precisely what happened to the hapless tobacco lobby in the summer of 1984.

But first the Public Health Lobby had to come of age.

COMING OF AGE IN WASHINGTON

In 1966 the first World Conference on Smoking and Health was held in New York. The principal host was the American Cancer Society. It was an impressive series of events. Robert Kennedy, who had attacked cigarette advertising practices, gave a passionate keynote speech. The media swarmed. The Cancer Society brimmed with pride.

Then in their midst appeared a dreadnaught: John Banzhaf, founder and baleful voice of ASH (Action for Smoking and Health). It was Banzhaf, the young lawyer whose petition to the Federal Communications Commission had provided the opportunity for advocates within the FCC (principally its general counsel, Henry Geller) to initiate the FCC's radical ruling that the broadcasters must air one antismoking commercial for every three cigarette commercials shown.

Like a picador, he had perfected the art of provoking the Cancer Society. So it was not surprising that he was not offered a place of honor among the international luminaries at the world conference, though he had a reasonable claim to such a place.

Banzhaf did demand, and obtained, space and a typewriter, upon which he hammered out a press release denouncing—not the cigarette companies—but the Cancer Society.

He called a press conference and lashed the voluntary health agencies as "gutless." He scorned as "outrageous, deplorable, and reprehensible" their diffidence in failing to *demand* the free time for antismoking commercials which had been mandated by the Federal Communications Commission.

For the next dozen or so years, the very mention of the name Banzhaf was sufficient to unsettle the phlegmatic calm of those staff members and volunteers who believed they were dedicating their lives to the cause of smoking control.

Banzhaf was wrong in attacking their good faith and commitment. But he was right in arguing that the existence of an economically and politically bunkered adversary called for a higher level of political aggressiveness than the public health community had mustered thus far.

But, like Chambers of Commerce, the organizational culture of voluntary associations like the Cancer Society is shaped by their dependence upon the support of business leaders. Much of the staff and many of the volunteer leaders are simply not comfortable taking an aggressive, adversarial stand against any segment of the business community, nor with any form of political advocacy other than support for research funding.

But Banzhaf was not the only one to see the need for greater political activism against tobacco by the voluntaries. Many who labored patiently within them saw it themselves. Finally, their temperate but persistent internal lobbying was rewarded in November 1981, when the associations, led by the Cancer Society, convened a national conference of "over 200 experts in the field of smoking control" to develop a "blueprint for action."

Banzhaf came, glowered, and left: another conference, another blueprint; surely nothing would happen.

But something did happen. Shortly after the meeting, the leaders of the "Big Three" voluntaries, the Cancer Society, American Lung Association, and the American Heart Association, met and proclaimed the birth of a new organization. Though it would be called the "Coalition on Smoking Or Health," it was far more than a coalition. What they agreed to create was a political lobbying organization.

The task of building the coalition fell to its steering committee, made up of the heads of Heart, Lung, and Cancer's Washington legislative offices. This was not a low-level commitment. Alan Davis, for example, was a senior policy maker for ACS.

In the years since 1966, though hardly keeping pace with the Tobacco Institute, these offices, and a small group of lobbyists who worked with them, had already grown increasingly sophisticated and aggressive in dogging the tobacco industry.

Scott Ballin of the Heart Association, for example, actually drafted the first version of the labeling bill, approached Representative Waxman offering support should he choose to take the lead on the legislation, and worked in tandem with his staff to build an early environment of legitimacy and inevitability for the legislation.

Another of the new breed of Washington "rep" was Bob Weymueller of the American Lung Association. Of the Big Three,

Lung had the longest tradition of public policy advocacy—and the least political fastidiousness. Weymueller had spent more than thirty years in a variety of staff positions at the Lung Association—none of them in lobbying. He had only recently arrived in Washington and had no illusions about his own lack of political experience. But Washington's levers of power challenged him (though it may have repelled some of his colleagues) and he set about his new tasks with rare openness and enthusiasm. He especially knew what he did not know.

Neither Weymueller, nor the other members of their steering committee (each of whom was to prove an adept lobbyist), needed convincing that the coalition required a coordinator, a keen legislative strategist and a politically deft spokesperson, independent of all the voluntaries—indeed a mutually trusted diplomat threading among the bureaucratic rigidities, crotchets, and competitive sensibilities of its sovereign constituent groups. As Weymueller recalls, "One thing we agreed upon is that we needed a single spokesperson; we had to break out of the mold that each one—Heart, Lung, and Cancer—would speak for themselves. Every time we did that we were outflanked by the Tobacco Institute spokesman."

They found Matt Myers. I would like to claim credit for Matt Myers. After all, he had come to the Federal Trade Commission (direct from the American Civil Liberties Union Prison Reform Project) while I was chairman, in September 1980. He had come just in time to take charge of our cigarette investigations—to hammer the labeling and advertising report to Congress into coherent, solid shape, ease it past the nervous commissioners, softly peddle it on the Hill, and quit before the Reaganites could find him and fire him.

After Myers left the commission, he joined a small law firm. But law was only marginally less appealing than service under the great regulatory nihilist in the White House. He was hooked on the smoking and health issue. He had offered his services as a volunteer. Instead, they hired him as staff director of the coalition.

Unhappily, I can't claim credit for discovering Myers. I didn't know him when he was hired by the commission, and I didn't even get a chance to recommend him when the coalition offered him the directorship.

By common agreement, both among the health lobbyists and "Deep Cough," our Greek chorus of anonymous tobacco lobbyists, he led the health lobby to an unaccustomed victory. And he proved shamelessly adept at taking advantage of the tobacco lobby's missteps.

While none of the voluntary agencies alone could be considered a political titan, together they were able to marshal formidable political resources.

Take the case of Senator Orrin Hatch of Utah, for example. As the new Republican chairman of the Health and Human Services Committee, Hatch was positioned to play a key role in any cigarette legislation. Conservative Hatch had been a persistent Senate champion of corporate regulatory relief, but was nonetheless a very good Mormon from a state with a large Mormon constituency. And Mormons detest smoking. So Hatch became a principal Senate sponsor of the labeling bill, and, as committee chairman, could virtually control its progress through the Senate. But conservative Hatch would experience periodic political heartburn in threatening the principal crop of such fellow moral majoritarians as Senators Jesse Helms and John East of North Carolina.

The Cancer Society, however, deftly drew upon its network of prominent Mormon volunteers to build a fire under Hatch when his passion for enacting the labeling law flagged.

Each of the voluntaries had a network of volunteer members, politically impressive both in quality and in numbers. Together, they counted nearly 5,000,000 volunteers. Of course, relatively few were policy activists, but in the state of Washington, alone, the Lung Association could generate 30,000 signatures on petitions urging their congressmen and senators to oppose tobacco price supports.

The Lung Association's volunteer president in 1983 was Conrad Fowler, an Alabama businessman. He and Alabama Senator

Howell Heflin were close friends (Heflin had been best man at his wedding). Heflin's door and ear were open to him. He'd also done some campaigning in Utah for Hatch. He was truly the kind of citizen resource which the Chamber of Commerce refers to, reverently, as the "golden bullet" of lobbying. Here, too, at a sticky moment when Hatch seemed evasive about his plans to move the bill, Weymueller remembered Fowler's connection with Hatch. ("It's serendipity, quite often.") Hatch sat still for a meeting, and the bill resumed its forward progress. Even Wendell Ford had a soft spot for a volunteer—his own cardiologist, Antonio Gatto, past president of the Heart Association, who persuaded Ford to meet (productively) with the health lobbyists at a critical moment late in the bill's odyssey. Weymueller celebrates the volunteers:

How do the volunteers help? Let me count the ways. The very first occasion for announcing our presence in the Capitol was a reception on the Hill the night before Mr. Waxman held the initial hearings on his bill. Each organization arranged to have a celebrity volunteer witness here: John Forsyth of Dynasty; Captain Kangaroo for the kids; and Miss Amanda Blake of Gunsmoke.

So right from the start the coalition was able to get the attention of the Hill. We had a roomful over in the House that night; it was jam-packed—a number of politicians, certainly a lot of staff, and our volunteer leaders.

And then the next day, these celebrities testified. And, when they had gotten everyone's attention, leading scientists from all the organizations spoke. For instance, for us, Dr. Stephen Ayres, an outstanding scientist from Washington University in St. Louis—and there were other scientist-volunteers. Sometimes we don't think of scientists as volunteers, but I do. And it was just excellent testimony from people who cared, and even after they went home, they stayed in touch.

And periodically, each organization would bring in other volunteer leaders depending on our needs, such as Dr. Fisher [Edwin B. Fisher], the psychologist, who could offer a different type of expertise added to the credibility of being chairman of our Smoking or Health Committee. He's not just a pretty face; he's a very effective witness—and he's a hard working volunteer.

And the voluntaries had professional staffs. Cancer, for example, though it had only one full-time and two part-time lobbyists, could draw upon professional researchers and others in New York.

So the public health lobby was not without its battalions and its cannon. And now it had its battlefield general.

GOLIATH STUMBLES

Yet Myers, his coalition, and his network of congressional allies could not match the political and financial resources of a well-led tobacco lobby. Matt Myers might not have had so many inviting opportunities to outthink his adversaries had Earle Clements remained at the industry's helm. But by 1981 Clements had long since retired to his home in Covington, Kentucky.

For a while, it didn't seem to make a difference. The tobacco lobby followed the same basic strategy in the eighties which had served it so well in the sixties: adopt a public posture of outraged innocence and studied lack of concern, lobby fiercely in the clinches, wear the Congress down, and let its antismoking contingent save face by reluctantly accepting a weak compromise.

"But why do you need to change the warning at all?" asked Earle Clements, of then House Commerce Committee chairman, Harley Staggers, in 1969.

"Because we have to bring something home."

So the industry had given an inch, as "Caution: Cigarette Smoking May Be Hazardous to Your Health" became "Warning: The Surgeon General Has Determined That Cigarette Smoking Is Dangerous to Your Health." Big deal.

It might have worked again. But it required a firm and deft hand; one deft hand. In 1965 and again in 1969, Earl Clements provided both; and though he faced persistent low-level grousing from his employers, he was their unchallenged leader. No comparable leader emerged for the eighties. Horace Kornegy, a former North Carolina Democratic congressman, who had served on the House Commerce Committee, was Clements's titular successor as president of the Tobacco Institute. He was rather well-liked among his former colleagues in the House and in the Senate ("Horace is a very decent fellow"), but he was not so formidable a force either within the industry or in Congress. Early in the campaign, he was succeeded as president by Sam Chilcote, who never quite got a grip on things while Kornegy remained active diffusing the focus of authority.

Tobacco lobbyists swarmed and wiggled all over the Hill: staff members and consultants to the Tobacco Institute; executives, general counsels and lawyer-lobbyists from each of the individual companies; and lobbyists for satellite industries, especially billboard advertising. The institute doubled its complement of well-connected ex-congressmen and senators: conservative Republicans and liberal Democrats, each to "deliver" their own kind.

But though they generously spread opportunity among this vast horde of lobbyists eager to ply their influence with the Commerce Committee, the industry did not exactly get its money's worth. Thus, the institute engaged David Satterfield, a former Virginia congressman who had recently retired as a senior Democrat on the House Energy and Commerce Committee, to commune with his former colleagues. Except that Satterfield had retired in part because he was so philosophically and personally out of tune with the other committee Democrats that they had taken the extreme step of denying him the subcommittee chair to which his seniority entitled him. On the other hand, Phillip Morris allowed Ben Palumbo, whose effectiveness (and beguiling candor) with liberal Democrats early bedeviled the coalition, to turn his lobbying talents to other, doubtless more benign, causes at a critical time in the spring of 1983. As his friend and a partisan of the health lobby, I was doubly delighted.

Kornegy and Satterfield talked several times with committee Chairman John Dingell (D., Mich.), their former colleague and "good friend." Dingell was unfailingly warm and courteous. But Dingell is almost always unfailingly courteous, even when he's plotting mayhem. Nevertheless, these two lobbyists confidently assured the cigarette companies that John Dingell's personal friendship had placed the bill in irretrievable congressional limbo, and that no serious compromise was necessary. They were wrong.

Dingell knew that he could not sit on the bill forever. He could only give the industry time to cut the best deal—and sign. That was the message he had tried to give them.

Kornegy, in particular, displayed a chronic tendency to hear only what he wanted to hear. Members of Congress habitually tell their petitioners what they want to hear. When they are fond of a lobbyist, especially an old colleague, they're even more inclined to effuse empathy.

Kornegy met with Orrin Hatch, the principal sponsor of the labeling bill in the Senate. He came away convinced that Hatch had pledged not to hold hearings. So the industry was shocked and unprepared when the hearings were promptly scheduled. Yet it should have been clear that Hatch was under pressure from his antismoking constituents (including Utah's Cancer Society activists). Besides, as Senate health committee chairman and a principal sponsor of the bill, he might be able to drag his feet imperceptibly, but he could hardly fail to schedule hearings.

Hatch also emitted what should have been an unmistakable signal: while he felt compelled to go forward as the public champion of strengthened cigarette labeling, he would look kindly upon any compromise the industry was prepared to bless. Thus at a committee hearing in the spring of 1983, Hatch publicly urged Kornegy and the assistant secretary for Health, Dr. Edward Brandt, to explore compromise. And, though Dr. Brandt plainly had misgivings, such a request from the chairman amounted to a command.

The negotiations took place in private, with no representative of the coalition present. Dr. Brandt was a committed physician but a woefully inexperienced legislator. When I learned how he was subjected to relentless bargaining sessions with Horace Kornegy, Sam Chilcote, and Stan Temko, a veteran tobacco industry lawyer, member of yet another of Washington's premier law firms, Covington and Burling, I was reminded of my days as putty in Earle Clements's hands. Brandt steadily gave ground. Finally, he notified the expectant Hatch that he had obtained an agreement from the industry—an agreement which would have abandoned the separate rotating warnings for, once again, a slightly strengthened single new warning, which would read: "SURGEON GENERAL'S WARNING: Cigarette smoking increases your risk of cancer and heart, lung, and other serious diseases."

It looked as if Hatch had found his escape hatch. Though Brandt did not urge adoption of the compromise language, neither did he repudiate it.

The health lobbyists despaired. They were convinced that Hatch would accept a compromise which they characterized as "abominable." They could fight Hatch, possibly collect the votes to override him in the committee, but, having thus turned upon one of their own nominal leaders, they could hardly have marshalled the votes to overcome tobacco state senators' obstruction and delays on the Senate floor, including the dreaded filibuster.

Matt Myers recalls that moment: "Had the tobacco industry played their cards right, that would have doomed us in the Senate."

But the tobacco industry did not play their cards right. Indeed, the day before the committee was to meet in executive session to vote on the labeling bill, a swarm of tobacco lobbyists flitted back and forth among the staff members of each Health Committee senator. To each, they confidently passed the news—relevant, but untrue—that a group of senators on the committee had already agreed to support the compromise warning, suggesting that any senator who failed to climb aboard the compromise would be left in lonely solitude.

By the end of the day, the tobacco lobby's collective nose had grown to Pinocchian length. Apparently under the bizarre misapprehension that the staff members would not compare notes, they had left a messy, bipartisan trail of conflicting, fanciful tales depicting platoons of senators poised to champion their compromise. Yet none of these reports could be confirmed. Indeed,

Myers and the coalition spent most of the day quenching the fire-storms of misinformation spread by their adversaries.

Utterly confused, the staff members, Republican and Democrat alike, convened themselves in an extraordinary session that night. They sifted through the various representations made to them, seeking in vain for grains of truth. In fact, none of the committee members had agreed to support the compromise. The staff members and the senators to whom they reported were not pleased.

Particularly not pleased was Senator Don Riegle of Michigan, whom the tobacco lobbyists had touted as posed to play a leading role in support of the compromise scenario.

Still, it was with some trepidation that Myers and his colleagues watched Riegle seek the floor the following morning as the committee convened. But Riegle soon made clear that he did not support the compromise. Then he warmed to his task. He was even less happy at being falsely identified as its champion. And he called for the labeling bill's passage, undiluted.

But Hatch was plainly still groping for a compromise. Dramatically, he called out to Kornegy, seated in the audience. Would the industry support the bill with the compromise label?

Myers held his breath. He still feared the chronic congressional itch for painless compromise. If the tobacco industry offered to drop its opposition to the bill with the proposed compromise language, the health lobbyists would be defeated.

No, said Kornegy, the moment of truth upon him, the compromise language was unacceptable to the tobacco industry.

The health lobbyists were greatly relieved—and delighted. As one of them later observed, "Even Orrin Hatch can't stand to be publically humiliated. He was livid; he was absolutely livid, and from that point on, Orrin Hatch was committed. He was going to get his bill out of committee, and nobody was going to stand in his way."

So, the committee was not sundered by conflict over an abominable compromise. Instead, on June 22, 1983, with Hatch at the helm, a 15–1 bipartisan majority voted out an amended bill with a single, but full-throated dire, graphic warning. That warning was proposed by tobacco critic—and self-confessed addicted smoker—Democractic Senator Tom Eagleton of Missouri, who also took the occasion to even a political score or two with Helms and his sharp-tongued North Carolina colleague, East. He was not the only one. The warning read: "WARNING: Cigarette Smoking causes Cancer, Emphysema, and Heart Disease; may complicate pregnancy; and is addictive."

TWO MOUNTAINS

Publically, the coalition rejoiced, exuding confidence; privately, concluded Myers, "we were still dead."

Why? Because in the Senate, there remained Jesse Helms and Wendell Ford, each ready to remind their sympathetic party colleagues that the last thing tobacco state politicians needed was an election year vote imposing new cigarette health warnings.

Myers knew that "Our act was going to be the last one in an election year." Even the threat of a filibuster would surely inhibit the unenthusiastic Senate leadership from scheduling Senate debate on the bill.

So Matt and the coalition now concentrated their efforts on the House, because forceful action there would create pressure on the Senate to act. And, with Henry Waxman in charge of the House Health Subcommittee, they had a strong leader. Waxman is one of the few members of Congress who confesses that his sole professional ambition is to legislate well in the public interest—and really means it. So, despite straying members enticed by siren calls of false compromise, and the wearying obfuscations and procedural delays generated by the subcommittee's tobacco district congressman, Virginia Republican, Thomas Bliley, Waxman steadily steered the bill through his subcommittee. On September 15, 1983, he corralled a majority of the subcommittee's members to report to the full committee a bill with a series of rotating warnings even stronger than the bill he had first introduced!

But the House remained strewn with pitfalls, stumbling blocks, and two formidable mountains: House Energy and Commerce Committee Chairman John Dingell; and the leader of "the tobacco boys," North Carolina Democrat Charles ("Charlie") Rose, chairman of the House Tobacco Subcommittee.

Dingell's support was crucial. As full committee chairman, he controlled the scheduling of all votes in the full committee. Worse, even if a reluctant Dingell could be pressured or shamed into bringing the bill before the committee for a vote, his lack of enthusiasm could infect the committee, inviting spurious compromise or evasion. Only with Waxman and Dingell as enthusiastic partners could the coalition hope to build the necessary legislative intensity and momentum.

And in September 1983, that seemed as illusory as the prospect of Helms and Ford actually voting for the rotating warnings.

Myers and other representatives of the coalition met with Dingell in December 1983. It was not an auspicious beginning, Myers remembers:

Dingell was skeptical: "I don't believe labels make a difference." He added, "I've talked to my wife, and I've shown her the labels and she's a chain smoker. She told me that even if the labels appeared on the cigarette packs tomorrow, she'd continue to be a chain smoker." He said he'd asked her whether, had she known the facts spelled out on these labels at the time she began to smoke, would she still have started smoking. She said, "Yes."

It was a troublesome meeting, though Chairman Dingell left the door ajar for further discussion and cordially invited them back to talk again.

Myers recalls that, "You walked out of the room thinking, 'He really doesn't believe that. There's something else there. I don't know what it is, but there is something else there and we've got to figure it out!'

John Dingell is a maddening legislator. He cannot be pigeon-holed. One evening in June of 1984, he received the Consumer Federation of America's public service award, to the accompaniment of paeans and cheers. He had stood fiercely in the path of the Reagan administration's battering of the nation's consumer and environmental laws and agencies. The award was just and earned.

At the same moment, outside, a group of protestors, led spiritually by Ralph Nader, were denouncing Dingell's obstruction of auto safety standards, especially the automotive safety air-bag. They were right, too.

If it could ever be said of a legislator that he was splendid in his rectitude when right, but dreadful when wrong, it could be said of John Dingell. And it was not at all clear that John Dingell was going to be right on cigarette labeling.

Myers' nose was scenting accurately: "something else" was there; some things else, to be precise.

First, having spent much of the last decade defending his Detroit constituency against what he saw as the "consumerist" auto safety regulatory oppression, Dingell had a reservoir of sympathy for all safety-beleaguered industries, even tobacco.

Next, Dingell was not in a generous mood toward Henry Waxman. Waxman is to clean air as Ralph Nader is to auto safety. Waxman was not only Dingell's arch adversary on auto emission standards, he was an effective adversary, and had, for three years, effectively frustrated Dingell's plans to take advantage of the Reagan administration's deregulatory mania to relax auto pollution standards.

But, most of all, the "something else" was Charlie Rose. Rose represents the growers of "The Golden Leaf" in Fayetteville, North Carolina. To do that, Rose has risen determinedly to chair the Tobacco Subcommittee of the House Agriculture Committee. And for Rose, all issues, all votes are an extension of the defense of tobacco.

In his powerful chronicle of tobacco's successful resistance to the dictates of civilization, Peter Taylor *(The Politics of Tobacco)* quotes Rose's assistant, John Merritt, on their North Carolina constituents' view of New Yorkers:

People in North Carolina don't like New Yorkers. One, they beat us in the Civil War; two, they talk funny; three, they're not very genteel and courteous. It's worse than the Argentinians and the British.

After all, when Ed Koch was still a New York congressman, he was reported to have said, "Who needs farms when we've got grocery stores?"

But Charlie Rose voted for federal fare subsidies for the New York metro. And nine of New York City's congressmen voted to continue the tobacco price support program.

Charlie Rose voted for earthquake and disaster aid to California, and special Brucellosis protection for cattle in Texas. And Democrat Charlie Rose supports the National Democratic party at a time when Republican Jesse Helms has become the symbol of a surging right wing Republicanism in North Carolina and all the old Democratic South. In 1974, when Tip O'Neill was the leading, but indelibly northern and liberal, candidate for House Speaker in a contested race, Charlie Rose was the first newly elected freshman congressman publicly to announce his support for O'Neill.

Rose was personally close to John Dingell, very close.

Rose was personally close to Speaker O'Neill, very close.

Rose was liked and respected by virtually every Democrat in the House. He had paid his dues as a loyal Democrat; he had paid his dues as a reciprocating colleague. And he was skillful enough to claim his debts with a minimum of ill-feeling and discomfort.

The North Carolina delegation had stood firm—a bulwark against the defecting conservative "Boll Weevils" who joined House Republicans to override Democratic resistance to Reagan's early initiatives. Now, says Rose to his friend and colleague, John Dingell, is the time for all good Democrats to come to the aid of the party—by sparing its faithful North Carolina brethren needless electoral pain. So long as Rose remained adamant against the labeling bill, its House passage remained in jeopardy.

Ten or fifteen years earlier, it would have occured to no one from the Cancer Society, or Lung, or Heart, that there was any point in reaching out to Rose—or to any tentacle of the tobacco lobby. Manufacturers and farmers, retailers and advertising agencies—all were viewed as indistinguishable parts of a monolithic evil empire (just as I had first viewed Earle Clements from a safe distance as the embodiment of evil). And to deal with the devil is dirty work.

There was, of course, a genuine risk in seeking any accomodation with tobacco interests, the same risk I stumbled on two decades earlier. In negotiations, the clarity of our own vision of right and truth can blur. We may slip into understanding, then sympathy, even for our adversary—and lose the essential edge of outrage.

But maintaining an antiseptic distance also has costs. For one, it enables your adversary to maintain an equally demonic, or at least dehumanized, image of you—as a mindless, puritanical zealot hell-bent to consume innocent tobacco farmers in the flames of righteousness. And it forecloses the possibility of discovering genuine common ground.

Almost from the first days of the coalition, Myers and the members of the coalition had been searching for the key to soften Rose's opposition to the labeling bill.

The coalition fought Rose hard in seeking an end to the price support program—and they had substantial congressional support. But they also welcomed Rose's sudden initiative—at the moment when he began to sense the political potency of the coalition and to fear for the future of the price support program—to open up a dialogue.

The first meeting, and it was the first time Rose had ever met with anyone from the health community, consisted in large part of a passionate plea from Rose that the price support program was not a health issue, but an agricultural one. Myers responded that tobacco economics could not be divorced from health issues. They could not, of course, agree.

But they were able, at that meeting, to work out a modest procedural agreement, in which the coalition agreed not to object to Rose's timetable for votes on the price support program, and Rose, in turn, agreed for the first time to hold public hearings in non-tobacco regions, and to hear non-tobacco witnesses testify against the program.

Myers and his colleagues were determined to build upon this opening to Rose. Weymueller recalls:

Once we started talking to Mr. Rose, we were hoping that he would be able to see the merits of the labeling bill, and that if we were reasonable regarding the price support program, he would be reasonable. The great lesson we've learned, is that you look out not only for what you're out to get, but listen to what the other fellow is saying, see if there is any kind of give in your position that is honorable. But mostly, you keep talking.

And they kept talking. It was not an easy relationship. The coalition continued to fight the price support programs—and Rose continued to lean hard on Dingell to hold up the labeling bill. At times their conflict provoked hard feelings, and hard words.

[Myers] *The dialogue with Rose really went up and down: one day he'd call us in to harangue—and the next day he'd call us in to talk.*

But one thing that happened in those meetings ultimately proved important: sitting down with us, face-to-face, gave a very different feel to him of who his opponents were—and to us, as well, I suspect. Charlie Rose now saw real live faces and human beings on the other side; faces which sometimes got him very angry, but faces which he also, I think, respected and felt he could deal with in a crisis.

And there did arise an issue on which the interests of the tobacco farmer and the health coalition came together—against the cigarette manufacturers: tobacco imports. The farmers found their markets severely eroded, not by smokers quitting, but by low-priced foreign tobacco purchases by the manufacturers.

By the spring of 1983, Myers recalls, Rose had become increasingly preoccupied with imports. "Listen," he'd say to Myers, "your concern is health. What really concerns me is imports. They're ruining my farmers, destroying them!"

To which Myers quickly responded, "That's something we can talk about—if you can find us an angle."

And Rose found "an angle." His staff conducted a survey of foreign agricultural practices, and produced evidence that foreign tobacco was commonly and liberally treated with pesticides barred for use within the United States.

And so, with delicate irony, Rose and the coalition joined forces in support of legislation to protect the health of American smokers—by banning the import of tobacco treated with forbidden pesticides.

Rose got what he wanted—support from a source concerned for reasons more noble than economic self-interest. But, like Br'er Rabbit, Rose had become increasingly entangled with the health lobby, though there was, as yet, little tangible benefit to show for the energy expended upon the outreach to Charlie Rose.

Indeed, in the winter of 1983, Rose was not only not helping the coalition, but was holding Dingell to his commitment to obstruct the labeling bill.

Something else had to be done to budge John Dingell.

GOLIATH OVERREACHES

Once again, the tobacco lobby itself provided the opportunity —by a course of conduct so shoddy as to alienate even its most faithful congressional allies.

Whether the industry was deliberately feinting compromise, hoping to forestall any legislation, or merely proved breathtakingly inept, will probably never be known. Twenty-five years of operating in political Washington have left me with a handy rule of thumb for divining such matters of intent: such behavior is the product of diabolic conspiracies, except where it isn't.

My guess is that the industry's behavior reflected a little of each. Some companies (probably Reynolds and Phillip Morris) wanted to negotiate the best deal they could, get a bill through, and be done with it for another five years or so.

Others (most certainly, Brown and Williamson) believed they could string out negotiations long enough to kill the bill. The picture is not made any clearer by the fact that the companies were simultaneously engaged in a contest at the FTC, in which Reynolds and others were nagging the FTC to punish Brown and Williamson for cheating on low tar and nicotine claims. This internecine wrangling did not contribute to the atmosphere of clubby good feeling at the Tobacco Institute, where they met.

Dingell, as we have seen, was determined to allow the industry an opportunity to work out its "problems" with the Waxman bill. So long as the industry lobbyists held out the prospect of reasoned negotiations, he would not schedule the bill for a vote.

This pregnant pause in the legislative process posed a serious threat to the coalition. Since the avoidance of hard choices is most congressmen's daily pursuit, there is nothing that satisfies the congressional soul better than to reel in a live compromise.

At one time or another, no less than ten individual members of the House Commerce Committee, the chairman of the Democratic Congressional Campaign Committee, other House leaders, and at least as many eager staff members were enticed into intense negotiations with one or more of tobacco's emissaries. All believed, at times, that they were on the brink of compromise, only to have their hopes dashed—either by the principled resistance of Henry Waxman and the outcries of the coalition, or, where a decent compromise actually appeared imminent, by new problems raised at the last moment by the companies.

After the Hatch committee had passed out a strong bill in the Senate, and Waxman had plowed aside the obstacles to report his bill out of subcommittee, the tobacco industry collectively decided to put a new face on their negotiations. The Tobacco Institute hired two new lobbyists with reputations for moderation and trustworthiness: Howard Liebengood, who had enjoyed a reputation for straight dealing as a key aide to Senate majority leader, Howard Baker, and Chuck Mehren, a liberal Democrat who had lobbied for labor. Liebengood and Mehren were told, and confidently told others, that the industry was embarking upon a new course of statesmanship, genuinely dedicated to reaching an honorable compromise.

What the coalition needed to meet this challenge of a promised new era of sweet reason was a congressional leader simultaneously trusted by Waxman to maintain the integrity of the labeling bill and by Dingell, as an honest broker. Such a negotiator could test the industry's good faith, either by successfully negotiating a worthwhile compromise (unlikely), or by unmasking the industry's disingenuousness.

Myers quietly put out the word, along the network of smoking control advocates, that help was needed in identifying and recruiting one or more moderate members of the committee to test the industry's good faith, and thereby help budge Dingell.

Now it just so happened, shortly thereafter, that a Friday breakfast group of pastured former Democratic Senate staff barons, to which both Ben Palumbo and I belong, provided an auspicious opportunity. I was still a member of the FTC, largely isolated by the Reagan-appointed majority, cheering for Myers and the coalition largely from the sidelines. Just about everybody in the group, deprived of the opportunity for public service by the Reagan landslide, had ended up, prosperous, if unsatisfied, lobbying for corporations and trade associations. But they never stopped being loyal Democrats. Since many of them managed Political Action Committees (PACs), for their companies or trade associations, in election years we would be joined from time to time by the hungrier of the Democratic senatorial candidates.

So it was, on a Friday morning in October, 1983, that our guest was Albert Gore, then a congressman from Tennessee—and a subsequently successful candidate for a Senate seat.

I knew that Gore had been an aggressive fighter for consumer and environmental rights on the Investigations Subcommittee of the House Energy and Commerce Committee. I also knew he had tobacco in his district (and state). I thought I'd sound out his feelings about the labeling bill for Myers, but there was a slight complication: Ben Palumbo and I were the co-hosts. Though Ben had left Phillip Morris, I still thought it prudent to wait until he was distracted.

I waited until the meeting was about to break up. Then, as Ben was momentarily pulled aside into a whispered corner conversation, I struck.

"How do you feel about the cigarette labeling bill?" I asked Gore.

Gore, whom I had always admired, did not disappoint. He was, he said, reluctant to do anything to harm (or alienate) the tobacco farmers—he had 10,000 of them in his district alone. He himself had inherited a tobacco allotment and could wax nostalgic without prompting about the patriotic glories of tobacco farming. But he knew that smoking was a grave hazard, and he wanted to be as helpful as possible within the constraints which bound him politically.

I grew bolder. The labeling bill needed an honest broker. Would he talk to Matt Myers? Sure. Ben rejoined us, unaware.

Myers didn't need any more help. He set up a meeting with Gore, almost immediately. Gore's administrative assistant, Peter Knight, commented on that first meeting:

Matt handled himself with professionalism and a great deal of character. You know, sometimes your public interest lobbyists go a bit too far and go crazy. Matt didn't. He was reasonable and realistic and soft spoken and reassuring.

If he had come in to Al [Gore] and said, "Smoking is the worst thing in the entire world!" and, "God! There's just no room for compromise" and all that stuff, it would have been more difficult, because it might have seemed, if that side was going to be intractable, God knows what the tobacco industry is going to be like! But he didn't. I think he's one of the best people I've come across on all aspects of lobbying.

Myers didn't have to wait for a response to his visit:

That night—between 7–8 o'clock—I get a phone call. It's from Al Gore. He'd called my office and tracked me down at home. He had a very excited tone in his voice. After our meeting, he had decided that the bill was too important to languish. There was no good reason the tobacco industry ought seriously oppose it.

So he had called the Tobacco Institute (probably Howard Lieben-good), and said to them, basically, dammit, why are you opposed to this bill? There really isn't that much in it you ought to be violently opposed to. Cutting out all your rhetoric, is there room for compromise? And they said, "Yes," and he said, "Okay, tell me precisely what it is about this bill that you can't live with—not that you don't want to live with, but that you can't live with."

The institute lobbyists told Gore that their primary concern was that the bill be worded in such a way that the tobacco compa-nies not be exposed to product liability suits, and that the FTC not inadvertently be given greater regulatory authority over them. Myers had anticipated these concerns. He had talked with the coalition's members about a compromise which would alleviate the companies' concerns, while preserving the strength and clar-ity of the warnings.

Gore says to me, "Matt, can you agree to changes that would deal with those issues?" And I said I hadn't cleared it with my people, but that, if he could bring me home a deal on that basis, I would promise him, sight unseen, that I could get my people to go along.

And he hung up euphoric; absolutely euphoric, saying to me, "I think we've got a deal!!"

The euphoria was doomed to be short-lived. But Myers knew that Gore would have to experience for himself the pain of deal-ing with the tobacco lobby. The next call disappointed but did not surprise him. It came from Gore's administrative assistant, Peter Knight, who told Myers that Liebengood had suddenly come up with a list of ten or fifteen additional problems that had to be solved. Despite his profound misgivings, Myers felt that the health lobby "had to appear reasonable, willing to compromise if the other side was acting in good faith":

I sort of went out on a limb on that because I wasn't sure my clients were willing to make the compromises that now were being discussed. But I also felt they had to overcome the image they had on the Hill of being zealots, and that they had to win people over by convincing them that, if there was going to be no deal, it was the industry—not the health community—that was going to force them to vote on an unpleasant to-bacco bill. The health community had to go up there and say, very solidly, "The reason you've got a political problem now, in voting on this tough bill, isn't us. We were willing to go this last mile."

Gore now had a good sense of what he was up against. He moved to strengthen his bargaining position by drawing into his negotiations Representative Mike Synar of Oklahoma, a well respected moderate member of the Energy and Commerce Committee, who had, quietly, supported the labeling bill from the beginning. In turn, Gore and Synar solicited the help of three other moderate-middle committee members: Al Swift of Washington state, Dennis Eckart of Ohio, and Gerry Sikorski of Minnesota (the latter two, having been briefly tempted by a weak compromise peddled by the billboard lobbyist). Swift, Eckerd, and Sikorsky essentially gave Gore and Synar their proxies.

Gore gingerly touched other bases. He made certain that his negotiations were not obnoxious to Waxman or Dingell. (Waxman was skeptical). Waxman's able staff man, Ripley Forbes, saw the negotiations not as an opportunity to cut a deal, but to demonstrate to the committee members the industry's perfidy.

The negotiations were predictably maddening. As they dragged on, Myers's steering committee members grew increasingly restive and indignant—and Myers was bearing the brunt of their frustration. He recalls the litany of their complaints:

"We can't make these deals, these concessions!"
"We can't have a bill that doesn't have a warning on addiction in it!"
"We're being kicked around, you know. We're the only ones who are making concessions. We're tired of it. You've come back to us three or

*four times with new proposals, and every time we say, "Okay—if this
will end it, we'll go along." Then, there's a new proposal; there's a new
this, a new that—and we've had it. No!"*

Myers confesses that, by this time, he was himself "getting very
antsy." He also worried that he himself might get caught up in the
pressure to reach a compromise: "There is a danger to the negotiator—the more hours you spend, the more intensity you put into it,
the more you want to deal. Sometimes, I'd go back to the office,
and say to myself, 'Have you fallen into that trap—you just want
a deal for a deal's sake.' "

Myers was increasingly certain that the industry would agree to
no compromise, no matter what concessions he was to make, but
that it was essential to keep talking. The meetings with his steering committee grew increasingly hostile. But he insisted:

*"We need to play it out. We've got a lot to lose. We're winning; we're
getting commitments from more and more congressmen. They now
know that it is the health community that is being responsible, and the
tobacco companies who are jerking them around."*

*By now, it was early February; we were losing time. I didn't know how
much further we could go. My people were totally beside themselves.
Every meeting I held with my clients was hostile, because they were
wondering what was happening.*

*And the only thing that was saving me was the sense, "Despite all
your irritation, all your aggravation, you are making some very good
friends whom you need to pass this bill—as well as other bills!"*

In mid-March, after months of negotiations, Gore called
Myers to tell him that he thought he had finally reached a compromise with the industry. Like all true compromises, it was
painful.

The warnings would not be as prominent as in the Waxman
bill. The required statement disclosing the tar, nicotine, and carbon monoxide content of each brand was deleted. Most painful,
the specific warning of the addictive quality of smoking was deleted.

But four strong labels survived. They were much more detailed and specific than their predecessors, and they would rotate. Henceforth, the smoker would find that the pack in his or her hand revealed at random, as in an ill-tempered fortune cookie, one of the following messages:

SURGEON GENERAL'S WARNING: Smoking Causes Lung Cancer, Heart Disease, Emphysema, and May Complicate Pregnancy.

SURGEON GENERAL'S WARNING: Smoking by Pregnant Women May Result in Fetal Injury, Premature Birth, and Low Birth Weight.

SURGEON GENERAL'S WARNING: Cigarette Smoke Contains Carbon Monoxide.

SURGEON GENERAL'S WARNING: Quitting Smoking Now Greatly Reduces Serious Risks to Your Health.

The next day, the deal fell through. Myers received a call from Gore, whose voice was "quivering" with rage. The cigarette company executives had met and disavowed the compromise. Gore asked Myers to withhold public comment for 24 hours because "he had made a commitment to me that he was going to do certain things, and he wanted me to give him a little time to do them."

Later that night, Myers heard from Peter Knight, Gore's assistant. It turned out that Gore was not the only member affronted by the industry's behavior. Gore had sought out tobacco champion Rose to tell him of the companies' arrogant game playing. Rose was so disgusted that he agreed to go with Gore to see Dingell, and said he could no longer justify asking Dingell to hold up committee action on the bill.

As Myers recalls, "It was at this point that Dingell got involved and that really was a crucial turning point. I mean, an absolutely crucial turning point."

So Dingell was finally aroused, not by an epiphany drawing him to the splendors of rotating labels, but by an insult and affront to his committee. And Rose walked away in disgust from an industry which he had exerted every waking moment to defend, because he saw it overreach, and thus dissipate the enormous reservoir of influence and reciprocity he had built up.

Dingell then unleashed his most awesome legislative weapon, William Michael Kitzmiller, once a Chaucerian scholar at Yale, now staff director of the House Energy and Commerce Committee. Actually, the qualities of the "parfit gentil" scholar are not readily associated with Kitzmiller. To the tobacco lobbyists who were to find themselves largely in his hands, "John Dingell's killer," as he is known in certain House circles, perhaps comes closer to capturing his effect.

Throughout the circuitous odyssey of this bill to date, the tobacco lobbyists had been treated with unfailing, and undeserved, patience and respect. That ended when Kitzmiller took charge.

Dingell himself confessed to me that the only complaint he had with Kitzmiller was that they spent so much of their time together laughing, they sometimes had difficulty settling down to the work at hand. Dingell did not tell me, but I knew, that what doubtless provoked their utmost glee were the heights of their own invention in devising schemes for delivering mischievous and painful justice to malefactors. ("Bring me his liver!" Dingell is reliably reported to have cried with regard to one, only partly in jest.)

Kitzmiller had taken little interest earlier in the labeling bill. When he describes Dingell's attitude to such legislation generally, he plainly speaks also for himself:

Dingell, as he's gotten older, has developed a very keen sense of the unintended damage that can be caused by crusading for good things. For example, one of the things he always worries about, even when he's doing his legislation to save fish—which he loves—is what kind of burden is this going to put on the taxpayer—how does this pass back down the line? Will the aluminum company actually close its doors and move to Osaka? And so his resistance in any of these things is not so much reluctance as it is care, caution. He also, by the way, is not wild about crusaders anymore, having been one in his youth.

Kitzmiller, neither by inclination, nor by the derivative nature of his staff position, looks upon himself as a crusader. And, as he is himself a heavy smoker, he is especially no crusader against cigarettes.

But both Dingell and Kitzmiller have a low threshold of indignation when it comes to those whom they perceive as toying with the Congress, and most especially with the Energy and Commerce Committee.

And, as the reports of the frolics and detours of the various tobacco lobbyists began to filter into the committee's HQ, first Kitzmiller, then Dingell, did not like what they heard. And as Kitzmiller gradually took a more active role, his regard for them did not rise. "They are an absolute case study of how to shoot yourself in the foot. They did absolutely everything wrong. . . . You've got ten or fifteen people saying absolutely contrary things. . . . How can you help fools? You can't make the system foolproof against fools."

Of one lobbyist he said, "There was this guy, he's about 5'6', maybe, lots of jewelry, black suit you could see at night without the aid of light, dark hair that was clearly dyed, and the look of a friendly rattlesnake."

Once unharnessed, Kitzmiller devised a delicate strategy for further negotiations with the tobacco lobbyists. "I figured the way to deal with these people is to have at them with an axe. . . ."

Kitzmiller knew that he could follow through. The tobacco lobbyists had finally alienated everyone who could possibly have helped them. He summoned them and announced: "Either come to heel within the next 24 hours or the committee will just vote out the original Waxman bill with all its warts!" Kitzmiller prudently kept in constant touch with Rose:

I told him, when they kept stalling, "I'm really now mad at these people."

Finally Rose said, "I don't care what you do to them. I'll hold your coat. As a matter of fact, I'll hold their arms." He was absolutely livid with them, and still is.

The industry now had no choice, and Kitzmiller exacted a hard bargain. In exchange for Dingell's forbearance in not voting out the original Waxman bill, the industry's negotiators not only agreed to remove their opposition to the Gore compromise. They also promised to do what was necessary in the Senate with Wendell Ford and their other allies, to make certain that the bill would not be stalled by a filibuster or other parliamentary trickery.

That is the essence of our story. But, as Matt Myers might say, "there's something else"—something so sweetly satisfying that it justifies extending this moral fable a few paragraphs. In the last act, the tobacco lobbyists even succeeded in alienating—and publicly embarrassing—Wendell Ford.

Kitzmiller recalls that, "The Tobacco Institute was now in fear of their lives because Dingell had said, 'You know, if Henry's (Waxman) bill doesn't go through, I want to tell you that I will support unseen on the floor of the House any bill that Henry reports out of his subcommittee next year. I will not read it, but I will fight for its enactment.' They were in mortal terror."

Myers and his colleagues seriously debated whether it might be worthwhile to let the bill die and try for an even stronger bill in the next Congress. But they knew that anger fades quickly in Congress and new issues arise to preoccupy the members. They were close to obtaining a strong bill—a stronger bill than any "seasoned observer," including this one, thought they had a prayer of achieving. And now they were treated to the spectacle of the tobacco lobbyists lobbying their own tobacco state allies in the Senate to let a strong labeling bill pass without a fight, without a filibuster.

It was painful—and delightful! Among the senators there was anguish and resistance, but gradually, with the threat of Dingell and Kitzmiller's vitriol spurring them on (and hundreds of calls and letters from health volunteers), most of the tobacco state senators agreed to let the bill pass.

Except Wendell Ford. Apparently, Brown and Williamson's lobbyists still held out hope for killing the bill. Evidently, they assured Ford that no deal had been made. So, while other tobacco senators were quietly removing their "holds" on the bill (an informal but strong custom that permits one senator to hold up action on a bill, at least for a while), Ford had gone ahead and publicly vowed to block passage of the bill with all his might, keeping his "hold" on the bill, which, since it was very late in the congressional session, would have effectively killed it. And so Ford publicly boasted.

Only then did Ford hear the anguished cries of the rest of the industry, who feared Dingell's redoubled wrath. But now Ford's formidable pride was on the line, and none of the tobacco lobbyists could figure out a graceful way for Ford to back away.

Ford was acutely distressed. One day he met with a delegation from the coalition, and, seething with outrage, subjected every provision of the compromise bill to his undiminished calumny. To boot, he accused Myers of deliberately undermining the chances for the passage of a reasonable compromise so that Myers could continue to be paid for lobbying the bill in the next Congress.

Then, at a meeting the very next day, he appeared transformed into the embodiment of sweet reason. He asked for very little beyond clarification that cigarette wholesalers and retailers were not to be held liable for non-conforming labels—a principle that Myers and his colleagues had always agreed to. "He couldn't have been warmer or friendlier," recalls Myers. He asked calmly if Myers could solve the problems he had with the bill:

> I [Myers] turned to him and said, "I think we can solve your most serious problems. But I'm going to be straight with you, we can't solve some of the others. This is what we can do and this is what we can't do, and it's too late for me to be playing games with you.
>
> "I'm not authorized to tell you I can do even this, but I've been working this issue a long time, and I know what my people think. And if you can tell me that we can solve the problem with me making these changes, I'll get on the phone and I'll get the agreement of my organizations for them."

Ford readily agreed. He graciously offered Myers the use of his office and phones, so that Myers could check with the coalition members and with his allies in the House, while Ford himself checked with other tobacco state senators. Within an hour they had reached an agreement. And then Ford had one favor to ask of Myers: "The 'Tobacco Boys' didn't talk to me when they struck their deal. I'm not telling them I've struck my deal, and I would appreciate it if you didn't tell them."

Myers had nothing but praise for Ford's conduct from that moment on: "He was a man of his word. He delivered completely.":

He appeared at exactly the time he said he would. He had made all the calls he promised he would make. We said, "We have a slight problem with how these compromise amendments will be introduced. Senator Hatch seems to have a preference for his name being on the amendments." Ford laughed and said, "I know Hatch and I'm sure he wants his name first on the amendments, and I don't care." We had some concerns outside the wording of the amendments, about what they meant, and we asked that in his floor statement on the bill he say certain things, which he said precisely and accurately.

The woeful miscalculations of the tobacco lobbyists and the patience of Myers and the coalition had accomplished the unthinkable: wedded Wendell Ford to the Coalition on Smoking Or Health, as Ford graciously removed the last obstacles to passage of the strongest smoking control law in history.

The Comprehensive Smoking Prevention Education Act, almost exactly as provided in the Gore compromise, passed the Senate on September 26, and was signed into law, quietly, by the president on October 12, 1984.

AFTERMATH

The new labeling bill, while nettlesome to the cigarette companies, was not the most painful casualty the industry suffered in the course of defeat. Their most severe loss was the destruction of their image as monolithic and invulnerable.

Congress responds to myths of power. Tobacco used to enjoy mythic repute; no more. No more is defiance of the cigarette companies an automatic invitation to retribution at the hands of the congressional "Tobacco Boys." There is no "tobacco lobby" any more. There is a still powerful, though chastened, tobacco *farm* lobby. And there is a cigarette company lobby, still potent, but isolated, thrashing about, and running scared.

The tobacco lobby was in large part the victim of economics. Nothing has more divided farmer from manufacturer than the companies' massive purchases of cheap imported tobacco. And nothing has undercut the economic viability of the tobacco price support program more than the vast oversupply of domestic tobacco caused both by imports and by slowly shrinking consumption.

But tobacco's lobbyists made a heroic contribution to tobacco's own downfall. Hatch had offered them a compromise better than any they could foreseeably have negotiated. They had rejected it and alienated Hatch. And they ultimately were forced to swallow a bill substantially more onerous.

Had they heard John Dingell clearly, they would have jumped early at the Gore-negotiated compromise, thereby gaining credit for corporate statesmanship—and respite from further legislative assault on their marketing practices. Instead, they angered everyone—and still had to swallow the Gore compromise.

In the months that followed the passage of the labeling law, it became clear that the companies had spawned an era of ill-feeling.

The industry's major legislative concern for the next Congress was keeping the cigarette tax down.

[Kitzmiller] *I think they may have blown their tax issue, too. They annoyed a lot of people who could be expected to help them. Charlie Rose isn't going to help them; Gore isn't going to help them.*

We went and sat down with Jesse Helms and Jesse was very charming, had one cigarette, and said he'd cut down on his smoking. Then he said,

"Quite frankly I don't care about these bastards [the companies]. You can do anything you want with them."

It is said that Wendell Ford refused to talk to any of Brown and Williamson's lobbyists for at least several months after the bill's passage.

When the fight was all over, Weymuller wrote Kitzmiller a note expressing his appreciation for Kitzmiller's help. He cherishes the hand scrawled response:

Dear Bob,

Thank you for your extremely generous words regarding my role in resolving the tobacco bill problems. It was really a cooperative effort and we are especially grateful for the efforts of Matt Myers, without whom nothing would have happened, and countless people whose names I don't know who individually provided information and parsed the shifting sands of tobacco industry policy.

As a confirmed, 'tho regretful chain smoker, nothing wedded me more firmly to your cause than exposure to the leadership of the opposition. They turned a job into a labor of love and labor of love into a crusade which I fully intend to pursue in the future.

4

WHO SHOT THE AMA?

IT WAS 6:15 in the morning, Friday, December 17, 1982. The Senate of the United States was plodding through an all-night session, with visions of a Christmas respite driving it relentlessly to its close. Some senators hovered in small groups on the Senate floor. Others napped in makeshift bunks in the Senate cloakrooms. Gradually, through the night, the Senate had ground out decisions on a series of controversial "riders" to the simple resolution to appropriate funds so that the government could pay its bills while Congress went home for the holidays.

And what matter of great national moment now stood between the Senate and its adjournment? Freedom. Freedom from regulatory oppression. Freedom from regulatory oppression of the caring professions, especially our doctors, by the Federal Trade Commission, a "rogue agency gone insane." The Federal Trade Commission, uninvited by the Congress, was threatening the nation's health by challenging the medical practice of price fixing (agreeing upon minimum fees). Worse, the FTC had so overreached, as to order a group of obstetricians distressed at threats to expectant mothers to cease their boycott of a hospital that allowed nurse-midwives to make deliveries. (Never mind that the state licensed midwives to perform deliveries, or that their safe-delivery record was superior to that of obstetricians). Worst, the FTC had attacked American Medical Association rules which barred physicians from advertising (a medically essential restraint to forestall soft-hearted healers from informing the public that they were content to accept medicaid fees as payment in full).

Freedom, in this case, was embodied in a pending amendment which would grant a special exemption from antitrust and anti-fraud prosecution by the Federal Trade Commission of any member of a "learned profession."

The AMA, with great fervor, had carried on its crusade for this exemption since the late seventies. (For simplicity, I will refer generally to the "AMA exemption" and the "AMA lobby," for the human doctors were in the vanguard, though veterinarians, dentists, optometrists, engineers, accountants, and caring lawyers' groups played modest supporting roles).

In 1980, in the waning days of the Carter administration, what was then known as the "professions" amendment was first sprung upon the Senate as a late-blooming rider to a routine bill authorizing the FTC's activities for the next several years. The rider was offered by a Republican libertarian from Idaho, Senator James McClure, and by a Democratic veterinarian from Montana, John Melcher. So taken were senators by the evident justice of their cause, that the rider failed by only two votes—though it had never been the subject of hearings, had never been considered by the appropriate committee, and was heatedly opposed by the Carter administration and just about everybody else.

Now, with a Reagan administration and a sympathetic Congress intent upon dismantling all forms of regulatory restraint, the AMA and its allies seemed poised on the brink of triumph. In fact, the more Democratic, more liberal House had already passed the exemption. And, this time, the Senate Commerce Committee, over the fierce opposition of its chairman, Senator Robert Packwood of Oregon, had voted by a 2–1 margin to support the exemption.

Just to make sure, a dozen or so lobbyists from the AMA had also spent the night in the Senate's antechambers, as the *Washington Post* reported, "importuning sleepy legislators who shuffled in and out of the chamber."

Now, just before the vote, Warren Rudman, a junior Republican senator from New Hampshire who had been elected to the Senate in the conservative Republican tide of 1980, rose to speak. The senators who had gathered for the vote actually listened. Step by step, Rudman unmasked the AMA's spurious case for relief. Then he paused and added:

I noticed something very interesting in the last week. For the first time in twenty years doctors are making house calls. They made house calls in the Dirksen [Senate] Office Building. . . . They made house calls in the Russell [Senate] Office Building. They are so concerned about our health that the reception room is packed with them. . . .

As they trudge down the steps discouraged and disheartened because we did the right thing, as they get into their Mercedes and Porsches and drive back to their suites in the Madison, let us give the American people a break. Let us regulate those things which need regulation. Let us regulate anticompetitive practices.

Mr. President, I do not get excited by my own rhetoric. I get excited when I see someone attempting to perform a frontal lobotomy on the free-enterprise system, which is precisely what is going on here.

Rudman was not just speechifying. In a virtuoso performance he had, in the previous 48 hours, personally lobbied every member of the Senate. A former boxer, the fit and aggressive Rudman had barely rested throughout the previous day and night.

It showed. The Senate voted 59–37 to table the McClure-Melcher amendment. It would not rise to plague the Republic again.

In the 25 years (as bit player or fan) in which I've been observing Senate battles, I can't recall another in which the work of one member so influenced the outcome. Senator Packwood, who himself had fought sturdily against the AMA, largely in vain, called Rudman's lobbying achievement "stunning."

But the stage for Rudman's achievement was set by an equally remarkable public interest lobby, both within and without Congress.

RASHOMON ON THE HILL

There are several dozen individuals who, setting aside modesty, could claim with justice that their own skillful (or heroic) efforts were the *sine qua non* of the AMA's downfall. I'm one of them, myself, as our small band of legislative guerillas at the FTC did our mischievous best to undermine the AMA in the press and on the Hill.

Or take, for example, the American Association of Retired Persons (AARP), many of whose members saw themselves as exploited by MDs whose greed could not be satisfied by Medicare payments. They proved a sturdy ally.

Its 20,000,000 members might not all be trigger-ready citizen lobbyists, but they provide the material underpinning for a serious lobby. And they were becoming more and more skilled in the lobbying arts.

As the vote in the Senate neared, Kent Brunette, who had been directing the AARP's lobbying effort, illustrated the wonders of AARP's new phone bank system, organized by congressional district:

> *I have this very enthusiastic member on the line, and he says to me, "Look, I'm going to be in Washington, and I'm going to see Senator —— (a member of the Senate Appropriations Committee). I want to talk to him about Social Security, and while I'm there, I'll just have a little talk with him about this AMA stuff."*
>
> *I began to worry that he might overstay his welcome, so I gently reminded him that senators are busy men, and his senator might not have time to hear all he had to say.*
>
> *"He'd better," came the caustic rejoinder, "I'm his Daddy."*

The senator's "daddy" certainly qualifies as that most sought after of all grass-roots lobbying resources, the well-connected "golden bullet." And there were others, though few quite so well-connected. But I'm not going to catalogue or celebrate them here; not any of the other senators, congressmen, nor their intrepid staffs; nor the diversified assortment of consumer, para-professional, and business groups which came together in an effective coalition to preserve the FTC's authority; and not me, nor my staunch allies at the FTC (except one).

For you will find in other chapters equally rich examples of the interweaving of members, staffs, and grass-roots coalitions that make up every legislative tapestry.

But you will not see so extraordinary a model of media lobbying. For what prepared the Senate for the Rudman assault on the doctors' cupidity was a "non-paid"—meaning free—media campaign which relentlessly undermined the legitimacy of the AMA's cause.

It was Ralph Nader who taught us how the skillful priming of the news media can serve to turn the economic resources of powerful private interest lobbies back against themselves. So it seems apt to study the work of his own lobby, Congress Watch, and more specifically, the work of lobbyist Jay Angoff, architect and craftsman of the anti-AMA media campaign. Because that's exactly what Angoff was.

Ironically, Angoff's work proved particularly telling because it complemented the principled defense of the FTC by its Reagan-appointed chairman, James Miller III, who, as we shall also see, proved himself no slouch at working the media.

To be sure, to the AMA itself must be granted a generous share of the credit for its own defeat. It is true that the AMA's lobbyists were neither as colorful, nor as steeped in flim-flammery as the tobacco lobbyists we visited in earlier chapters. And the tobacco lobby ran afoul of Congress by offering what proved to be a constantly vanishing compromise out of several sides of its several mouths.

The AMA, on the other hand, refused to talk, or contemplate compromise at all. Such uncompromising rigidity might have been appropriate while it was riding the crest of congressional support. But as that support began to wane, the AMA's intransigence perfectly mirrored the portrait of moneyed arrogance that its adversaries sought to draw. Besides, there is little doubt that the AMA could have gained at least a partial exemption at almost any point up until its final defeat. By holding out for unconditional victory, they helped to bring about their own unconditional defeat.

The AMA was, nonetheless, a formidable lobby, the Croesus of campaign contributors. For many decades, it had handily kept the spectre of "socialized medicine" from its members' doors. And until the summer of 1982, its juggernaut was rolling to crush the FTC and its rag-tag coalition.

The basic ingredients for a smooth legislative campaign appeared comfortably in hand: a seasoned Washington lobby, backed by an extensive grass-roots network with money and motivation. Indeed, the AMA's grass roots were the envy of all lobbies. Who could match the potential for trust, respect and affection of a congressman's fond family practitioner? (Recall the congressional doors opened wide to the Cancer, Heart, and Lung associations by their volunteer physicians and surgeons.)

Physicians and their PACs poured more than $3,000,000 into the congressional campaigns of the medically enlightened (or educable). "The all-world champion distributor of political campaign money," the *Washington Post*'s Ward Sinclair and Thomas B. Edsall called the AMA.

And the AMA lobbyists proved skillful, at first, in associating their cause with the reigning symbols of debate, making the most of a shamefully weak case. Indeed, the uninitiated citizen must wonder just how congressmen and senators, however grateful to the AMA, or good old Doc Whatsisname, could nonetheless justify, to themselves—or to everyone else—their support for so bare-faced a special interest vote.

The answer lies partly in the manipulative skill the AMA used to connect itself to the regulatory reform crusade, which reached its zenith in the late 1970s and in those first years of the reign of Ronald the Deregulator.

You've had a preview. The FTC, as we have seen, was a prime

target for deregulatory buffs. Though I have argued elsewhere that corporate charges of FTC's power-hunger and bullying were largely sham, that image had taken hold in Congress.

One spirited congressman who raised anti-FTC invective to an art form was Republican William Frenzel of Minnesota (upon one of whose medical associations the FTC had imposed a modest, though prickly questionnaire). As the House in the fall of 1979 debated various proposals to restrain the FTC, Frenzel gathered up the available themes of FTC's abuse and recast them in this stirring diatribe:

> The FTC is such a mess that one hardly knows where to begin discussing its problems. It epitomizes all the things that Americans find excessive, unnecessary, wasteful, duplicative, and repugnant about regulatory agencies.
>
> But the FTC is more than just your ordinary pain-in-the-neck. It is a king-sized cancer on our economy. It has undoubtedly added more unnecessary costs on American consumers whom it is charged with protecting, than any other half-dozen agencies combined.
>
> It is bad enough to be counterproductive and therefore highly inflationary, but the FTC compounds its sins by generally ignoring the intent of the laws and in writing its own whenever the whimsey strikes it. . . .
>
> Ignoring Congress can be a virtue, but the FTC's excessive nose-thumbing at the legislative branch has become legend. In short, the FTC has made itself into a virulent political and economic pestilence, insulated from the people and their representatives, and accountable to no influence except its own caprice.

Put simply, the FTC had become "a rogue agency gone insane."

The AMA and ADA (American Dental Association) lobbyists knew a good thing when they saw one, and they set about seizing the symbolic high ground.

To appreciate the skill (and disingenuousness) with which they distorted the FTC's challenge to the professions, please recall that the FTC's purpose was not to regulate the practice of medicine, but to challenge excessive economic regulation—by the profession, of the profession.

Yet in testimony, press releases, statements drafted for willing congressional proponents, TV debates, and in-house newsletters fanning their own indignation, they portrayed the commission as poised to station FTC regulatory SWAT teams in every operating room, or as insisting that janitors (or FTC lawyers) be given equal access to the scalpel. They studiously avoided noting that the commission had confined its enforcement activities to challenging such "quality of care" self-regulation as bans on honest price advertising of eyeglasses, or gold fillings.

So the chief lobbyist for the dentists raged at the FTC's "assumed rule-making authority to nullify state laws that were enacted years ago to protect the public from the unfettered provision of health care by anyone who chose to offer it."

Once the FTC's efforts were characterized as seizing "authority to decide who is and who is not qualified to deliver services to the public," then it would follow that " . . . among all agencies of government, state or federal, the FTC probably has the least expertise to decide such questions."

After all, who is better qualified to practice medicine, the FTC, or the faithful family practitioner?

The true public interest lobbies are the medical societies: "For the protection of American patients-consumers and the benefit of taxpayers, Congress should pass legislation to keep the FTC out of already regulated areas where it did not belong in the first place and does not belong now." That was the AMA talking.

Indeed, the doctors, dentists, and their trade associations disappeared entirely from their own rhetoric. Even in discussing the course of the lobbying campaign, the defender of the good appears not in the guise of the AMA, but the anthropomorph "Medicine." As the *AMA News* told it, "Medicine's fight is in the public good. . . . Medicine faces a massive challenge if it is to prevail in the U.S. Congress."

"I don't want the FTC to practice its brand of quackery in

regulating medicine!" thundered another of medicine's advocates, Congressman Thomas Luken (D., Ohio).

This crude, but artful rhetoric, probably did not convince many congressmen, though it may well have touched a responsive chord among those already predisposed to sympathize with the victims of energetic regulation. But it furnished safe rhetorical cover for those ready, for whatever reasons, to sign on with the AMA. The AMA exemption had become, if not motherhood and apple pie, at least a legitimate cause. And that's all the AMA needed.

So if the anti-AMA forces were ever to prevail, they had not only to challenge, but to destroy that legitimacy. Only then, overriding sympathetic vibrations and even commitments, would senators and congressmen be shamed into shunning the AMA's cause.

In one of the choicer ironies of this series of studies, so subversive a task could only be achieved by the fortuitous, tacit partnership of political extremes embodied in the personas of Reagan's FTC chairman, James C. Miller III, and Nader's Congress Watch lobbyist, Jay Angoff.

And, curiously, at a time when lobbying *cognoscenti* were heralding the advocacy power of the electronic media and computer generated and targeted direct mail, the lead medium for accomplishing this task proved to be the old-fashioned editorial—indeed a phalanx of editorials, marching in an ideological pincer from far right to middling left—all condemning the AMA and its misbegotten venture.

ON THE RIGHT FLANK

I'm not exactly a Jim Miller fan. For those who might be curious as to the causes of my disaffection, I offer up the 268 page report which I filed with the House Oversight Subcommittee as I departed the Federal Trade Commission in the fall of 1984. About five pages of that report are devoted to the good things Miller did at the FTC; the rest are not.

But first among the good things was Miller's spirited defense of the FTC's jurisdiction over the professions.

It was not exactly surprising that economic conservatives and liberal consumer advocates should have found common ground in the FTC's professions program: the conservatives, nurtured in the Chicago School of Economics, abhor all forms of market regulation, including self-regulation, because such regulations impair the free market. Liberal consumer advocates abhor such rip-offs as price fixing and monopolization. The learned professions managed to breach both thresholds of obnoxiousness simultaneously.

But it was Miller who could speak to conservative opinion. As a notorious knee-jerk liberal, I could plead (as I tried) that the commission's challenge to the profession was to free up honest competition, not to impose more regulation. I could mouth the appropriate conservative rhetoric; but it was Miller who was credible.

For the six months prior to the Senate vote, Miller unleashed the FTC's aggressive press office to propagate his view that FTC action against professional restraints on competition was essentially conservative. This message was beamed to every conservative editorial ear. As a result, editorial support for the FTC boomed forth from quarters which never before, at least within living memory, had a kind word to say for the FTC. Miller's deregulatory credentials opened the door. From the *Honolulu Star Bulletin:*

The (exemption) bill is being touted as consistent with President Reagan's philosophy of returning powers to the states and shrinking federal regulatory interference.

A clue that the bill is not really that at all is given by the identity of the bill's chief foe.

He is none other than a conservative, the passionately free-market economics professor whom President Reagan initially chose to head his regulatory reform task force. The President later made James Miller III chairman of the FTC, presumably to fight the deregulation battle right up in the front lines.

Miller says he's still fighting it, but finds that in this case the name of deregulation is being used to shelter anti-competitive practices from federal oversight. . . . He has the backing of conservative publications like the Wall Street Journal.

Yes, the *Wall Street Journal,* for whom the sun arose and set many a day without a good word for a federal bureaucracy! The *Journal* swallowed hard: "Generally, more power to the FTC has meant more punitive and unnecessary regulation." And then transcended its instincts, "But this time the Commission is on the side of the markets. . . . On this one we are on the side of the Feds."

Other conservative precincts chimed in, from the *San Diego Union* to the *Chicago Tribune* to the Reverend Moon's Washington D.C. conservative bulwark, the *Washington Times* ("James Miller's opposition . . . is the truly conservative position.").

Miller also hit hard at the (somewhat strained) connection between rising health care costs and the FTC's efforts to expand competition. That message also took, as other conservative papers found virtue in the FTC's "fight to contain sky-rocketing," or "spiraling," or "soaring" health care costs the old-fashioned way —by enforcing "the rules of fair and open competition that other businesses take for granted."

Miller's advocacy reached beyond exposual of the doctrinal conservatism of the FTC's position and the miraculous cost savings potential of competition. Though the AMA's members have ever been good and faithful Republicans, Miller introduced an un-Republican note of class warfare which mined a populist vein. For example, the *Christian Science Monitor* (perhaps a shade less tolerant of doctors than others), spoke harshly under the headline "Don't exempt the 'privileged class' ":

Even Federal Trade Commission Chairman James Miller III—a conservative who has led the fight for a smaller, less activist FTC—expressed dismay [at the exemption] . . . because "it sets aside the privi-

leged class in this country . . . from laws and enforcement efforts that
govern everyone else's behavior."

As a debater, Miller scored a knockdown on the nation's editorial pages. The Miller press office calculated, with justified satisfaction, that the final tally of newspaper editorials (not counting
the AMA and ADA *News,* of course) scored 154 for Miller and
the FTC; 0 for the AMA.

But winning the public debate is not winning the heart and
soul of the Congress, especially the soul. By June of 1982, 219
members of the House were hanging out in public as committed
sponsors of the AMA bill, which had come to be known by the
names of its two principal House sponsors, Democrat Luken and
Republican Gary Lee of Syracuse, N.Y., as the "Luken-Lee bill."
And their commitments were shored up, not by the power of reason or symbol, but by the influence and money of the AMA and
its lobbying allies.

Miller had taken the high road in his rhetoric, vigorously attacking the logic and public policy of his AMA adversaries. He
deliberately avoided attacking their lobbying campaign, their
campaign contributions, and the whiff of corruption that attended their otherwise inexplicable progress in Congress. Typical
was this exchange with a *Wall Street Journal* reporter:

*Mr. Miller doesn't blame lavish contributions for turning lawmakers'
heads on this issue, as many critics do. But he does fault legislators, including Republican ones, for falling for what he regards as a none-too-
subtle manipulation of political labels. "You have a Republican Congressman or Senator who's very oriented to states' rights and someone
comes in to him and says, 'The FTC is trying to over-rule the states,' "
Mr. Miller says, "and this legislator's gut reaction is, "By God we've got
to stop the FTC from doing that.' "*

Of course, it's prudent for the head of an agency which is ac-
countable to Congress to avoid accusing his overseers of corruption—just as consumer leaders within the Congress hesitated (at
least publicly) to embarrass their congressional adversaries by

drawing unwelcome attention to the AMA's PAC contributions.
To suggest that one's colleagues are on the take does tend to dissipate collegial comity. (And may invite retribution in kind; who,
among them, is entirely free of electoral venality?) Besides, nothing so excites Congress's pompous self-righteousness as the sug-
gestion that the hundreds of thousands of dollars they each have
to grub every two years influence their behavior!

But Jay Angoff was not so inhibited. And where Miller would
not tread, Angoff trod.

BRASS KNUCKLES IN THE PUBLIC INTEREST

About the only attitude that Jim Miller and Jay Angoff shared
in common was their disaffection with the FTC of the late seventies—except that Miller was offended by what he perceived as his
predecessors' hyperactive, "star-trek" law-enforcement adventurism, while Angoff was frustrated at the FTC's constraints!

Angoff had joined the FTC in 1977 right out of law school,
because he had greatly admired Ralph Nader since he was thirteen and "either wanted to enforce the antitrust and consumer
protection laws or go after the Mafia."

After two years, Angoff took a 60 percent cut in pay and went
to work as a lobbyist for Nader's Congress Watch. He recalls the
events that led to that decision:

*I really liked what I was doing at the FTC, which was antitrust, and
it was fun, too. But I got bummed out when Congress put the squeeze
on and the FTC ran out of money for a couple of days. It was nuts: here
were these directives coming around saying you had to pack up boxes;
you've got to act as if we're closing.*

*I never had any desire to work in or with Congress whatever, but I
remember going over to watch the hearings of the Senate Commerce
Committee [investigating FTC "excesses"], and then watched the debate on the floor. I was absolutely amazed. You can't believe these guys
are saying this stuff, it's so without foundation.*

I knew some of the guys at the FTC working on the "cereals case" (a major FTC antitrust case). They had spent eight years of their lives on this one case, which I really believe they would have won. And then Congress, in one day, can wipe out what these guys had done for eight years.

I thought that was really a disgrace, and I thought if there was any way I was going to make a difference, I was going to do it with Congress. I thought Congress was where things really got done, and I still do, and that's why I came here.

Congress Watch proved hospitable to both Angoff's convictions and metabolism.

Angoff would not be counted among the more gracious of public interest lobbyists. He is tough, prickly, righteous, slow to compromise.

Ralph Nader does not coddle those who choose to work with him. Paid little, they are nonetheless expected to devote every waking hour to the public interest. And they do. But even among them, Angoff soon acquired mythic status as an indomitable worker. One day work stopped at the Congress Watch offices, a rabbit warren of bare offices on a third floor walk-up flat, close by the House office buildings. There had been a smoldering electrical fire, and acrid fumes permeated the offices. The building was evacuated—of all, it seems, but Angoff, who could not be bothered—or deflected—but remained at his desk. Why not? At last the single long distance WATS line, jealously sought after by the dozen or so Nader lobbyists and interns, would be free. Before the building was declared fit for habitation, five editorial writers and four call-in radio talk shows could be told the truth about the AMA, money, and the FTC.

Angoff possessed a hefty set of lobbyist's tools. He was a good lawyer and a careful analyst. His knowledge of the issues relating to the AMA amendment ran deep, and he understood well how to shape his arguments to the forum. After he testified before the Senate Commerce Committee, Chairman Packwood circulated Angoff's testimony to the committee staff as "an especially effective" model.

Angoff also understood that even testimony of matchless logic and eloquence would not shake the AMA's grip on the Congress. Of course, the members had to be persuaded that the AMA's quest was bad public policy. But they had also to be made to feel shame for casting an AMA vote; and, if shame were not a sufficient deterrent, then fear—fear of a disturbed and potentially rebellious electorate!

Angoff understood that the only way to derail the AMA campaign was to cast the AMA's lobbying campaign and its lavish campaign contributions into coarse symbols of vote-buying, and hammer away at the corrupt nexus between money and votes.

And it was here that he gained an involuntary assist from the National Automobile Dealers' Association.

The first campaign Angoff engaged in for Congress Watch, was defense of the FTC's proposed rule to require used car dealers to disclose serious defects in the cars they offered for sale. Naturally, the used car dealers ran to Congress for relief from this un-American regulatory effrontery. They succeeded in May 1982, despite Angoff's best efforts.

Angoff had known from the beginning that the used car dealers (the most powerful of whom were also new car dealers) were likely to win. The automobile industry was in the midst of a severe depression; many dealers had gone bankrupt. The dealers were able to trade on a wave of congressional sympathy. ("Ralph used to yell at me for spending so much time on it, because it was such a hopeless issue.") But Angoff was determined to fight as hard as he could. And, in losing, he discovered the value of money:

The whole thing started with Tony Capaccio [an investigative reporter with Jack Anderson]. He was the one who really first touched on the money. It was before we did anything on it. He named four or five congressmen who had gotten a tiny bit of money from the dealers. That's how we first got the idea. We thought, there's probably a lot more here.

Nader may not furnish his lobbyists access to the most advanced computers with which Angoff could scan campaign contribution tapes. But Angoff was not bereft of resources:

There's no substitute for slave labor. We had a few interns go down to the FEC [Federal Election Commission]—you don't need computers and high tech stuff—and copy down the contributions by hand. The used car dealers filed quarterly—the AMA each month—and we just told which congressman got how much from each. Our interns were very enthusiastic, and it was a lot of fun.

Angoff and his interns packaged and repackaged their data, updating it periodically. Each time they collected new data, they'd put out a press release tying the dealer contributions directly to the used car veto proposal.

To at least one paper in each major city, Angoff and the interns sent out ("with our computer-like efficiency") a used car package, including their first used car PAC study and editorials from the *New York Times* and the *Washington Post.* A persistent secretary followed up the mailings with calls to make certain the material was received and noted.

"We got a tremendous response," recalls Angoff. "We really didn't have to do too much. The *New York Times* rarely runs our stuff, but our first PAC study on the used car rule was a featured news story in the Sunday *Times.*"

More important, the Associated Press put the story on their wire, setting out the contributions separately by congressional district, so that the media in each district could turn it into a local story.

Nader may have been skeptical about wasting lobbying energy on the used car rule, but he saw clearly the long-term benefits of the PAC studies.

"When we lost," Angoff remembers, "I was real upset. But Ralph said, 'Don't worry about it. It's going to help us on the AMA fight.' " And it did.

Angoff and his interns then turned their full attention to the AMA:

When I was at the FTC in 1979 and 1980 and when the AMA issue started, it was always referred to as the "professions exemption." Who cares about the "professions exemption?" We just all the time called it the "AMA exemption." We didn't talk about the lawyers, dentists, ar-

chitects; this was the AMA. And that fed on itself, not just with the press, but with members, too. That's why Rudman struck a chord when he got up and talked about all the AMA lobbyists outside.

The interns were ready to pounce on the AMA's monthly PAC filings, though they also watched for contributions from the dentists and optometrists. They compiled both gross and individual contribution totals on contributions made between January 1, 1979, and December 31, 1981. These then became the "hard news" of a Congress Watch study released in early March, 1982, titled "FOLLOWING DOCTORS' ORDERS: The Medical Profession's Campaign Contributions to Cosponsors of Bills Exempting Doctors from FTC Prosecution."

The study began with a terse, but not cursory, review of the issues. It did not neglect the brisk and compelling specifics which caught Packwood's eye, especially the commission's prime exhibit: eyeglass deregulation.

Today, contact lenses are much cheaper than they were before 1978, and the price of eyeglasses has increased at less than half the rate of inflation. The prices of glasses and contact lenses are routinely advertised now; just a few years ago they were rarely advertised. The explanation? In 1978 the FTC ruled that restrictions on advertising the price of eyeglasses and contact lenses were unlawful. Such advertising then began to appear, and price competition broke out. According to the FTC's Bureau of Economics, consumers saved well over $100 million dollars in 1980 as a result of the FTC's ruling.

There followed similar concrete examples of ADA and AMA restraints on competition, and the cost reduction blessings of FTC intervention. Then concluded:

In short, the FTC wants doctors, dentists, and optometrists to live by the laws the rest of us must live by. The "professionals" don't like it. They have therefore been lobbying heavily for legislation that would prevent the FTC from suing, investigating or studying them, and that would make it impossible for the FTC to enforce any of the orders that it has already issued against them.

They have also been contributing heavily to congressional campaigns, as the following data show:

There followed text and tables formulating and reformulating the contributions, calculated to bring home the massiveness of the total contributions received by the sponsors of the Luken-Lee bill. The study noted that the AMA had contributed more money to congressional candidates than any other organization except the National Association of Realtors. Focusing upon both House and Senate sponsors, and, of course, naming names, the study singled out the big winners among key committee members, but took care to note that a very few committee leaders who had received such contributions nevertheless opposed the bill. The study contained a table tracking the contributions of each member of the House. The study concluded:

The $863,810 contributed by the AMA, ADA, and AOA to 157 House and Senate co-sponsors of bills that would exempt them from FTC challenge is an investment that has already paid off; the $281,810 they have contributed to the members of the committees that will be considering the FTC authorization bill is an investment they hope will pay off in the future. Whether that investment does pay off—or whether Congress will have the strength to say no to moneyed interests seeking special treatment—will be determined by May 15, when the Senate and House Committees must report out the FTC authorization bill.

The study, as intended, unleashed two waves of AMA-scarring publicity: first news accounts, then critical editorials. The report was treated with respect by the press. The AP and UPI wires treated the report as hard news, though the *Washington Post* did not bite.

Stimulated by the wire stories, and by mailings and calls direct from Angoff, by April and May several editorials appeared throughout the country, plainly influenced more by Congress Watch's dollar signs than by Chairman Miller's economic rationality. From the *Topeka Capital-Journal:*

*There are 181 House co-sponsors of the bill to exempt professionals.
It just so happens that 96%, or 155, of the co-sponsors have received a
total of $800,000 in campaign contributions from. . . .*

*Three Kansas Congressmen who are co-sponsors of this legislation
have received contributions from these organizations. Rep. Jim Jeffries
has received $6,250; Rep. Pat Roberts, $15,700; and representative Robert Whittaker, $16,350. . . .*

And from the *Birmingham, Alabama Post-Herald:*

*The relationship between large campaign contributions and an indi-
vidual congressman's support of legislation favored by the contributors
has long been plain to anybody who cared to look. And as campaign costs
have escalated, the relationship has become even clearer. . . .*

*The second highest recipient was Rep. Richard Shelby of Alabama,
who received $18,500. . . .*

*There is nothing illegal under current law about the contributions.
But the strong correlation between where money goes and the legislative
actions of recipients doesn't do much for public confidence in Congress'
dedication to the public interest.*·

And from the *Lewiston, Idaho, Tribune* (in sponsor McClure's
own state):

*. . . And the U.S. Senate—bought and paid for by many of those the
FTC would keep under control—is apparently ready to check the FTC.
It's the Senate's way of saying thank you for all those contributions.*

*But there is no price fixing on the purchase of Senators. Some of them
will sell out more reasonably than others.*

*Congressmen may wince when they read attacks on Congressional
venality. But they pale when such attacks single them out and list their
price!*

Congress Watch was back in June, with another report, and
another release: "Following Doctors' Orders—II." The big news?
Campaign contribution totals from the three professions' trade
associations to AMA exemption cosponsors had escalated to
"more than $1 million." Of the now 192 cosponsors, "186 re-
ceived an average of $6,145 each from the three trade groups.

Forty-four members received $10,000 or more." The study listed the top ten and the amounts.

Angoff also took direct aim at the AMA's claim that "contributions from our own political action committee, as well as those from other PACs are made far in advance of any knowledge of specific proposals on which the Congress might act." Plainly, the vote-buying charges were beginning to bite.

"This statement is simply not true," the Congress Watch study argued, noting that the exemption amendment was first introduced in October, 1979.

Angoff relentlessly bound the doctors up with the used car dealers. The June study began:

When Congress voted 286–133 to kill the FTC's used car rule on May 26, some legislators stated that the auto dealers' campaign contribution/lobbying effort to have Congress kill the used car rule would be just the first of many similar efforts by other business groups to kill FTC investigations they didn't like.

The editorial outrage escalated. The tone became increasingly sharp as mainstream newspapers combined the Miller and Angoff themes in a rich porridge of reason and outrage.

"Following Doctors' Orders—III" was ready in early September, as showdown votes in the House appeared imminent. This time the report concentrated on AMA contributions.

Angoff, himself, could not have written more provocative news stories than those that flowed from this latest study. So, while the editorial pages of the *Wall Street Journal* never mentioned campaign dollars, the news pages ran a detailed account of the Congress Watch report, under the headline, "Doctors and dentists prescribe donations for some in House; medical groups give sponsors of bill on FTC exemption $1.7 Million for campaigns."

Other headlines were even less subtle, such as the *Chicago Tribune*'s, "Medical lobby gifts linked to FTC bill."

The network news shows, while careful to provide opportunity for AMA spokesmen, would not grant the AMA the high ground of a genuine debate over regulatory policy. On May 18, Bill Moyers lashed the AMA in his nightly CBS News commentary. And, on September 24, Dan Rather led into a Susan Spencer interview with Miller and AMA's Executive Vice-President James Sammons, thus:

It's no secret that the American Medical Association has a big say on matters of medicine. Less well-known perhaps is the AMA's political clout, and lately the AMA has been paying House calls, and Senate calls, too. . . .

And Susan Spencer wrapped up:

On Capitol Hill . . . the AMA has portrayed itself as the underdog, fighting big government. Critics note, however, that the underdog has contributed over $700,000 to incumbent congressmen over the last year and the bets are that, despite Reagan Administration opposition, the AMA may very well win this one.

The AMA was losing the struggle to portray "Medicine" as a selfless calling. Steve Aug, "Good Morning America's" business reporter, covered the story on September 22:

The image of the physician: the man of science . . . healer of the sick . . . but medicine is also big business—worth about $300 billion a year . . . it's the medical lobby with its large supply of cash that's doing most of the arm-twisting on Capitol Hill.

By September and October, the flow of critical editorials had become a torrent. And deepening cynicism inspired a rash of scornful puns in such headlines as "Doctors in the House," "The Doctors' Bill," "AMA's tourniquet squeezes consumer," "Doctoring the antitrust laws," "Wrong prescription," "Unhealthy exemption."

On September 28, Angoff issued perhaps the most mischievous release of the campaign. It began:

Medical doctors, who are seeking a special exemption that would allow them to fix prices and restrict competition without fear of FTO prosecution, earned an average of $86,210 in 1981, according to a study

in the latest issue of Medical Economics, a journal devoted to the business aspects of the practice of medicine.

This was not exactly hard news; the report had been out for
several weeks. Besides, the income levels of the nation's doctors
bore only the most tenuous relationship to the issue of FTC exemption for physicians. But so successful had Congress Watch
been in portraying the exemption campaign as the child of physicians' unadulterated greed, that the press soberly treated this release as news.

Angoff credits Sidney Wolfe, who heads the separate Nader
Health Research Group, with the inspiration for this sortie:

*I went up to Sid's office and saw a three- or four-year-old survey done
up like that, and I said, "Hey, do they do these every year?"*

*It turned out that a new one had just come out, so we put it out and
the timing was great. Not only was it in the midst of the debate, but it
was an off-day for news—I remember this because it was Yom Kippur,
but I just figured, "Look, God wouldn't mind if I worked on Yom Kippur
just that one time!"*

On October 29, one week before the 1982 congressional elections, Congress Watch announced that the AMA's total direct
contributions for the 1982 election campaign was "$1,723,335
more than any other PAC. . . ."

This study not only documented AMA contributions to sitting
congressmen, but singled out forty congressmen and challengers
who had benefited by a sleazy AMA subterfuge for getting around
legal limits on PAC contributions. The Federal Election Commission, in its peculiar wisdom, had ruled that opinion polls de-
preciate precipitously: 50 percent after fifteen days; 95 percent
after only sixty days. But, if framed carefully, they remain of great
use to candidates. So the AMA conducted polls costing up to
$56,000 for 40 candidates; held the results for either 15 or 60
days; and contributed the results, depreciated to slide under the
$5,000 limit for PAC contributions. And so Congress Watch dis-
closed—naming names and the original costs of the polls.

That revelation actually originated with Congressman Mike

Synar, of Oklahoma, who had become increasingly appalled at his colleagues snickering private revelations of the AMA's crude stretching of campaign financing restrictions—and his fellow congressmen's shamelessness. Synar helped lead Tony Capaccio, the investigative reporter for Jack Anderson—who needed little leading—to the story and an Anderson column blasting the AMA and its beneficiaries. Angoff decided to make more of a good thing:

Very few of the things we did were our original ideas. Other people did them and we just extended them.

The AMA was a perfect target. They made three different kinds of contributions: the direct contributions, the polls, and the independent expenditures in support of a candidate. So the amount becomes huge, because some members got $10,000 in direct contributions, a poll that was worth $60,000, and an independent expenditure of $20,000. The press really picked that up. A whole atmosphere was created so that the AMA's strength really did work against them . . . when you can pin it on one group with a lot of money, it makes things so much easier.

And Angoff again harvested some choice headlines: "AMA labeled biggest political donor," "AMA prescribes $41,126 opinion poll for Rep. Snyder," "AMA kind to Molinari as bill waits," "Schneider praised in AMA brochure; receives donation."

In October came *Time* magazine's semi-official certification that PACs had become a national nuisance. In its October 25 cover story portraying an omnivorous PAC-man, *Time* clucked in vintage *Time* simile and rhetoric:

The question of whether PAC donations actually buy votes or only reward members who tend to vote properly is akin to that of the chicken and the egg. One thing is certain: the combination of chicken and eggs fertilizes the process.

Angoff's strategy was not subtle. The October 29 release was unabashedly timed to influence the elections scheduled for the following Tuesday. By hammering away at the tie between AMA money and cosponsorship of the AMA amendment, Angoff had hoped to make political lepers of AMA exemption cosponsors, and to create a realistic fear of voter retribution. The editorial campaign, of course, was designed to remind congressmen that there was at least the potential for such voter retribution. But what Angoff and his colleagues needed most were a few political corpses whose electoral demise was certifiably attributable to a fatal dose of AMA PAC money.

By divine providence and through the accidents of congressional redistricting, Congressman Gary Lee of Syracuse, who enjoyed the doubly dubious distinction of authoring the used car rule veto resolution and the AMA exemption, was thrown into a primary campaign with another popular incumbent Republican, George Wortley (who had not endorsed the AMA amendment—and would vote against the AMA). If Lee could be defeated, and if his defeat could be tied to his espousal of the AMA exemption, his defeat might deflate congressional enthusiasm for the AMA's bidding.

GARY LEE: AMA MARTYR

Angoff spent many hours on the Congress Watch WATS line that spring and summer. The interns, scouting, would search out radio call-in shows in selected congressional districts, scheduling "live" guest appearances by "a spokesman for Ralph Nader's Congress Watch." And, at the appointed hour, Angoff would call, and through the wonders of electronics, participate in the gentle deception that he had journeyed all the way to Syracuse, say, to speak directly to the local folks. Angoff recalls:

The usual presentation was about the same. We went out of our way to say the used car rule, the AMA exemption were not Democrat vs. Republican issues. You know you can be 100 percent for President Reagan; you can believe in a balanced budget amendment. We'd go out of our way to say the administration supported the FTC. We're not anti-Reagan, but for the people against the special interests.

The issue is simple: somebody from Syracuse, or some other place, comes to Washington and votes for the special interests that contribute to his campaign—whether it's used car dealers or the AMA—and against the interests of the folks back home.

We emphasize, number one, even more than the money, the fact that here's a guy doing the worst thing he can, which is to come to Washington and forget about the folks back home. That is what we hammered on.

One city targeted was Syracuse, the population center of Gary Lee's district. Angoff hardly expected to shame Lee into abandoning his advocacy of the AMA exemption, but he sought to make certain that Lee experienced sufficient pain to check others who might be tempted to follow his example. The ultimate pain, of course, was electoral defeat. Angoff knew that Washington perceptions of political power were often grounded in myth, such as the prevailing myth that a popular senator, Maryland's Joseph Tydings, was defeated in 1968 solely through the organized wrath of the National Rifle Association. Political savants believe that Tydings was an extremely vulnerable candidate that year, with a multitude of other political liabilities, but the myth of NRA political potency still draws upon the Tydings legend. Though beating Gary Lee might create a similar myth, it seemed only a remote possibility.

But once again, Angoff could build upon a foundation laid by Jack Anderson and his investigator Tony Capaccio. On October 31, 1981, in a column carried by the Syracuse *Herald-Journal,* Anderson attacked the used car lobby—and Gary Lee:

On the House side, the No. 1 water boy for the dealers is the obscure Gary Lee, R. N.Y. In 1980, he received one of his largest contributions: $3,000 from the used car lobby.

Then, on February 18, 1982, Capaccio and Anderson unearthed more about Lee's relationship with the auto dealers:

The usual response of legislators caught accepting favors from an industry representative is that their votes are not for sale—at least not for the price of a fancy meal or a weekend in the sun. Yet the buddy-buddy relationship between lobbyists and lawmakers can't help but look suspicious to the public.

Take the case of Rep. Gary Lee, R. N.Y., the car dealers unabashed waterboy in the House. Last month, at the height of the Caribbean tourist season, Lee and his aide, Harry Bellardini, spent ten days with their wives in Freeport, Bahamas, in a condominium partially owned by an upstate New York attorney named Richard Malcolm. The party of four paid a bargain rate of $300 for the condo.

The landlord-tenant relationship also extends to Lee's district office in Auburn, N.Y. He rents the office from a company in which Malcolm is a partner.

What makes this interesting is that Malcolm is the co-owner of University Toyota of Syracuse, N.Y., which is a member of the National Automobile Dealers' Association. This industry group has led the fight against the proposed used car regulation—and has contributed heavily to congressional campaigns through its political action committee.

Malcolm denied that he has lobbied against the FTC rule, and told my associate Tony Capaccio, "I haven't talked to Lee for a long time." The Congressman said there was no conflict of interest, because he paid his share of the condo rent and hadn't talked to his landlord about the used-car rule anyway. His aide, Bellardini, said Rep. Lee had had nothing to do with the vacation arrangements, and added, "I have known Malcolm for a number of years."

Angoff set out to make Lee less "obscure," at least to his constituents. He searched out Washington-based reporters for newspapers in Lee's district and called editorial writers to chronicle Lee's relationship to the dealers and doctors. In Syracuse, the *Herald-Journal* was also hearing from local representatives of the American Nurses' Association, a strong pillar of the coalition.

On August 3, 1982, the *Syracuse Herald-Journal* delivered itself of an untempered editorial labeled: "Phony: FTC exemption legislation not really deregulation." The editorial hit all Miller's themes (and even quoted me as calling the Senate committee vote "a tribute to the naked political power of the American Medical Association . . ."). Then it concluded:

And who is one of the two prime sponsors of the House legislation? None other than central New York's own Congressman Gary Lee. A group called Congress Watch, which monitors campaign contributions, says that over the last three years, 155 of the 160 sponsors in the House received more than $800,000 from medical and dental associations and related groups.

Obviously, our question to Gary Lee is, "What gives?"

When the smoke of the primary battle cleared, Wortly had defeated Lee—by 256 votes!

No newspaper in the country had expressed more exquisite outrage at the AMA campaign than the *New York Times,* which, on this issue, had spoken with a passion and earthiness, more characteristic of the *Daily News,* likening the AMA campaign to "Abscam-style bribery," citing the upcoming AMA votes as a contest of "conscience or cash," and concluding, "This is one doctor's bill there is no reason to pay."

Angoff and I conferred, and it was my pleasant task to call Peter Passell of the *Times's* editorial board to draw his attention to Gary Lee's defeat—and the Congress Watch-inspired activity that had preceded it. On September 28, the *Times* editors summed up "The lesson of Representative Lee: Opportunistic congressmen who flack for special interests may wind up paying for their jobs."

I was, of course, delighted. Angoff was also delighted, but sheepish. He wasn't convinced that we really could claim credit for Lee's defeat. I argued that the news and editorial flack and the radio barrage that Angoff had generated must have influenced at least 256 votes.

On October 2, the *Syracuse Post-Standard* reproduced the *Times* editorial, and concluded with its own postscript: "We couldn't have said it better, ourselves."

The FTC's public affairs office reproduced heavy stacks of editorials and Angoff and his interns made the rounds, ensuring that every congressional office saw them:

You don't want to be heavy-handed. We just had a big package of editorials which, wherever we lobbied, we would take with us. We'd put the local paper on top. So, for example, if we wanted to see George Wortley, the guy who beat Lee, we'd put the Syracuse paper on top, and we wouldn't have to say much.

It had to get around.

Angoff's media campaign, amplified by direct calls, visits, and mailings to each member of Congress, began to take firm hold by mid-summer. Erosion of AMA support had set in. Congressman James Florio of New Jersey, a fierce and effective opponent of the AMA's grab, told the Associated Press that, "he knew of at least 12 congressmen listed as co-sponsors of the bill who have now decided to vote against it."

[Angoff] *There was a two-tier strategy. On the one hand, the strategy in the press was to talk about the money as much as possible and to make that the issue. On the other hand, when we were lobbying people face to face, we never mentioned the money. But, a lot of times, members would bring it up. There were many guys who said, "The AMA doesn't support me anyway, so the money is nothing." The members were so aware of the money.*

On September 18, the *National Journal*'s Michael Wines, who had kept a close pulse on the FTC's prospects in Congress, reported that, "the exemption is still popular, but its success is far from assured." He quoted "consumer lobbyist" Jay Angoff as predicting the AMA's defeat, and concluded:

If Angoff is right, his victory will be due not to high pressure lobbying but to the adept use of that rarest of political weapons: public opinion. Foes of the exemption have been masterful in generating public awareness of an issue that few had heard of six months ago. And supporters of the measure were slow to react.

Unhappily, the chronic congressional aversion to biting the bullet—this time for fear of antagonizing either the doctors or aroused citizen constituents—led congressional Democrats to convince Speaker O'Neill to postpone the AMA amendment vote until after the election.

This greatly disappointed the coalition, since they feared that by the time the bill came to a vote in the lame duck session, the immediate pressure on AMA supporters would be off, and defeated lame ducks could vote for the AMA without the slightest fear of retribution.

Nevertheless, while the decision to put off the vote may have vitiated the pressures of an imminent election, the damage was more than offset by the still rising crescendo of editorial indignation. Nowhere was this more palpable than at the *Washington Post.*

MEANWHILE, BACK AT THE *POST*

Washingtonians, especially new or uneasily settled ones, ritually revile the *Washington Post.* The Right knows that the *Post* is the Enemy. The Left is convinced the *Post* has been seduced by Yuppie neo-liberalism or has otherwise subordinated its journalistic creed to the cash flow needs of security analysts. I, myself, love and hate the *Post.* I hated the *Post* when, with its profitable TV stations tucked under its corporate wings, it scorned our efforts to restrain children's advertising and cursed the FTC indelibly as the would-be "National Nanny."

But I loved the *Post* when it roundly condemned the concept of an FTC exemption for the professions, just as soon as that initiative surfaced in 1979 and thereafter, with commendable vehemence.

Yet it took Angoff's priming to stimulate the *Post*'s perception of the AMA campaign as an emblem of campaign financing corruption.

As the AMA effort took root in early 1982, its progress through committee was amply monitored by the *Post*'s FTC beat reporter Caroline Mayer, who, in stories on March 11, March 24, April 27, and May 12, faithfully sampled quotes from the measure's opponents—but recounted neither AMA lobbying nor campaign contributions. Angoff's March study and release had evidently not yet breached the *Post*'s consciousness.

And on June 2, when the *Post* delivered itself of its first critical editorial of the season, it demolished the arguments of the AMA in workmanlike fashion, dismissing the amendment as a "terrible idea," but, again, mentioning neither lobbying nor money.

Angoff struck gold ink, however, with his June update. Under a two-column head, "Medical Societies Aided Backers of FTC Curbs," Caroline Mayer laid out the numbers, and counterposed quotes from Angoff and AMA's Executive Vice-President James Sammons, uttering the ritual, tepid disclaimer that it was " 'a disservice' to members of Congress to link their actions with campaign contributions."

Mayer's article was the first of no less than fourteen news articles, columns, op-ed pieces, or editorials highlighting or condemning the AMA's lobbying and campaign contributions, which would appear in the *Post* before that fateful morning when Rudman rose to slay the AMA dragon.

There was a generic lobbying story on business PACs, by Paul Taylor, on July 27, which featured AMPAC (the American Medical Political Action Committee) as the top PAC contributor.

There were separate op-ed columns on September 12 and September 17, by Senator Howard Metzenbaum and Congress Watch's Joan Claybrook and Nancy Drabble entitled, respectively, "Monopoly for Everyone" and "It's Harvest Time for the PAC-men."

On September 15, under the wry headline, "Doctors Want the Federal Trade Commission to Take a Powder," the *Post* gave skeptical coverage to the AMA's responses. The *Post*'s Paul Taylor and Caroline Mayer reported verbatim such scholarly responses by the AMA's leaders to criticism of its campaign, as "pure, unadulterated nonsense" and "a bunch of baloney."

On September 28, Angoff scored again, as the *Post*'s Christine Russell, under a three-column head on page 2 ("Typical Doctor Earned Over $86,000 in '81") reported on Congress Watch's recycling of the Medical Economics study "publicized yesterday by Public Citizen's Congress Watch."

That article, in turn, led to an editorial the following day extol-

ling the virtues of medical competition, and highlighting "the average doctor's income at $86,000," a figure well calculated to
evoke the latent populist animus of congressmen and women
whose annual salary was only $60,662.50.

On October 20, *Post* columnist Judy Mann (echoing the well-
wrought arguments of my FTC colleague Pat Bailey) devoted an
angry column to the effort by physicians at a local hospital to deny
delivery room privileges to certified midwives. Mann related this
medical restraint of trade to the FTC's program and the AMA's
lobbying campaign, concluding:

> And when all is said and done, there will be two important lessons for
> consumers and voters: one is how the elite professions, faced with chal-
> lenges in the marketplace, fought back by trying to buy protective legis-
> lation from Congress. And the other will be how Congress, afloat in
> political contributions from these professions, reacts.

Two days later, Mann again went on the offensive, this time
taking off from the ratings by citizen groups, including Congress
Watch, of congressional voting records. Once again, Mann
stressed the relationship between money and votes, and, once
again, the AMA quest ranked high among PAC outrages.

As December and the lame duck session opened, Helen Dewar,
the *Post*'s House correspondent, reported the December 1 House
vote narrowly adopting the AMA exemption. By contrast with
the reporting of such action by the Senate committee earlier in
the year, her description of the action, while brief, did not fail to
include the now standard reference to lobbying and money:

> The doctors' exemption, for which the AMA lobbied with thousands
> of dollars in campaign contributions to supporters of its position, was
> approved after a 208–to–195 rejection of a substantially less-restrictive
> compromise.

The next day came a glorious Herblock cartoon. The scene was
a doctor's office: the patient, a befuddled congressman, knelt on
the examining table before a besmocked, smirking figure bearing
the sign: "AMA POLITICAL QUACPAC." In his left hand, the

patient held a jar containing a roll of bills, labelled "Take regularly." With his right hand, he was signing a receipt, promising "Whatever you fellows want." On the side, his nurse was explaining to a puzzled onlooker, "IT'S A MIRACLE DRUG CALLED MONEY."

On December 8, another editorial swipe. On December 15, another ferocious column by Judy Mann. And the same day, yet one more *Post* editorial was devoted to a critique of the AMA exemption: "among the worst legislation before Congress." The editorial did not fail to note that "the political action committees of the American Medical and Dental Associations have been among the biggest contributors to congressional campaign." This time the *Post* also sang the praises of the Rudman position as "entirely sensible to us."

Just in case anyone in the Senate might miss the point, Angoff issued another release that day, analyzing the votes in a preliminary Senate Appropriations Committee skirmish between Rudman and AMA supporters:

> Senators . . . supporting the AMA/ADA position—received an average of $10,014 from the AMA and ADA during their most recent election campaign; Senators voting [with Rudman] against the AMA/ADA position—received an average of $4,407 from the AMA and ADA during their most recent campaign.

Angoff considerately had copies of the release hand-delivered to every Senate office.

So, when Warren Rudman rose up on that chill December morning to share with his colleagues the nostalgia evoked by the spectacle of doctors making House—and Senate—calls, he did not speak to the unknowing. Though he spoke with ironic humor, the shadow of Congress Watch's single-minded evocation of money and votes darkened the debate. The AMA exemption had acquired, over the past six months, the unshakable odor of corruption. And the Senate, reacting, shunned it.

In celebration of the AMA's unaccustomed comeuppance, dreadful puns pealed out all over:

The *Washington Post* noted slyly that "for the first time in recent years, the vaunted AMA was reeling from severe legislative contusions."

"The doctors were lacerated," proclaimed the *Miami Herald*.

"Congress makes a healthy move," welcomed the *Atlanta Constitution* despite efforts by the AMA to change its motto to "Physician, well-heel thyself!"

I, myself, at a grateful FTC, was moved recklessly to predict that, thanks to Warren Rudman, Jay Angoff, Jim Miller, and their allies, the 97th Congress would go down in history as the "lame-Doc Congress" (though I prudently cautioned against the temptation to label the Senate's action "a bitter pill for the AMA, but a tonic for the Consumer").

And Mary McGrory wrote in the *Washington Post* that "the lame duck's shining hour meant so much to so many. It said, against much contrary evidence, that money isn't everything."

5

A "RATTLE-SNAKE INFESTED, INACCESSIBLE, _____ING PLACE"

SEDUCTION is a lobbying technique not normally embraced by public interest lobbyists, but the most seductive lobbyist in the campaign battle to save the wild Tuolumne River in California proved to be the Tuolumne River herself—though she needed a little help from her friends.

Ask Hope Babcock, normally a clear-eyed, sober lobbyist for the National Audubon Society. Audubon had always been ambivalent about opposing hydroelectric power, since it was a clean alternative to nuclear and coal—until, that is, Babcock fled Washington in late summer, 1982, for a white-water rafting vacation down the remaining wild stretch of the Tuolumne, where it flows out of Yosemite National Park through the Stanislas National Forest.

As she emerged from three days immersion in the wild, the crafty guide handed her a pamphlet, headlined: "The Tuolumne River—there are those who would stop its flow forever. But with your help, we can keep it alive!"

There followed a baleful tale of greedy dam builders and power developers poised to run amuck. And at the very bottom, the plea, "Join us," with a telephone number.

Still mesmerized by the river, Babcock called the number, found John Amodio, executive director of the Tuolumne River Preservation Trust in San Francisco, and volunteered Audubon's support and her services as Washington lobbyist. She still has that crumpled, once-soggy pamphlet tucked among the artifacts of a lobbying campaign that was to prove only slightly less bumpy— and exhilarating—than the ride down the river.

One of Tuolumne's great congressional champions, Don Edwards, remained unshaken in his commitment, though the river unceremoniously dumped him as the raft he was riding lurched into one of its most feared falls. He fought for the river, one of his staff members was to confess, because, "he really loved it." Most whose lives touched the river were smitten.

Actor Richard Chamberlain fished the river with his grandfather as a boy, rafted it as an adult, and, never before a political activist, was moved to come to Washington to speak in its defense. This is what he said:

About a year ago a bunch of my friends and I went white-water rafting down the magnificent Tuolumne River and I fell in love with her.

This feeling of deep caring for the river took me by surprise. I've had the good fortune to travel widely throughout the world, living and working in Europe, trekking in the Himalayas, traveling through the Orient, Indonesia, Australia, South America, Canada, and our own wonderful country. And I've rafted on the Rogue, in Oregon, and the Salmon River, but I didn't lose my heart until I experienced the unique and ravishingly beautiful Tuolumne.

Plunging down her rapids (some of the best and most exciting in the world), camping in the evenings along the gentle tributaries and lush forests, and fishing her abundant trout, I feel more whole and closer to the very source of nature than I'd ever felt in my life.

I don't want to see her destroyed.

To my eyes, God seems to have lavished a special abundance of loving gifts on the Tuolumne River and its surrounding wilderness. We have the power to destroy it, but never, never in our wildest imagination could we ever recreate it.

But not all were enamored. Ernest Geddes, the general manager of the Turlock Irrigation District, had never ridden down the river. But when he thought of it, which was often, he thought of untapped, low-cost power for the farms and homes of his rural county.

And there was little hope for my old friend Lee White, an otherwise estimable public servant and citizen, who, early in life, marched under the banner of public power and the grand New Deal vision embodied in the Tennessee Valley Authority. Alas, White's vision of social progress dimmed his aesthetic. As he confessed:

> When I first left Nebraska and went to work for TVA, I'd go to see those beautiful reservoirs in the Smoky Mountains. They are really spectacular.
> I like rivers; I like streams. But this is a rattlesnake infested, _____ing inaccessible place. The fight's all over now, but if you'll take a look at that river, you'll think, "Jesus Christ, they've got to be kidding!"

And so he readily took up the cause of California's Turlock and Modesto Irrigation Districts who hungered to gain access to the Tuolumne's low cost electric power still unharnessed, by becoming the chief lobbyist opposing "wild and scenic" status for the Tuolumne.

As White saw it, his clients, the irrigation districts, were public bodies with public interests to serve; many of the communities they served were economically stressed, and thus some of the benefits of new, low-cost power from the Tuolumne would have flowed to less affluent Californians (though their power costs were already among the cheapest in the nation). Of course, profit (some might say greed) doubtless spurred the would-be dam builders and developers, and tantalized congressmen who would benefit from their good will, expressed tangibly in the form of generous campaign contributions. And, as the campaign developed, it appeared that the benefits of Tuolumne power were likely to flow in largest measure to real estate developers.

The river had deep claims: it had already yielded much of its natural magnificence to water and power development. Shortly after the turn of the century, a new dam on the Tuolumne was proposed to Congress, a dam which would flood the great valley of the Hetch Hetchy to slake the thirst of an earthquake-parched San Francisco. The pioneer naturalist John Muir, who founded the Sierra Club, raged against the desecration of the Hetch Hetchy:

> *These sacred mountain temples are the holiest ground that the heart of man has consecrated. . . . These temple destroyers, developer devotees of raging commercialism, seem to have a perfect contempt for Nature, and instead of lifting their eyes to the God of the Mountains, lift them to the Almighty Dollar. . . . Dam Hetch Hetchy! As well dam for water-tanks the people's cathedrals and churches, for no holier temple has ever been consecrated by the heart of man.*

So John Muir smote the spiritual antecedents of Lee White. Muir was a determined lobbyist who stimulated the first (recorded) nation-wide letter writing campaign to Congress on an environmental issue.

But the dam builders struck back, artfully, in language worthy of White: "Convert the valley floor into a permanent mountain lake," they wrote, "and the valley will have a charm of its own." And far from diminishing the loftiness of the cliffs, the reflection from the waters would magnify the heights two-fold!

Muir himself was scorned by a scabrous-tongued Interior official as "so long in harmony with nature that he is out of touch with humanity."

In the grand American tradition of casual environmental exploitation, the consensus that "one Yosemite is enough" prevailed, and Muir was ignored.

By 1980, the Tuolumne had become a great workhorse of a river—harnessed to 90 percent of its potential. Its five dams provided two percent of California's electricity, irrigated hundreds of thousands of acres of agricultural land, and supplied water to one out of every ten homes in the state.

But 83 miles of free-flowing river and wilderness remained untamed—a haven for fishermen, rafters, and a handful of traditional family camps.

One might have hoped that the exploitive spirit would have modulated in the half-century since John Muir fought for the Hetch Hetchy. Indeed, in 1968, Congress passed the Wild and Scenic Rivers Act. This established a national policy and a legislative mechanism for selecting and designating the handful of remaining unspoiled rivers free from further exploitation.

Several were saved in the seventies. But none were protected by the Reagan administration, and none set aside by Congress since the fall of the Carter administration.

As those concerned about the fate of the Tuolumne surveyed the political terrain, they had before them a chilling precedent: the recent campaign to save the Stanislaus River, not far to the north of the Tuolumne.

For thirteen years, California conservationists had fought to save the wild Stanislaus River from the dam builders. They went to court, formed "Friends of the River" to campaign for a state-wide referendum. They lobbied, first the state legislature, then Congress—all to no avail.

By 1979, in desperation, one of their leaders chained himself inside the hidden cleft of a boulder on the banks of the river, daring the Army Corps of Engineers to flood the river and drown him. The corps was momentarily disconcerted and held back the flood, while Friends of the River seized headlines. It was heroic—and inspired! But it was not enough. Eventually, he was unchained; the Stanislaus Wild River Bill was not. The flooding was completed in 1981.

The champion of the dam builders was Congressman Tony Coelho from Modesto, whose irrigation district stood to benefit from the damming of the Tuolumne, as it had from the damming of the Stanislaus. White makes no bones about it; Coelho was their leader:

I've got to tell you. Tony was really heroic in the early stages. He was our leader, and he is one very, very bright cat. There's no question about it. The other congressmen liked Tony; especially they liked him when it came time to pass out the money.

Coelho was chairman of the Democratic Congressional Campaign Committee—"perhaps the most successful fund-raiser since Lyndon Johnson," judges the *Washington Post*'s Thomas Edsall. The land developers and dam builders were generous contributors to Coelho's campaign committee. There were few Democrats in Congress who didn't seek out Coelho's help at campaign time, and few who wouldn't look upon his views on a local California matter with grave respect.

The mostly young, somewhat anarchic, Friends of the River had proved no match for Coelho and the dam builders in the Stanislaus campaign. They never quite developed a coherent strategy. "Sometimes, it was bedlam," recalled one of their organizers.

Their zealousness was too often misdirected. They kept pressing those who were already committed, so that one staff member for a friendly congressman finally exploded, "Why are you seeing me again? Go see the opponents!" Yet, when they did reach out to conservative opponents and fence sitters, they failed to send reassuring emissaries. "You can't look like you're growing pot in Mendocino County," lamented a frustrated congressional supporter.

No one in Congress was more committed to their cause than the late Representative Phil Burton from San Francisco, but after a series of false alarms climaxed in a semi-hysterical late night phone call to Burton, whose wife was in the hospital, Burton almost soured on the campaign. John Amodio, a seasoned environmental campaigner who had played a peripheral role in the Stanislaus campaign, recalls:

The Stanislaus was a campaign run from the heart. But it didn't have the benefit of more experienced players to manage it. They were learning as they went along. They were doing a tremendous job, but they were always kind of desperate. The dam was being built and they were flailing away.

I knew the Friends of the River people who had led the Stanislaus campaign. I thought they had the most heartfelt spirit in that campaign that I'd ever seen. I loved them for their enthusiasm. But they had had

such personal relations with that river that they were going through a
personal grieving process. The organization as a result was diminished. A
lot of people had left.

Those that remained had too much luggage from that battle for them
to lead the Tuolumne fight. Even if they had the resources and retained
the staff, it could not have worked. The staff had become too controver-
sial. Friends of the River, as the lead organization, automatically would
have recast it as a replay of the Stanislaus.

Of course, most citizen campaigns are late starting, reactive,
and, hence, chronically frenetic. The campaign to save the Stanislaus didn't fully get under way until the dam was built, standing
there, beckoning to be filled.

There were those who thought the hour was equally late for the
Tuolumne. Though Congress had suspended development so the
government agencies could decide whether to recommend wild
river status for the Tuolumne, that suspension was scheduled to
expire at the end of 1982, unless Congress acted to designate the
river or extend the study period.

In the spring of 1981, a small group of environmental leaders,
remnants of the Stanislaus campaign, asked John Amodio to consider organizing a coalition or separate campaign organization
dedicated to the preservation of the Tuolumne.

Amodio might seem a curious choice. Though he had played a
minor role in the Stanislaus campaign, he was not a leader of any
of the organizations which had been prominent in the Stanislaus
battle. He had been an active leader of environmental causes, but
it was wild land, not water, which had engaged him. Amodio had
spent the last nine years in the far reaches of northern California's
Humboldt County, most of them in developing and coordinating
the campaign to expand the Redwoods National Park.

In turn, the wilds of Humboldt County and the Tuolumne
were a far reach from St. Anthony's High School in Trenton, New
Jersey, where Amodio held two school football records (most tackles in one game; most tackles in one season), and delivered the
student eulogy to the slain President Kennedy.

Before agreeing to take on the Tuolumne campaign, Amodio spent several weeks talking to environmental leaders and potential supporters. He met a good deal of skepticism.

I talked with one of our early key supporters in San Francisco . . . a county supervisor and she said, "Geez, our people in Washington tell us that this isn't going to go anywhere. There's no way it's going anywhere." They had their ears to the wind, and the word was "Hell, first of all you've got Tony Coelho, who's against you. You've got agriculture; they're not only the top economic special interest in California, but they have a lot of clout in Washington nationally. You know this just can't happen."

Amodio took the job, anyway, relying upon his "gut-level feeling that we could go against the odds and prevail. It had all the elements of a classic campaign. But I didn't think it was anything approaching a cakewalk. It had lots of problems."

Amodio didn't exaggerate when he concluded that the campaign he was about to undertake would not be a "cakewalk." If it were to succeed, it had to overcome the mood and expectation of failure: the legacy of the Stanislaus campaign. The campaign had to dispel the prevailing public and political perception that wild river preservation efforts were the special interest pursuit of commercial white-river rafters and their very elite clients, set against the broader interests of working, water-consuming, and energy-using peoples.

Aligned against the river, along with Coelho and the developers, were Reagan's secretary of the Interior, James Watt, who doubtless would have viewed John Muir as a dual agent of Satan and the Red conspiracy, and the new Republican leaders of the Senate Energy and Natural Resources Committee and its key Public Lands, Reserved Water and Resource Conservation Subcommittee: Senators James McClure of Idaho and Malcolm Wallop of Wyoming, no-nonsense westerners for whom land and water ached for development.

The campaign had also to contend with the other priorities—

even the ambivalence—of major environment groups, whose preoccupation with the hazards of nuclear power led them to view hydropower and the dams that produce "clean energy" almost as benignly as Lee White did.

Before signing on, Amodio exacted agreement on a series of conditions he deemed essential to success (and his sanity). Amodio had enough experience to know what he wanted:

I had run a primary campaign for a Democratic candidate for Congress. But the candidate was unwilling or unable to delegate authority and I had been frustrated because I couldn't get done the things that needed to get done.

By contrast, my first professional conservation work was as executive director of a very small non-profit up in the boonies. I had real authority with no real supervision. I could have done with some more training and guidance, but that wasn't to be had and so I had a lot of self-learning. I really came to believe in my abilities as an organizer. There's a part of me that's operating that doesn't necessarily lend itself to rational analysis. At some point you have to take those leaps of faith and act and you have to have the authority to do so.

Amodio had also worked for a while with the Sierra Club and he had observed the workings of Friends of the River, both of which were to be central participants in the Tuolumne campaign:

I left the Sierra Club partially because I found it a bit maddening to deal with the constant overview, questioning, justification that was structured into their volunteer leadership. Friends of the River was a consensus group. I mean, beyond the Sierra Club in some ways. They always wanted to discuss things and make sure everyone agreed. Both of those were far from my style and not what I felt was needed. What was needed was a lean, small organization—without the time or resources to go through these more elaborate processes.

They were going to have to view the director as kind of like the captain of the ship and, if they didn't like where I was taking it or how I was taking it, they would be better off getting a new captain and having a different structure.

Amodio recognized that it was a virtue that he did not come from any of the groups associated in the campaign. As a credentialed environmentalist, he would be substantively trusted, and no one would fear his tilting toward one or another of his constituent groups.

Amodio's model was the well-oiled political campaign, and to bring home the analogy, he first chose the title, "Campaign Manager." And he gained the authority he sought.

CAMPAIGN SNAPSHOTS

The Tuolumne campaign shared many of the same qualities as the campaigns we've already looked at—above all the salience of uncommonly committed congressional leaders. California's Democratic Senator Alan Cranston and Rep. Sala Burton, Phil Burton's widow, along with other members of the Bay area delegation, especially Reps. Don Edwards, Norm Mineta, and Ron Dellums—concerned about the preservation of family camps along the Tuolumne—formed a united Democratic bloc in opposition to Democrat Coelho. And the congressman newly elected to represent Tuolumne County, Rick Lehman, exercised no small heroism in supporting wild river status—defying the Tuolumne County Board of Supervisors and powerful development interests within the district. Relatively early in the campaign, two key Republican congressmen also took the plunge into wild river support: Robert Lagomarsino and Edward Zschau, from Santa Barbara and Palo Alto, respectively—a key bridgehead to uncommitted Republican Senator Pete Wilson.

They will, nonetheless, remain essentially unsung. For they simply could not have defeated Coelho and the dam builders' lobbying and congressional support network without the campaign conceived and deftly executed by the lobbyists, Amodio and Babcock, and the campaign organization, the Tuolumne River Preservation Trust. For it was a gem of a campaign, especially in the painstaking care with which the campaign organization was built and reached out for broad and diverse support, and in its thematic focus and media strategies.

As the campaign moved into high gear, Amodio seized upon successive tactical goals and pursued them relentlessly—especially the mini-campaign to gain the support of Senator Wilson, the tactical deployment of Richard Chamberlain to move the Senate subcommittee, and setting the stage for the felicitous self-destruction of Congressman Coelho. And these are the campaign snapshots we're going to take a look at.

THE CAMPAIGN ORGANIZATION AS ECOSYSTEM

Public interest lobbyists do not generally come in patient, reflective guises. Amodio surely didn't. But he restrained his impulse to flail against the bulldozer and set forth, instead, upon a deliberate, measured course. He concluded that the Stanislaus campaign had suffered greatly from being portrayed in the press, and perceived by policy makers, as "a white-water boating issue":

Stanislaus was far more than that but it never got recognized to be more than that. We needed to upset the stereotypes, to overcome the media clichés which unfairly described and terribly burdened the Stanislaus campaign efforts. The Tuolumne deserved and needed an identity of its own, not a knee-jerk reaction to it as "another river issue."

We needed to establish public support as broad and diverse as the river's own range of uses and values. We were committed to expanding our own support network. As with natural ecosystems, the more diverse the community, the stronger it is.

But to build such an "ecosystem" required time. And Amodio concluded that all of 1982 was needed. Even though the congressional restraints on Tuolumne development would expire at the end of '82, he determined that the campaign could not be fought in '82—but should be ready to emerge "strong and early" in 1983. "That made some people very nervous," recalls Amodio:

> Some of the people who moved from the Stanislaus to the Tuolumne were those who were most nervous and anxious to see us do something, "Okay, when's something going to happen? Come on John. Time's running out. Protection's expiring. . . ."
>
> So we had a little struggle within the organization to have people accept that we were much better off—not biding our time—but using our time for foundation building.

An early Amodio memo on recruiting for the executive committee suggests the care with which the group painstakingly built its new superstructure. He looked to recruit such political and financial ballast as "a partner in a large San Francisco law firm, well connected with the foundation world," "a *bona fide* 'fishing fool' who owned a 'little oil company,' " and "a major stockholder in American Motors, an avid fisherman, and active conservationist."

Amodio wanted board members "who possessed at least two of the three 'W's—Work, Wisdom, or Wealth." And he especially sought out "risk-takers" and those whose "can do" attitude would "infect others. . . . I really wanted people who were not only experienced, but experienced with winning."

The early campaign may have been publicly understated, but Amodio was indefatigable in his weaving of a supportive network:

> While I was hired in large part due to my experience in organizing, lobbying, and media work, I found myself completely over my head in certain aspects of the campaign. Even our board, with its diversity of experience and skills, lacked some insider political knowledge and experience. We compensated for this by development of a "kitchen cabinet" set of advisers whom we would informally keep in the loop—ranging from aides to several of our key congressional supporters to experienced strategists for major conservation groups to people whose identity we must still keep under wraps, such as "Deep Trout" and the "Shadow."

Amodio revealed that "Deep Trout" was "someone working within the state government when we were first organizing. On his own personal time, he was very instrumental in founding the organization, but to have been an overt founder would have compromised his position. So, respecting his needs, I just started to refer to him in memos as 'Deep Trout.' "

The Shadow was a "Washington lobbyist, although born in California, with roots in California conservation." He was to instruct Amodio on the political uses of the door-to-door canvass, which he had successfully employed in regional issue advocacy campaigns, and which he advocated as a means of softening up Coehlo.

In Washington, there was also Scootch Pankonin, a political consultant who had worked for Senate Energy and Natural Resources Committee chairman, James McClure of Idaho, and now represented western river guides. She was to make "critical connections" with McClure and other conservative western Republicans, hold small dinners for key staff, a gala reception for over 300 of the Capitol Hill star-struck, presenting Richard Chamberlain live in her home three blocks from the Capitol. She was, says Amodio, "an ace who was always available, and who provided access, insight, and credibility."

Amodio pursued his "diverse ecosystem" in ways that startled and troubled many of the pure at heart. Of course, no one was disturbed when such recreational users of the Tuolumne as the fifty-year-old Berkeley Community Camp Grounds were drawn in; or the fishermen's group, California Trout; or Native Americans concerned with preserving what the campaign would describe as "the most extensive and least disturbed archeological remnants of the Miwok Indians, whose other ancestral remains are largely buried under reservoirs"; or Rosa Guin, a determined senior citizen activist in Harden Flat, a small river community which would have been partially inundated by one of the proposed development projects.

But the more politically partisan participants winced at the special effort Amodio made to enlist some of the very people who had led the fight to flood the Stanislaus. Among them were two men whose testimony at hearings helped convince Congress to flood the Stanislaus. One was Don Moyer of California Trout. The other was Cliff Humphrey, who was the founder of the Ecology Action Institute in Modesto and the founder of the first recycling center in California. Their testimony in support of the damming of the Stanislaus had been particularly damaging because of their conservation credentials. But Amodio understood that their support for damming the Stanislaus in turn strengthened their credibility in supporting wild river status for the Tuolumne. Amodio sought out Moyer, in particular, as "one of our premier witnesses because he was so affable, down-home, just funny."

Recruiting the network was one thing, keeping it humming, quite another. Amodio set out not only to keep his board members and associated groups informed, but so informed that "they could not ignore us." Such "memo madness" was directed both at those who were already committed to the campaign and those Amodio sought to draw further in. To this hotshot list went twice-monthly bulletins with the latest strategic briefings, salted with news clippings selected to heighten excitement about the effort. After months of such barrages, even lukewarm recipients became *"de facto* members of our effort."

THE MEDIA CAMPAIGN

"Ink" is the public interest lobbyist's holy grail. Almost any media coverage of a campaign is panted after. Private interest lobbies often wince at publicity; but not citizen lobbies. All public interest advocates are confident that right would prevail "if the people only knew."

"Given the facts of the situation," says Amodio, "we know that the general public will strongly support preserving such special natural areas."

So for a citizen's lobby to gear down its media outreach is ordinarily unthinkable. But that is precisely what Amodio did, at first. "Of course, we were looking for any media exposure we could get in the right time frame. But for a long time, for that first year and a half, we avoided the media. We didn't even want the issue to become prominent because we weren't organized or strong enough."

It was first necessary to recast the image of the campaign, and the first step in that recasting was the choice of a name for the organization. This was the first major decision taken under Amodio's direction, and it was approached with the care Proctor and Gamble lavishes on a new soap. Discarded along the way were some sylvan and romantic contestants: "River of No Return," for example, and "Misty fjords," but romance gave way to pragmatism in the form of the stolid "Tuolumne River Preservation Trust." "Preservation" was a term which elicited a high positive response in public opinion polls. "Trust" evoked the conservative image of grey flannel-suited bankers conserving ancestral estates, not the Mendocino pot cultivators associated with the Stanislaus.

Next came the campaign slogan.

"There's too many god-damn dams in this country!" thundered the founder of Earth First, a militant environmental group, at a rally late in the campaign. "For Earth First, it's not enough to prevent further dams on the Tuolumne. We'd like to see O'Shaughnessy (the Hetch Hetchy dam) taken down!"

That millennial battle cry was not precisely the tone Amodio had in mind. So he took care to differentiate the Trust from the apocalyptic warriors of Earth First—though he valued their presence as a reminder to the recalcitrant of the potential disruptive civil disobedience, or worse, of the wild river lovers. He appeared at their rally, but proclaimed himself the square spokesman for the "namby-pamby, middle of the road."

Amodio's themes ran to balance, reasonableness, sharing: given that the Tuolumne was already a hardworking river, the remaining stretch should be preserved.

The chosen slogan of the "namby-pamby, middle of the roaders" "THE TUOLUMNE: LEAVE IT AS IT IS." There were good dams and there were bad dams. But now, for the Tuolumne, "Too much of a good thing can be very wrong and bad."

The irrigation districts were portrayed as the extremists. "They were the ones being greedy," Amodio would argue. "They were the ones seeking to have it all. It made people angry to think that the river could be so well-balanced, yet there were those who wanted to have all of it for their exclusive use."

Amodio could tell that his symbols were firmly in place when a California magazine headlined its account of the Tuolumne struggle, "Why not take all of me?"

By the fall of 1982, Amodio was ready to convey these themes and symbols both directly, to the public, and indirectly, through a systematic cultivation of the media.

The Trust developed a series of precisely targeted "propaganda" pieces: a boater's brochure, one for fishermen, and another for family campers. There was a sober document addressing economic and energy issues. There was a pictorially evocative black and white general purpose brochure designed by a professional graphics designer. And a slide show profiling the cross section of appealing Californians whose lives would be debased if the river were dammed. And there was an elaborate "Opinion Leader" information kit.

Much of the media work was contracted out to specialists, including graphic designers, direct mail specialists, and an allied environmental group specializing in door-to-door canvassing. For "major media cultivation," the Trust relied on Don Briggs, a well-known environmental activist, journalist, and photographer, who was so creative and energetic in pursuing favorable press coverage that Amodio labelled him the "Reggie Jackson" of the campaign.

They sent carefully picked teams to talk to editorial boards. To the chauvinist, reactionary *San Francisco Chronicle* they dispatched the conservative president of the San Francisco Board of Supervisors. She was hardly a typical supporter, but she had, discovered Amodio, "grown up on the Tuolumne and loved it." That sortie would be followed up by a visit from "one of the most successful businessmen" in San Francisco.

They didn't fully succeed in binding the *Chronicle* to their cause, but they did gain its editorial blessing for their basic theme of fairness and balance—and gained the full support of every major paper in the state, except for the *Modesto Bee,* in the heart of the irrigation districts.

Towards the end of November, 1983, a series of slightly bizarre headlines began appearing in newspapers all over California, and, the next week, there was an outbreak of similar news tidbits throughout the country:

CORNNUTS TO THE RESCUE OF THE TUOLUMNE

CORNNUTS MAKER WARNS 20 MILLION OF TUOLUMNE DAMS

CORNNUTS ENTER FIGHT OVER TUOLUMNE RIVER

CORNNUTS JOINS FIGHT FOR RIVER

RIVER PRESERVATION BROUGHT TO YOU BY CORNNUTS, INC

FOR $2, YOU CAN SPONSOR A TROUT

A NUTTY PLAN TO KEEP MORE DAMS OFF A RIVER

SNACK FOOD FOR THOUGHT AND PROTEST

The Cornnuts campaign was a direct outcome of Amodio's methodical board-building process. He had persuaded Maurice Holloway, a strong conservationist and the owner of Cornnuts, to be on the board of the Trust. Holloway and his advertising agency came up with the idea of putting the Tuolumne message on the packages, and about 20,000,000 such messages were printed and distributed. And by the time the labels made news—and highlighted the Tuolumne campaign—the campaign in Washington had gathered momentum and now, says Amodio, "any type of general publicity was in our favor."

As an unexpected dividend, the Cornnuts proved as handy a Washington door-opener as a hefty campaign contribution. "It was fun to take them around in Washington," recalls Amodio. "There were a few congressional offices that wouldn't talk to me unless I brought them their box of Cornnuts."

Where did Amodio get the money for so sophisticated a campaign? Mostly, imagination substituted for cash. The Cornnuts campaign cost the Trust nothing; it even raised a few thousand dollars in contributions.

Of course, unlike many citizen campaigns, the Trust could count on the modest, but direct, financial stake of the Commercial Outfitters—which was crucial in funding the campaign's start-up costs. But the outfitters' share dropped from 80 percent during the first six months to less than 10 percent in the second full year. How did they raise the rest of the $400,000 dollars needed for the full three-year campaign? By risking limited funds on the hiring of a fund raiser; by hustling small fund-raising dinners, and large; by raffles, river trips, and a T-shirt; and by professional direct mail and targeted foundation and large donor outreach.

The Trust would probably have been crippled without the $100–150,000 a year it raised. But that sum was dwarfed by the $130,000 each month that the irrigation districts were spending on lobbying and public relations. A reminder of the relative sparseness of material resources available to the Trust leaps out from the pages of an elaborate battle plan in which, as Amodio spells out the need to meet in Washington "to refine our legislative strategy," he pauses to note, "It is also a cheap flight time, being only $99.00 each way."

The dam builders paid well for public relations counsel and advertising, but their campaign dissipated into the air. Coelho became so frustrated at the contrast that he challenged witnesses for the irrigation districts, in hearings, to defend the quality of their campaign: "[They] have been able to out-P.R. you, and out-manipulate the facts."

FOR THE HEART AND MIND OF PETE WILSON

By January 1983 Amodio was ready. Out went a memo to the "Hotshot List:"

To: BOARD AND SPECIAL FRIENDS
From: JOHN AMODIO
Memo Subject: FOCUS! FOCUS! FOCUS! 1983–1984: THE
                 YEARS OF THE TUOLUMNE

The overriding message of this outline of our campaign strategy is that our time has come. A combination of good work on the parts of many and good luck has made the issue "ripe" for political action.

It is my very firm belief that if we effectively mobilize and efficiently harness the widespread beneficiaries of the natural Tuolumne, that we can succeed this Congress. Conversely, if we fail to focus our attention and resources now, then the protection effort shall languish. As with any harvest, if you don't work while the picking is good, the fruit rots. Enough allegories. Down to the specifics.

Amodio's memo spelled out a comprehensive strategy. It included not only lobbying targets but media initiatives, organizational and fund-raising imperatives, and the pursuit of a major foundation grant to the prestigious Environmental Defense Fund —to a grant support a technical study of possible alternatives to meet the genuine energy and water needs of the irrigation districts.

The political objective of the campaign was the isolation of Coehlo. This was to be achieved by continuing the process, already well under way, of gaining the support of every possible member of California's congressional delegation.

In 1982, quietly and painstakingly, Amodio and Babcock had coordinated targeted campaigns tailored to each remaining uncommitted member.

Lee White acknowledges, "they did a little bit better job in discovering the need to work the California House delegation a little bit quicker than we did."

Now, in the center of the political cross-hairs was the single most important uncommitted California legislator, newly elected Senator Pete Wilson, the former Republican mayor of San Diego, who had just defeated a strong environmentalist, former Governor Jerry Brown. With Republicans in control of the Senate, Wilson's support, coupled with the ongoing support of Democratic Senator Alan Cranston, was essential to Senate movement, and a key to the isolation of Coehlo within the California delegation.

By February the Trust's paper barrage was rolling: "Newsflashes" to journalists and editorial writers; "urgent" calls to action to all friends of the Tuolumne; op-ed pieces, magazine stories, letters to the editor, packets for editorial writers. And all were focused on Pete Wilson. A February "Newsflash" contained the headline: THE NEXT STEP: SENATOR PETE WILSON

The centerpiece of the Wilson campaign was "Republican Friends of the Tuolumne."

Here is where Amodio's conservative outreach came into play. One letter from prominent Republican hotshots went out to all Republicans living in areas demographically identified as "environmentally supportive" who had contributed more than $500 to Wilson's campaign—and another, thanks to Babcock, went to all Republicans in California on Audubon's membership roles.

The Republican Friends letter was signed by William Penn Mott ("Director, California Department of Parks & Recreation under Gov. Reagan, 1967–75") and Republican State Senator Peter Behr. Individually word-processed and warmly personalized, it was to elicit a higher response than even action alerts to Sierra Club members.

Imagine yourself a rock-ribbed, moss-backed Republican conservative, sitting down to a letter which began:

The Republican Party introduced Conservation to American Politics. We are the Party of Teddy Roosevelt and Gifford Pinchot, David Packard, Bill Ruckelshaus, and Laurence Rockefeller. In many respects, we have a better environmental record than the Democrats. Under Teddy

Roosevelt, we brought reason and restraint to the logging of America's forests and created millions of acres of National Parks and Monuments. Republicans opposed New Deal-era projects that turned out to be costly and destructive boondoggles.

Without a discernable missed beat, it even managed to invoke, for positive reinforcement, the environmentally dreaded James Watt:

Republicans have consistently opposed government subsidies to development in environmentally critical areas, such as barrier beaches, flood plains, and wetlands (as Secretary Watt has just done again).

There follow a few bars of "free enterprise" directed towards the socialistic public irrigation districts:

Nowhere, however, does the Republican Party have a more honorable conservation record than in its steadfast resistance to hydro-electric dams that sell dirt-cheap, uncompetitive public power at the expense of the nation's rivers, fisheries, and the private power market.

The praises of the Tuolumne are sung in muted terms of "balanced resource management."

The role of current California Republican statesmen is called:

To our party's credit, other prominent Republicans such as Congressman Robert Lagomarsino (the senior California Republican on the Interior Committee), Congressman Ed Zschau (who represents one of the irrigation districts) and Republican State Chairman Ed Reinecke already support protection of the Tuolumne.

And Pete Wilson is summoned front and center:

Yet, Senator Pete Wilson will play the decisive role in determining the future of the Tuolumne.

Pete is well aware of the issue, and has taken considerable time and effort in studying it. His office reports receiving more mail on the Tuolumne than on any other issue during his first year in office (over ninety-nine percent of the letters have supported preservation). We are increasingly optimistic that Pete is inclined to support the Tuolumne's protection. On the other hand, the two irrigation districts are financially and politically powerful, so it will not be an easy decision.

*At moments like this, the opinion and counsel of friends and support-
ers means much. We want Pete to know that those who support him also
support this key leadership commitment on his part.*

The letter closes with a word of reassurance from "a notable
sage of our party, George Will":

*Only 1.2% of the 'lower 48' states is wilderness; only 4% could ever
be so designated. Surely the nation's vitality and maturity are not so
marginal as to depend on that 4%. The same is even more dramatically
true for the few remaining wild rivers we can leave as a legacy to our
children.*

Enclosed was a card with a box to be checked "to include me as
a Republican Friend of the Tuolumne River," and another to
note "I am writing to Pete Wilson to request his leadership commitment on this timely and vital issue."

The pace of major articles and editorials stepped up as summer
came. If any emotional chords remained unplucked, they were
struck in a half-page column by Bill Mandel in the July 10th *S.F.
Sunday Examiner* and *Chronicle*, headlined, "Choosing Life
Over Death For the Wild Tuolumne River." First, Mandel drew
a logically weak, but symbolically potent, parallel between the
scandal that "previously secret Dow Chemical Co. documents
proved the firm knew dioxin could be fatal as early as 1967, but
continued to manufacture and market dioxin products anyway,"
and "the effort by the irrigation districts to dam the Tuolumne to
keep already cheap local utility bills low.' " The parallel? In each
case the question is raised whether "short-term business gain was
more important than human lives." Mandel zeroed in on Wilson:

*Senator Pete Wilson is considering supporting inclusion, but hasn't
made up his mind. If Wilson decides in favor of saving the Tuolumne,
it will probably be saved. . . .*
The choice, then, is up to Wilson and the people he works for—you.

Then Mandel recounted—not the thrills of white-water rafting
—but "some of the people whose lives would be impoverished if
the Tuolumne dies."

First stop was Camp Tawonga, run by the United Jewish Community Centers of the Bay Area, which sits on the Middle Fork of the River. The planned construction would dry the Middle Fork to a rivulet.

Hundreds of happy kids were singing camp songs at top volume during lunch Thursday. Director Judy Edelson spread tuna salad on white bread and explained what the Tuolumne means to the 600 kids who summer at Tawonga each year.

A few miles away, on the South Fork, sits Berkeley's Tuolumne Camp. The camp consists of large canvas tents—with decks, of course—grouped on rocky promontories on both sides of the river. There's a handful of beautiful '30s-style main buildings, all burnished wood and dark green trim. Open to any resident of Berkeley, the camp has been in operation for more than 60 years. Construction plans call for it to be under 200 feet of water.

Standing on a domed gray rock in the bright afternoon sun, occasionally getting hit by mist as the Tuolumne pounded through the camp, Emeryville fireman Mike McEneany looked back over his years there. "I'm 36 and I've been coming up here with my family for 33 years," he said. "There's a special spirit here in the trees with the river. There's a majestic sense of peace and harmony. It would be a crime to ruin this for a project that isn't needed."

Emotions in the nearby town of Hardin Flat (often spelled "Harden" on maps) aren't as Berkeley-bucolic. Hardin Flat would also be under 200 feet of water if the builders have their way. Doug Guinn, grandson of community activist Rosa Guinn, was talking with a neighbor in the small general store.

"I'll be out there with a flag to stop that dam," the neighbor said.

Guinn, in his mid-20s, was unimpressed. "Flag, hell," he said. "Whaddya think God invented the .30–.30 (caliber rifle) for?"

You can help the Tuolumne much more peacefully—by picking up a pen and telling Pete Wilson you want to save it for future generations. It will be a sad day on earth when the last rapids around are Tiger Mountain Rapids—a plastic ride at Marine World Africa USA.

One of the loyal campers at camp Tawonga was the daughter of Lee White's cousin. White notes, ruefully.

Carolyn, my cousin, said, "I trust you, and I'll be glad to have you come out and talk to our camp's executive director. But listen, you've got a problem, not only with everybody else. But my daughter, who doesn't *even know you, heard that a relative of mine was involved on the other side. She came steaming out of a camp reunion, slammed the car door and cried, "I hate Tony Coehlo, and I hate cousin Lee!"*

By the summer of 1983, Wilson's office was reporting a flood of more than 2000 letters a week pleading for preservation of the Tuolumne, more than on any other issue (including the MX missile or social security)!

One, not exactly typical, came from Charlton Heston, romanced by the river itself (and by an assist from his son, a partisan of Friends of the River). Heston, a political soul-mate of former fellow actor Ronald Reagan, had headlined major fund-raising events for Wilson during his 1982 senatorial campaign.

His letter is intimate, ("Thank you for your birthday phone call"), rhapsodic ("awesome experience of white water, still close to the way God made it . . ."), and hard headed ("The projects for harnessing the water that's still wild on the Tuolumne are not planned to grow food, but to provide enough power so farm land can be converted into residential tract housing . . .").

Wilson expressed a need for hard, analytical data. And the Trust was ready. The Environmental Defense Fund had just concluded its cost/benefit study, that artifice beloved of neo-classical economists and hard-nosed business types (especially when it confirms their prejudices about the insufferable costs of regulation). This study concluded, sonorously, "Based upon a rigorous assessment, utilizing conservative assumptions and widely accepted methodologies, the analysis indicates that the proposed Clavey-Wards Ferry project [the big dam] would result in a net loss of more than $26,000,000 per year."

Lee White and his clients, the irrigation district officials, had ample opportunity to present their case to Wilson.

[White] *We had 45 minutes, uninterrupted, with Wilson; there wasn't a phone call. I had never done that with a senator before. I will say Wilson was fair to us, giving us an absolutely clean shot at him. As we left, I said to Ernie (Geddes), "Now we're in trouble; cause if we lose, we won't have any alibis." But we did lose, and he made his own decision.*

No one, probably not Wilson himself, knows what part sober analyses and what part constituent energy and intensity played in his final decision. But Amodio and the Trust had unleashed them all. And on February 9, 1984, a full year after Amodio had focused the campaign on Wilson, Wilson endorsed wild and scenic status for the Tuolumne. From that point on Wilson fought strongly to get a protection bill through the Senate.

CHAMBERLAIN PACKS A WALLOP

But he needed help. "Tuolumne" may have become a household, if garbled, word in California, but it was hardly on the national agenda. And the guardians of developer interest in the Senate, Energy and Natural Resources Committee Chairman James McClure, and Public Lands Subcommittee Chairman Malcolm Wallop, displayed no intention of moving a Tuolumne protection bill. Wallop had scheduled hearings in early July to consider California wilderness legislation, but not the Tuolumne legislation.

Amodio ran into a stone wall with Wallop and his key staff member, Tony Bevinetto: "He didn't like the Tuolumne at all." Amodio even tried to appeal to his fellow American of Italian extraction on an ethnic note, "I even changed the name to 'Tuolumne' (rhymes with Spumoni), but he didn't go for it."

Babcock and Amodio cast about for some way to stimulate national media coverage to focus attention on Wallop's intransigence and build pressure to free the bill. Had any potential media stars gone down the river who might be willing to lend a hand, asked Babcock?

Well, recalled Amodio, Richard Chamberlain had indeed gone down the river a while back and volunteered help.

Amodio was not too excited about Chamberlain. He had probably been rafting down the river when the TV blockbuster miniseries "Thornbirds" had aired earlier that spring.

But Babcock knew it had been a smash hit, and Chamberlain was its very hot star. As she describes it, she went slightly beserk.

" 'That's it! That's it!' I yelled. 'Get on the phone right away! I don't care what else you do, get on the phone!' " And Chamberlain immediately said yes.

When the Wallop hearings convened in July, Chamberlain was there. Wallop and his staff were not pleased. Wallop was also not pleased that a hearing which was to have been devoted to broad issues of California wilderness was to be dominated by witnesses pressing for the saving of the Tuolumne. And he was not pleased that the expected national inattention normally paid such a hearing was blown by the clamour of the national press.

As the hearings proceeded and witness after witness pleaded for the Tuolumne, his face grew stonier and stonier.

Finally, Chamberlain testified. He had studied the briefing materials Babcock and Amodio had prepared for him, and would strike solidly their themes, but he wrote out his statement simply and directly in his own words, and delivered it looking Wallop squarely in the eyes.

There are customarily sober witnesses who report that Wallop's stoniness visibly melted away. No one will ever quite know what later moved him, without public explanation, to release his grip on the bill. What is certain is that Chamberlain's impact on the media environment surrounding the bill was palpable.

Chamberlain was featured in the *Washington Post*'s Style section, to which all Washington turns with an interest as avid as any aroused by the front page. He was on the networks. He agreed to appear on "Good Morning, America," willing to endure the usual intrusions into his personal life, but only on the condition that he be given time to talk about the river. He was shown riding down the Tuolumne in a sympathetic twelve minute segment on the campaign on the CBS Sunday Morning Show with Charles Kuralt.

"He got us more Aloha—friendship and good feeling—on the Hill than anything else up to that point," says Babcock, "And then the media interest was enormous! When he came and talked about the Tuolumne, he talked personally from his experience—

why it was important to him. That genuine concern came through, and it caught people. He fashioned a lot of the phrases that we later used in our literature. He became, as John Amodio said, the 'poet' of the river."

The Modesto and Turlock Irrigation Districts had ample political resources, but no poet. Lee White expressed great respect, and affection, for the general manager of the Turlock Irrigation District, Ernie Geddes, the chief witness for the opposition:

> Ernie's sort of the inspirational leader of this whole effort—one of the very engaging, slick country lawyers from Tuolumne County, up in the mountains. I thought he was a very credible spokesman because he is an intelligent man and a very decent sort of guy. Yet, to look at him, he is not what you would call a counterpart to Richard Chamberlain. We used to kid the hell out of Ernie about it.

> The idea of getting people like Richard Chamberlain and thereby public attention is not something that hasn't been done before, but they did it very skillfully, very adroitly, and it worked.

With Wilson lobbying hard on the "inside," Wallop and McClure allowed wild river designation to be attached to the California Wilderness Bill, which glided through the Senate on August 9.

COELHO AT THE BRIDGE

Meanwhile, in the House, Tony Coelho and his continuously shrinking band of supporters still stood in the path of the wild Tuolumne. By gaining Wilson's support and that of key Republican House members, the Trust hoped to isolate Coelho, and to undermine his near-mythical influence with other House members.

But Coehlo was not easily undone. When Wilson cast his lot with the Trust in February 1984, Coelho privately vowed to use his influence to block the Tuolumne bill, as an object lesson in power, "breaking in" the freshman Wilson. When asked about the fact that a majority of the California delegation supported wild and scenic designation, he replied coolly, "Well, there may be a majority supporting it, but I'm on the committee and the subcommittee, and that's what counts."

Congressional Quarterly reported that many otherwise sympathetic House members shied away from supporting wild river designation "because they were afraid to cross the campaign chairman." Amodio recalls:

There was this big, deep shadow of Tony Coelho. Everywhere we went, people were saying, "Well, Coelho doesn't like this, and he may stop anything that it's part of. You could take the whole California Wilderness Bill down with you."

I remember one neutral congressman, after we'd given a little pitch on the Tuolumne, leaned back and the guy said, "Well, you only have one problem on the Tuolumne and it's spelled C–O–E–L–H–O."

In January 1983, after quiet subterranean burrowing in the depths of the Reagan administration, Coelho announced that the Forest Service, which had previously been on record in support of wild and scenic status, now "agrees that it would 'be premature to take action to designate the Tuolumne River as a component of the National Wild and Scenic Rivers system until completion of the current studies. . . .' "

In March, Coelho sought to defuse (or confound) the pressure for preservation of the Tuolumne by introducing his very own bill "designed," in his own words, to provide "strict protection of the Tuolumne River as a scenic and recreational area."

The bill would not have satisfied even a generous truth-in-labeling law. Thus the *Sonora Union Democrat* led its news story on the Coelho bill with perceptible irony:

Reaction has been predictably mixed to Congressman Tony Coelho's bill to bar dams on the Tuolumne River except where his constituents want to build a hydroelectric project. . . .

The dam builders . . . hailed Coelho's bill as a "masterful solution to a very difficult problem."

Amodio responded:

We're calling it "Orwell's 1984 Wild and Scenic Bill" because it is a perfect example of doublespeak. If Congress is cynical enough to pass this, they'll have to rename it the "Wild and Scenic Ditch System."

But if not too many close observers were taken in, the Coelho bill at least served to muddy the legislative waters.

By May, Coelho had gained an important ally. The Reagan administration ignored Wilson's entreaties and asked Congress to delay action on wild river designation until dam feasibility studies were concluded. That was just fine with Coelho, who never openly opposed ultimate wild river designation. His tactic was to study and delay that designation.

But Coelho was becoming increasingly testy. And his macho defiance of his fellow Californians began to alienate otherwise sympathetic (or intimidated) colleagues. He disdained to consult with the new congressman and fellow Democrat, Richard Lehman, through whose district coursed the entire 83-mile wild segment of the river. Lehman had given quiet support to the wild and scenic campaign—at substantial political risk—but Coelho's heavy-handedness provoked Lehman openly to introduce his own bill.

This was precisely what Amodio and his colleagues hoped would happen—that Coelho would self-destruct. And they soon had a splendid opportunity to bring out the worst in Tony Coelho. The first and only time Coelho and the river's advocates were to meet in open combat was at the Tuolumne hearings, held by the House Interior Subcommittee on Public Lands, on May 3rd and 4th, 1984.

Babcock and Amodio structured their panel of witnesses, the lead panel, with exquisite care. In addition to Amodio and Babcock themselves, experienced witnesses representing, respectively, state and national constituencies, the California-based witness from the Sierra Club—a strong, nonpartisan political force in California—they included Rosa Guinn, the *sympatico* respresentative of those whose homes faced destruction by flooding. Richard Chamberlain, says Babcock, came last, "batting clean-up." This phalanx evidently unnerved Coelho.

Babcock *Tony Coelho basically lost his cool. Coelho picked on Rosa Guinn. He just unmercifully bullied her. And you can get a sense of it if you look at the pictures of the hearing. You see Richard interposing himself between Coelho and Rosa. He was physically trying to block the questions, they were so bad.*

He just made a very serious tactical mistake in beating up on this little lady who'd come all the way from Hardin Flat, California, to stop her house from going under water.

Coelho also attacked both Wilson and Amodio.

Amodio *Wilson kept cool, and kept his sense of humor. Coelho was losing his temper in the process. I almost lost mine. Afterwards, my temper said, "I should have just swung back at him!" I could have said these really smart things, but, instead, I kept it cool, and kept on trying to give him a factual response, and he kind of hung himself.*

Coelho's nastiness plainly offended the subcommittee chairman, John Sieberling, who, while a strong environmentalist, had been concerned that efforts to save the Tuolumne might overburden and derail the major California wilderness legislation he was shepherding through his committee. But he sought out one of his Republican colleagues after the hearing, and said, "I must apologize for my colleague. I'm appalled at how he behaved!" After the hearing, Babcock and Amodio sensed a subtle shift in Sieberling's attitude—from troubled resistance to neutrality—and that was important.

But Coelho still retained strong allies and a position of leverage on the House Interior Committee, with its disproportionate representation of western, development-minded congressmen.

It was two freshman legislators, Wilson and Sala Burton, who ended up teaching Coelho a modest lesson in parliamentary legerdemain. Coelho's first hope had been to bottle Tuolumne legislation up in his stronghold, the House Interior Committee, keeping it from the House floor. But Wilson managed to have the Tuolumne legislation attached to the California Wilderness Bill, which had *already passed the House.* And when the bill returned to the House, Burton artfully persuaded the House Rules Committee to send the bill to the House floor under a "closed rule," which would not permit Coelho to offer an amendment striking the Tuolumne portion of the overall bill.

At that point, Coelho faced two equally unattractive prospects should he challenge the bill: either he would be beaten by a vote of the full House, a possibility which Coelho's pride and ambition for party leadership could not accept, or he would win—thereby defeating not just Tuolumne wild river designation but the whole California Wilderness Bill. That feat, observes Amodio, would have made him "the Darth Vader of the California conservation community."

Coelho chose not to fight. He voted quietly for passage of the bill.

Congressional Quarterly quoted one observer: "Coelho's a smart guy. If you're not going to win, why make a lot of Democrats walk the plank on an important environmental vote?"

EPILOGUE

Amodio and Babcock and their colleagues won more than 83 miles of preserved river. In 1982, the Stanislaus campaign had not only failed, but left its scars: discouragement and disarray among the embattled Friends of the River, emnity and disdain among their adversaries. In the Tuolumne campaign, Amodio and Babcock and their colleagues not only helped revitalize a movement, but gained the respect of their adversaries.

[White] *The people on the other side did a hell of a good job—first, by concentrating a lot of different groups and pulling them together into the umbrella group; centralizing eliminated a hell of a lot of the rivalry, and the jealousy, and the confusion and the inefficiency. Next, they hired an individual whose sole job it was to run the campaign. It's always nice to have an individual in charge, whose sole measurement of his or her success is one very discrete undertaking. If I worked for the Sierra Club, Christ, I got a dozen of these issues. But if I'm John Amodio working for the Trust, I've got one damn thing to be tested on: did I win or lose? Of course, since John's the winner, that was the right way to have gone; but I do think it was the right decision.*

And they won without leaving bitterness in their wake. A few months after the Tuolumne campaign, the *Oakland Tribune* reported that the general manager of the Modesto Irrigation District, Les Brooks, had appealed to John Amodio for help in winning support for an alternate, geothermal energy project. The *Tribune* quoted Brooks: "I don't think anything will be able to mature from it, but at least we can talk. I have a lot of respect for his [Amodio's] approach."

The campaign reaped other fruits.

[Babcock] *Part of the selling of the Tuolumne to the national community, politically, as a national issue was: "The system's dying, and if we don't break the log jam with the Tuolumne, it's as good as dead; it's over; it's not going to work. The National Wild and Scenic River System is a nice idea, but if you can't designate these rivers, it's worthless. And if we're not going to protect our rivers, we're going to lose them one by one."*

So the Tuolumne was seen as the dynamite to break the log jam— and indeed, there is now a lot of momentum out there to move other wild and scenic rivers. Lots of legislation is being produced. There's lots of bustling around at the local, state, and national level. It can be done.

Amodio believes they reached even further:

The campaign helped teach that the remaining natural and recreational values of the Tuolumne far outweighed its potential development value. As more people strive to meet their recreational and natural needs in an increasingly developed world, the value of these benefits will continue to rise. In the words of David Brower, we owe it to fu-

ture generations "to stop taking the easy trip and charging it to the kids."

A few days after the bill was signed into law, Amodio was talking on the phone with Ernie Geddes, his erstwhile foe. "I asked him if he'd had a chance yet to go down the river. He said he had been meaning to. I told him he'd better hurry up. Then I realized he had plenty of time."

6

A NOT SO SPLENDID MISERY

THE VOTING RIGHTS ACT of 1965 transformed the southern electorate. By 1981 black voters had asserted their rightful place in the political life of the South. In 1965 only 29 percent of the eligible blacks were registered to vote in the states of the Confederacy. By 1980, 57 percent of black voters were registered. In the minds of many who followed the civil rights movement, it had been the most important—and the most successful—of all the civil rights laws. Americans had witnessed the dramatic growth of black voting power in the South and the ascendancy of black elected officials (such as Andrew Young as mayor of Atlanta), and assumed the job was done.

But the job was not done. While crude voter discrimination had largely been rooted out, subtler forms had evolved to blunt the awakened political consciousness and aspirations of blacks. The sophisticated southern voting official of the 1980s would leave no trace of discriminatory intent, but voting discrimination persisted under a variety of guises.

In Medina County, Texas, there were four attempted gerrymandering plans in seven years, to thwart the growth of Hispanic voting power. In Montgomery, Alabama, it was the imposition of a "re-identification" procedure which required all voters to re-register—with registration hours limited to 9:00 A.M. to 4:00 P.M.—an especially burdensome requirement for working blacks. Polling places were often still located in white stores and churches, chilling black voters.

In Aliceville, Alabama, white policemen were stationed inside polling places, taking pictures of those who attempted to assist black voters. In Pickens County, Alabama, the vote was not secret —no booths, no curtains, just an open table under the watchful eye of white officials.

The 1965 act contained a series of "temporary" provisions, applicable only to jurisdictions which had systematically excluded black voters in the past. In its most aggressive provisions, it placed 15 states of the old South under the close administrative supervision of the Civil Rights Division of the Justice Department in a rigorous regime of voting process restraints and requirements, from which other regions were largely free. It was these provisions upon which civil rights lawyers relied to strike down the new generation of more subtle voter discrimination techniques. These provisions required all such jurisdictions to "preclear" with the Justice Department, or the Federal Court for the District of Columbia, any proposed changes in their voting practices or procedures. But those preclearance procedures were considered temporary. They were initially scheduled to expire in 1970, were then extended by Congress to 1975, and were now scheduled to expire. The Voting Rights Act had to be renewed before August 6, 1982.

As the expiration date neared, the civil rights community began to organize a campaign to extend the preclearance provisions again. Their vehicle of coalition was the Leadership Conference on Civil Rights. Formed in 1950 by A. Philip Randolph, Roy Wilkins, and Arnold Aronson, the conference had coordinated the lobbying campaigns that led to all the civil rights laws of this century.

By 1975, the older civil rights groups had been joined in the Leadership Conference by Hispanics, Asian-Americans, native Alaskans, and native Americans as the Voting Rights Act was broadened to ensure their access to voting equality.

In 1981, 165 organizations made up the Leadership Conference; virtually all civil rights, labor, education, minority, women, disabled, senior citizen, and religious organizations belonged. The AFL-CIO (American Federation of Labor-Congress of Industrial

Organization) provided financial resources, organizational muscle, and lobbying depth and sophistication; the NAACP (National Association for the Advancement of Colored People), the National Urban League, and NOW (National Organization of Women)—intensely committed, sophisticated grass-roots networks. Other membership organizations varied greatly in their strength and level of commitment, but groups like the National Education Association and the League of Women Voters were formidable allies.

Clarence Mitchell, the longtime legislative chairman of the Leadership Conference, was legendary as a lobbyist who could open both conservative Republican and liberal Democrat doors and minds alike. He, and the conference, had built a broad, bipartisan national consensus on civil rights.

In mobilizing grass roots; in structuring the media; in formulating and implementing legislative strategy; in substantive expertise and legislative draftsmanship; in building and sustaining a close and trusting relationship with its congressional leaders; in seeking out, packaging, and coaching a knockout array of witnesses at a hearing—the Leadership Conference was unmatched. As we shall see in the next chapters, when the arms control community sought to organize to fight the MX missile, they turned to the Leadership Conference on Civil Rights as a model.

So the Leadership Conference of the 1980s seems more giant than giant killer—and that was due in part to the very success of the Voting Rights Act. In the South and Southwest, fear of minority voter reprisal now reinforced the abstract principle of equal access to the vote. Indeed, but there was no organized constituency opposed to the Voting Rights Act extension.

So why should the effort to gain a simple extension of the Voting Rights Act's temporary provisions qualify as "giant killing"?

First, the effort was burdened by public—and congressional—perceptions that civil rights "was done"; what was broken had been fixed. Congressmen who were neither southerners nor bigots questioned the continued need to stigmatize the old South with burdensome federal supervision.

Worse, the late seventies and early eighties had produced growing reaction to some aspects of civil rights reform, especially affirmative action, which in turn led to the rise of politicians for whom opposition to aggressive civil rights legislation was a central political cause.

That is why the conference suffered a major loss in the last months of the Carter administration as an important, but hardly radical, effort to strengthen the enforceability of the Fair Housing Act (by establishing an administrative remedy for individual victims of discrimination) fell victim to a skillfully implemented filibuster. In 1982 this filibuster was led, not by a leader of the vestigial segregationist South, but by an aggressive, ideological missionary of the New Right, Senator Orrin Hatch of Utah.

We witnessed Hatch in slow motion as an uninspired sponsor of the cigarette labeling bill. But as an opponent of effective civil rights enforcement, Hatch struck with the zeal of an Old Testament prophet. Simply because a pattern of discrimination existed, Hatch argued, was no justification for invoking the law. Only where an intent to discriminate could be proven should the dreadful hand of the federal government be invoked. He would not be moved by the learning of three decades of civil rights enforcement that piercing the minds of real estate agents or voting officials to establish their discriminatory intent to the satisfaction of courts and juries was a monumental, and often vain task. So Hatch had stood vigil and forestalled the Fair Housing Act amendments in the last days of 1980.

In January 1981, the civil rights community confronted the political ravages of the 1980 elections. They had lost a president, Jimmy Carter, with a commitment to civil rights, while the country elected Ronald Reagan who had opposed every civil rights act. And the new president, within a month of his election, signaled his doubts about those voting rights provisions which subjected the states of the old Confederacy to special supervision.

In the Senate, the Leadership Conference had been able to count on the unwavering leadership of Democrats Ted Kennedy of Massachusetts as chairman of the Senate Judiciary Committee, and Birch Bayh of Indiana as chairman of the Constitutional Rights Subcommittee. Now Bayh was gone, defeated. Kennedy had lost his chairmanship, as the Republicans gained a majority and took charge of the Senate. In Kennedy's place as committee chairman now sat Republican Strom Thurmond of South Carolina, leader in 1948 of the Dixiecrat rebellion against the civil rights policies of the Democratic party. From his new eminence, Thurmond vowed that either the preclearance procedures or the entire Voting Rights Act must go.

And that very same Orrin Hatch, who had employed such mastery of parliamentary mischief to lead the sidetracking of the Fair Housing Bill, was now chairman of the Constitutional Rights Subcommittee.

In the spring of 1980, the Supreme Court delivered a heavy blow to civil rights litigators. In the *Mobile* case, the Court held that a Voting Rights Act violation could be established only by evidence of an actual "intent" to discriminate, not simply by a pattern of discriminatory "effects."

Hatch and his fellow conservatives would draw strength and legitimacy from the Court's decision in their single-minded crusade to eliminate *effects* tests in all civil rights laws—and to prevent an *effects* test from being applied to voting rights.

In gaining the extension of the Voting Rights Act unimpaired and in persuading Congress to instruct the Supreme Court to apply the *effects,* not the *intent* test, the Leadership Conference faced one of the most formidable tasks in its 30-year history.

The conference was, however, in transition. Its long-time leaders, Clarence Mitchell and Arnold Aronson, were about to retire. Marvin Caplan, the director, had retired and had not yet been replaced.

The conference also bore the scars of recent conflicts. In the Voting Rights Act extension debates of 1975, some members of the conference, fearing that the whole act would be jeopardized, had balked at backing the extension of the act to mandate bilingual ballots and otherwise extend coverage of the act to areas of the Southwest where Hispanic voters had been systematically disenfranchised. Though these provisions survived, there lingered distrust of the conference among Hispanic leaders, a residue of the internal conflict.

Because the conference harbored within the folds of its umbrella moderate groups such as the AFL-CIO, as well as black and Hispanic activists, and new feminist and handicapped advocacy groups, each with divergent priorities, it had experienced increasing inner stress.

In the voting rights campaign, there was another source of tension: the tension between litigators and lobbyists. So crucial were the expiring *preclearance* procedures to the success of voter discrimination cases, that a group of lawyers who had been fighting these cases, often in remote rural areas of the South and Southwest, had come to Washington to work for the extension—and would stay there until it was ensured. These litigators had often been forced to try their cases before skeptical, sometimes hostile judges, often coming from the very communities whose practices were being challenged. So they pressed for explicit legislative language that would make it impossible for a reluctant judge to twist ambiguities in the law to thwart voter discrimination cases.

The lobbyists, while sympathetic, had learned over time that the broad congressional consensus on civil rights principles could break down when embodied in harsh detail—and that ambiguity was often the key to legislative movement.

The litigators, however, remained convinced that, coming (as most did) from the communities they served, they were closer to the people than the Washington-acculturated lobbyists. They suspected they would have to bear the burdens of the lobbyists' chronic urge to compromise.

The persona of the new executive director would be critical in resolving, or at least neutralizing, these fragile fault lines. The conference's executive committee's choice, Ralph G. Neas, did not reassure everyone. Far from the civil rights movement, Neas was a white male Republican Catholic who had grown up in an all-white middle- and upper-income community with a burning ambition to play third base for the Boston Red Sox. He was a Notre Dame graduate whose sixties campus activism took the form of a meteoric ascent to Cadet Lt. Colonel of the Notre Dame Army ROTC unit.

But for those on the executive committee who had worked with him, Neas was exactly right for the job. Clarence Mitchell and his colleagues understood and valued the singular role Neas had played for almost a decade, first as chief legislative assistant for Senator Edward Brooke of Massachusetts, the black Republican civil rights advocate; then, for Minnesota Republican Senator David Durenberger.

In November 1973 Brooke became the first national figure to urge Nixon to resign; Neas drafted that speech, the first major speech he had ever written. With Brooke, Neas had played a central role in shaping the Senate voting rights victory in 1975. And he continued to pursue a passionate commitment to civil rights with Durenberger. His last task before taking the directorship of the Leadership Conference had been to conceptualize, then to draft for Durenberger, the comprehensive Economic Equity Act, a bill to eliminate sex discrimination in key economic sectors.

Bill Taylor, the former staff director of the Civil Rights Commission, who had served the conference for many years (and campaigns) as a key legislative strategist, had great faith in Neas's skill and commitment. He knew he could work in close tandem with him. The newcomers, and the litigators who left their homes to come to Washington to save the Voting Rights Act, were not so sure, however.

The task that Neas faced was predestined to aggravate these tensions—perhaps even to risk the dismantling of the Leadership Conference.

The first decision made by the conference was to seek not only extension of the act, but affirmative action to reverse a Supreme Court decision—an action Congress ordinarily shies from.

The conference was a strong lobby. There was no doubt that

they could line up majorities of the Democratic House and, probably, even the Republican Senate in support of a strong bill.

But Neas also knew that majorities would not be enough. A bill which passed the House with a bare majority against conservative opposition would be stopped dead in the Senate. Hatch and Thurmond, as the designated committee "generals" responsible for marshalling the bill through the Senate, would be afflicted with what Lincoln diagnosed in his generals as "the slows." They would make certain that no bill reached the Senate floor until late in 1982, whereupon it would fall easy victim to the filibuster.

And, even if the conference could overcome the filibuster, the bill would get the veto of any bill which troubled President Reagan, a veto which could be overridden only by a two-thirds vote of both houses.

What Neas needed was timely passage in the House by an overwhelming majority—a majority so large as to convey a sense of inevitability to wavering senators, incipient filibusterers, and a reluctant White House.

But to achieve that goal, Neas had to reach out not just to Republican moderates, but to hard-core conservatives. And that meant not only talking to members whom the activists neither liked nor trusted, but remaining open to compromises which might allay the reasonable concerns of conservatives.

The litigators, however, knew that a majority of the House would support a strong bill without compromise. Why explore compromise before it was clear that compromise was necessary? If the bill ran into trouble in the Senate, then compromise could be explored. For the litigators, even the early exploration of compromise presaged sell-out.

Neas's dilemma, and its resolution, is one good reason this campaign belongs in this book. To be sure, the campaign's coalition building, grass-roots stimulation, and media strategies were exemplary. But we have other, equally enlightening exemplars.

What we do not have is so powerful—or painful—a study in

the obstacle course of timely compromise—and resistance to untimely compromise. And it is on that, we concentrate.

Neas started the job on March 31, 1981. By then, precious time had already lapsed and a campaign had to be wrought. He plunged ahead. His first task was restoring cohesion to the coalition which made up the Leadership Conference.

Neas moved firmly to reassert the leadership of the conference at the helm of the voting rights campaign. In this, as in other delicate matters of leadership and conflict, he was guided by Althea Simmons, a black lobbyist for a black organization, the NAACP, who saw clearly both Neas's strengths and the need for his undisputed leadership. It was Simmons who urged Neas to move aggressively to fill the leadership vacuum and arrest the consequent unease and competing challenges for control of the campaign.

At a meeting in late April to discuss voting rights strategy called, not by the conference, but by South Carolina civil rights litigator Armond Derfner, Neas made his move. He proposed the formation of a steering committee to formulate strategy, coordinate, and lead the 25 Leadership Conference organizations which would be most actively involved in the campaign. As the executive director of the conference, Neas was the logical choice to serve as its chairman, and so he did.

The steering committee was to meet almost every Friday for the following sixteen months; during the heat of the campaign, it would meet four or five times a week. Its deliberations, sometimes rancorous, would often last several hours.

On one of the first issues to occupy the coalition, Neas sided with the risk takers. Several of the more cautious congressional leaders feared that the reactionary climate in Congress and the administration barred any chance of overturning the *Mobile* decision's *intent* test—so much so that even the attempt to include an *effects* amendment in the bill would jeopardize the extension of the act. They had pleaded for seeking only a simple extension of the act.

But Neas and others on the steering committee were convinced that Hatch and his allies were prepared to seek the substitution of an *intent* test in all civil rights legislation. They knew that of all civil rights, voting rights enjoyed the broadest popular—and congressional—support. If they were ever to beat Hatch, they argued, it would be on voting rights. And they believed they could win.

The first task for the steering committee was the shaping of the House hearings. They had the good fortune to be working with House Judiciary Committee chairman, Democrat Peter Rodino of New Jersey, and the chairman of its Subcommittee on Civil and Constitutional Rights, Don Edwards of California. Both Rodino and Edwards were strong civil rights champions, and both had worked closely with the Leadership Conference for decades. The Rodino-Edwards bill, on which the hearings would be held, embodied the conference's legislative objectives.

Edwards had instructed the subcommittee staff to work closely with the conference in developing a set of hearings, both in Washington, and in the South and Southwest, which would demonstrate the persistence of systematic voter discrimination, as well as broad support for the act.

Here the diversity of interests and skills within the coalition played a positive role. The major membership organizations could draw upon their roster of "stars," prominent civil rights spokespersons such as Benjamin Hooks of the NAACP, Vilma Martinez of the Mexican American Legal Defense Fund, Vernon Jordan of the National Urban League, and Harvard Law Professor Archibald Cox of Common Cause.

The community-based litigators on the steering committee were able to identify and prepare local witnesses from the South and Southwest who could tell powerfully in their own voices of the nature and extent of the discrimination which they directly experienced.

The underlying tension between lobbyists and litigators surfaced briefly as the litigators, committed to exhaustive documentation of the subcommittee records, sought more time to identify and prepare witnesses, while the lobbyists nervously watched the legislative clock reach May 1981, and pressed for a speedy conclusion to the hearings.

That proved, in this instance, a creative tension. The depth and quality of the hearings provided compelling evidence that systematic, though disguised, voter discrimination persisted where it had historically been acute, in the old South and parts of the Southwest.

Almost 120 witnesses testifying in support were orchestrated by the steering committee. And the hearings were completed by the second week of June, within the timetable set out by Neas and the steering committee.

At that moment, the conference experienced a breakthrough, an opportunity, and a risk—all simultaneously, and all in the person of Henry Hyde, an unlikely benefactor.

The Republican Hyde represented the conservative, mostly white citizens of Cicero, Illinois, and some black and Hispanic voters on the west side of Chicago. His national fame, or notoriety, rests almost entirely on his zealous and canny leadership of congressional efforts to stamp out abortion.

On the Judiciary Committee, he served as the senior, or "ranking," Republican on the Civil Rights Subcommittee. Hence, his vote for the Voting Rights Act would send an important signal to conservative Republicans in the House and Senate, and to the White House. His opposition meant trouble.

And trouble he appeared to be, as the Edwards's hearings got underway in early May. In his opening statement, Hyde deplored the mandatory preclearance provisions imposed upon the southern states: "For sovereign states to go through that procedure," he declared, "was demeaning, like sitting in the back of the bus." Indeed, the expiration presented "a perfect opportunity to lessen federal involvement and enhance local responsibility."

Then, on June 12, Neas was on the phone with Bill Taylor, when he was interrupted by an urgent message relayed from the League of Women Voters' representative in Montgomery, Alabama, where the last hearings were concluding. Henry Hyde had changed his mind.

"You're not going to believe this," he came back on the line to Taylor, "but we're on a roll!"

Hyde, who had attended every hearing, had grown increasingly restive as the testimony unfolded. That morning, he had erupted:

I want to say that I have listened with great interest and concern, and I will tell you, registration hours from 9 to 4 [are] outrageous. It is absolutely designed to keep people who are working and who have difficulty traveling from voting.

If that persists and exists, it is more than wrong.

The lack of deputy registrars—only 12 counties have them—demonstrates a clear lack of enthusiasm for getting people registered, obviously.

The location of voting places is a subtle intimidation of black people and is also wrong.

The lack of blacks working as polling officials is also wrong.

[Now] we have all heard where it is all done on the table; there is no privacy.

That is outrageous, absolutely outrageous.

Ironically, Hyde's sensitivity was heightened by his own youthful experience of voter abuse as a minority—a Republican—under the political thumb of Mayor Daley's Democratic Chicago machine.

Hyde announced that he would support extension of the preclearance provisions. He also had no objection to the substitution of the *effects* test.

"You're being dishonest if you don't change your mind after hearing the facts," Hyde told the *New York Times*. "I was wrong and now I want to be right." Since, as *New York Times* correspondent Steven Roberts observed at the time, "Congressmen admit making mistakes about as often as they admit taking bribes," Hyde's turnaround was not exactly a commonplace event.

That was the breakthrough.

Neas and Taylor also believed that they could persuade Hyde to cosponsor the Rodino-Edwards bill. That was the opportunity.

The risk materialized in the form of a concept called "bailout." The act provided that jurisdictions covered by the preclearance procedures because of past discriminatory practices could escape supervision, or "bail out," if they could convince a federal court in Washington that their hands had been clean since 1965. The burden of proof on the covered jurisdictions was so heavy, however, and the incentive to escape from the *status quo* so slight, that few jurisdictions had invoked the bailout provisions.

Hyde was convinced, both as a matter of fairness and as a positive inducement, that the bailout provisions should be substantially revised. Specifically, he proposed that jurisdictions should be allowed to escape supervision if they could demonstrate that they had not discriminated for at least 10 years, and that they had made affirmative efforts "to enhance minority participation in the electoral process."

Hyde's proposal threatened to sunder the Leadership Conference. The moderate members believed it was not inherently troublesome, but could be shaped, through good faith negotiation, to achieve a positive result.

The litigators viewed it with dark suspicion. They saw Hyde's conversion as a cynical ploy to disarm the civil rights community with sympathetic rhetoric, while engineering the escape of the South from supervision through a loosely-worded sieve of a bailout provision. Hispanic groups were wary of any compromise. They doubted the commitment of the conference to the bilingual provisions of the act, and feared they would be abandoned in the heat of negotiations. Few of the newcomers trusted Republicans. Fewer still, trusted Hyde.

But Neas, Taylor, and a handful of others on the steering committee saw Hyde's move as an opportunity not because they trusted Hyde, but because they had watched him and knew him. Neas, in particular, had a finely tuned appreciation for subtle variations among conservative Republicans with whom, as legislative assistant to two Senate Republicans, he had lengthy, if not entirely rewarding, dealings. He was, in any event, prepared to look at his adversaries, even conservative Republicans, as something other than fire-breathing dragons:

There is a tremendous difference between Henry Hyde and Orrin Hatch. Hatch has a very intense philosophical commitment to his point of view on these civil rights issues. He doesn't expect to gain anything more than the respect, at the most, of the civil rights community. He knows that we're adversaries and that we'll always be fighting, and he had won, once, and he hoped to win again.

Now Henry Hyde was someone I had watched carefully over a long period of time. Philosophically, he was not uniformly against positions of the Leadership Conference. He had been very effective, for example, in support of the Legal Services Corporation fight, and on certain civil rights issues he prided himself on leaving the fold of the conservative Republican administration; he didn't want to be pigeon-holed solely in the extremist camp.

Also, when you're working with representatives and senators, you've got to take into consideration their statewide ambitions, their national ambitions, and their felt need to expand their own constituencies.

I believe he does have statewide, if not larger ambitions. The Hyde [anti-abortion] amendment made him a national figure, and he wanted to compensate for that Far Right image by doing well on the Voting Rights Act. From the beginning, I think he perceived himself as the architect of some type of grand compromise. This was an historic bill. He was playing an historic role.

Part of the pressure working on Hyde to exercise leadership was the presence, in the wings, of moderate subcommittee Republicans ready to step into the gap, if Hyde were to leave a gap. A little competition and rivalry can play a significant role. He might be more flexible under these circumstances than under conditions of partisan combat.

So what if Hyde had reasons other than sabotaging the Voting Rights Act, asked the skeptics. Why should we meet him halfway, when we've got the votes to pass an undiluted bill out of the committee and the full House? Why compromise now? Later, in the Senate, then was the time to talk compromise!

There was irony in Neas's emergence as the advocate for dealing with Henry Hyde. There was no great love lost between them. While working for Brooke in the mid-seventies, Neas had spearheaded efforts to derail Hyde's anti-abortion initiatives. And, when Neas's name was floated in the Reagan administration as a possible candidate for assistant secretary for Fair Housing, Hyde had balked, grumbling to one senator, "How the hell am I going to explain Ralph Neas to Cicero, Illinois?!" The nomination was not sent forward. But Neas viewed the Hyde strategy unsentimentally:

The way I saw it, without Hyde, we could win in the Judiciary Committee and we could win on the House floor, maybe with 250 [out of 429] votes, maybe fewer on a couple of key amendments.

Hyde's was a very appealing argument. He was raising some valid points—why couldn't we come up with something to let those counties which either had no minority population or had conscientiously eliminated their discriminatory practices get out from under preclearance.

We had to think through the consequences of the course he was embarking upon and how it would effect our general strategy. The right question was, what did we pick up from dealing with Hyde? The answer was that if we could get out of the Judiciary Committee with a 3–1, 4–1, even a 5–1 margin, that would begin to give us the irresistible force that otherwise couldn't be counted on, on the House floor.

If we had, on our side, an ally as vocal as Hyde, especially someone who's been labeled the opposition for so many weeks, it would be difficult for our opponents to rebound—like a Hatch launching a filibuster at the last minute. Hyde was playing into our hands.

Central to Neas's strategy was "building public perception that the reasonable position was pro-voting rights extension, and that only isolated extremists were against extension." If they could win over the likes of Henry Hyde, they could withstand any future challenge by the administration.

Lurking in the shadows was the specter of the Reagan administration, still preoccupied with such pressing national priorities as relieving the tax and regulatory burdens of oppressed corporate citizens, but beginning to formulate an administrative position on the Voting Rights Act extension. The Leadership Conference had made some effort to gain the support of the attorney general, but discovered, in their brief live encounters, a near-total vacuum of knowledge or understanding in Reagan's attorney general, William French Smith.

Pulled in several directions, the president did what presidents often do: he ducked for a while. The White House announced that the president had asked his attorney general to study the history of the Voting Rights Act's enforcement and come back in a few months with a recommendation.

Some members of the Leadership Conference, recalling the benign leadership of past administrations, expressed disappointment, even outrage at this buck passing. But others, including Neas and Taylor, were delighted. They knew that nothing good could be forthcoming from this administration on civil rights. "Some people regarded the delay as a major setback," recalled Taylor, "but I think most of us regarded it as the opportunity to capture and continue the initiative, without the administration coming in."

By the first week of July, Neas had hammered out a brittle consensus within the steering committee: They had agreed on a firm memorandum of understanding, listing eight critical requirements that had to be met in any bailout compromise. Though it was contemplated that the lowest priority points might be yielded in order to secure the rest, neither Neas nor Taylor nor anyone else was to be authorized to yield on any point without the express approval of the steering committee.

Neas set out to execute this extremely delicate tactical manuever. In theory, as the executive director, he was the battlefield general. In truth, he was more like the untested successor to a Grant or Washington, whose dubious troops stand scowling, with their arms crossed, waiting for him to stumble into the Delaware. And he was forced to rely upon an assortment of imperfectly matched allies, each absorbed in his or her own set of priorities, allegiances, constraints, ambitions, and egos: good congressmen, bad congressmen; a plethora of congressional staff guarding all the key joints of the Congress, the Black Caucus, and those friends within the coalition who would take it into their own hands to help in their own way.

The steering committee entered into a succession of "tumultuous meetings," Neas remembers:

> The stress was rampant. There were several people who were very fearful that we would sell out the Hispanic community by not adhering to our commitment on the bilingual provisions. Others feared that, somehow, we would give up too much on a bailout.
>
> A lot of these people were new to the process, while we were really getting into the nitty-gritty of the legislative process: could we actually come up with a new bailout formula that would not harm the interests of minority voters throughout the country? And, if it could be done, was it something that would be worthwhile politically?
>
> We were into personalities, trying to figure out the psychology of a Hyde, trying to figure out how supportive and how resolved were the Rodinos and Edwardses, trying to figure out our proper role. How much can the Leadership Conference push? How much control of the process can we legitimately take without having it all backfire on us? Of course, the dominant question was how you keep the damn coalition together.

Next, Neas had to persuade Edwards of the wisdom of pursuing compromise with Hyde. Having done so, he then had to let his congressional leaders know that they would have to do so without public support from the steering committee, which wanted to maintain its public opposition to all compromise to avoid weakening its bargaining position. Third, the negotiations should remain secret (in a town where intended secrecy makes even a bad joke newsworthy), and, finally, that it was the considered wisdom of the steering committee that no negotiations should be initiated with Hyde until the subcommittee had made a show of its civil rights strength by reporting the unamended bill to the full committee.

Ralph Neas was not exactly ego-less—and he also knew he still had to convince the skeptics that he was a leader worth following. It was only his third month on the job. He had never made a presentation to Rodino or Edwards before, and he knew he would be debuting as a spokesman for the conference before the conference's veterans, such as Joe Rauh, a lion of the civil rights movement, as well as the newer members of the steering committee who did not yet hold him in high regard:

I didn't want to blow it. I didn't want anyone, the next time to say, "Well, why don't we have so-and-so give the presentation." So I spent about 15 minutes in the john rehearsing in my own mind. I always make an outline of a presentation I'm going to make, but I rarely refer to the notes. And this time, I didn't want to read.

The presentation went well. Indeed, it went almost too well. Rodino was so persuaded of the virtues of negotiating with Hyde that he rushed off to open negotiations with Hyde, ignoring Neas's counsel that he wait until the subcommittee had voted out an uncompromised bill in a show of civil rights strength.

Then Joe Rauh decided on his own that the Leadership Conference should not only act reasonably, but be publicly perceived as reasonable. So he leaked to columnist Bill Raspberry of the *Washington Post* the news that the conference looked with favor upon a fair bailout provision—thereby shattering the fragile consensus that the conference's willingness to compromise was to remain secret. Throats tightened; Neas recalls phlegmatically, "People were now a little bit nervous."

Since the steering committee had insisted that there be no direct negotiations with Hyde, they had to carry on negotiations indirectly, with the committee staff as conduits between the conference and Hyde—except that the committee staff did not choose to serve as conduits, but (in the classic manner of willful, ego-enhanced congressional staffers, of whom I was once one) preferred to "Do it ourselves!"

The principal Judiciary Committee staffer was Alan Parker, who had been, for some years, chief counsel for the full committee. Parker was not about to serve as the water carrier to the steering committee. As Neas put it:

Alan did not appreciate working with what appeared to be an excessively democratic group of people. To him, it looked leaderless, disorganized. To a degree there was some legitimacy to this point of view. It certainly did appear to be an unruly mob at times. This was our formative period; trust relationships hadn't been established. We hadn't won anything really significant yet. And we were not speaking as one. Althea Simmons, in particular, had been concerned that the Leadership Conference was speaking with too many voices, and urged that I try to assert more of a leadership role. At the same time, I was being criticized by others for being too autocratic. Parker would scorn us, later, as the "Leadership Circus on Civil Rights."

Meanwhile, Hyde was proving an unaccomodating negotiating partner. Believing that he held a strong bargaining hand, he refused to accept safeguards, such as the requirement that "saintly jurisdictions" show that no fewer than 60 percent of its minority citizens register and vote, and that judges in the District of Columbia, not in the petitioning jurisdiction, make the decision. On the critical importance of these provisions, there was no division within the steering committee.

Parker was not the most diffident of staff members; he had unbounded confidence in his own ability to negotiate a compromise with Hyde that the Leadership Conference could not refuse—whether or not it was cleared in advance by the steering committee. He seemed to be heading resolutely in the wrong direction.

[Taylor] *It was clear that he viewed us, the civil rights groups, as knee-jerk, uncompromising liberals. He did not understand the process that was going on within the civil rights community. He saw Ralph and me as so pressured by the hard-liners as to lose independence. He very much underestimated our substantive ability and, more important, our legislative ability, our understanding of the process. So he didn't understand our strategy and he wasn't really willing to listen to us.*

Ralph Neas, with unbounded irony, marks Wednesday, July 29, 1981, as "the brightest day of my professional life." The Judiciary Committee was within a few days of "mark-up" (deliberating and voting), and negotiations between Parker and Hyde's staff had intensified.

At midnight on the 28th, Neas received a call summoning him, Althea Simmons, and Laura Murphy (of the American Civil Liberties Union)—all perceived as among the least contentious steering committee members—to a meeting with Parker at 11:00 the next morning. Neas had a number of queasy sensations, among them that they ought not to meet with Parker without at least one of the litigators present. But it seemed more important to find out what Parker was up to than to fight over the make-up of the delegation, a decision Neas was later to regret.

Early the next morning, he alerted Taylor to stand by, close to the committee staff offices. And he scheduled a meeting of the steering committee at noon, so that he could brief everyone on the substance of the Parker meeting.

Parker greeted them with the news that he had forged the best compromise that could be worked out and that it ought to be satisfactory to all reasonable parties. He was, Parker noted, not asking, but telling. He had cleared his compromise with key black congressmen and the subcommittee and committee chairmen, Edwards and Rodino, had signed off. It was a *fait accompli.*

The three quickly caucused with Taylor, who had been waiting outside Parker's office, and hurriedly reviewed the Parker compromise.

It was patently unacceptable—again, not just to the litigators but to the others, the "moderates," as well.

At this moment, Neas faced a difficult choice. The members of the steering committee were waiting, restlessly he knew, for a briefing on the Parker meeting.

On the other hand, there was at least a chance that they could convince Edwards, before it was too late, to withdraw support from the compromise. Yet to do so, they had to persuade Edwards to repudiate the committee's own staff, a rare event.

They went directly to Edwards's office. He would see them. Alan Parker was already there, waiting.

[Neas] *Now, this may be the key moment, at least for the House. In front of Alan, we said to Edwards, "If you accept this, it will be rejected unanimously by every member of the Leadership Conference on Civil Rights, not just the litigators. Bill, Althea and I, and everyone else, will reject it out of hand. A disastrous mistake has been made."*

Alan was ready to go crazy, just ready to go crazy.

But Edwards agreed. He informed Parker that he had only tentatively agreed to the compromise, contingent upon its being acceptable to the Leadership Conference. Since it plainly wasn't, he would not support it. Then he turned to Taylor, with whom he had worked closely for almost 20 years, saying, "You now have to stay here and try to put this thing back together again." And he set Taylor to work, along with Simmons and Murphy, drafting an acceptable counter-offer to Hyde.

Finally, Neas was ready to meet with the steering committee. Having now scheduled, cancelled, and rescheduled the meeting twice that day, he was prepared for some unhappiness. But he was not prepared for what greeted him, for it turned out that, at the very moment Edwards was repudiating the Parker compromise, Parker's colleagues on the Judiciary Committee staff, unknowing, were distributing a memorandum detailing the terms of the compromise.

[Neas] *I walk into this group of 25 people, five of them with their hands on their hips, the memorandum in their hands. I'm just about ready to explain that we've really come up against a formidable problem and we are in the process of reversing a decision that has already been made. And, of course, they've got this memorandum, and they think everything had already been agreed to, so they're saying, "What the ___ is this, Ralph?! You've been with Edwards the last two hours and here's the memorandum."*

And I said, "Listen, all we've done is reject out of hand that memorandum you have in your hands and now we're trying to figure out how to incorporate our agreed upon eight points into the next stage of the negotiations."

But they complain, "How come it's just you and Bill and Althea and no one else?"

Of course, it was just a series of circumstances in combination with the urgencies of the moment. When Bill, Althea and I are in with Edwards, the overriding issue is, "Reverse this horrendous decision, which is going to break everything wide open." Sure, I had in the back of my mind, "Buy some time, and you'll just have to take the risk; some people are going to be upset." But I must admit I certainly did not estimate correctly the wrath that was awaiting me.

I have never been attacked in my entire life as I would be in the following hour. My integrity was impugned; I was basically called a liar.

And Neas stood there and "took the beating," knowing that, in the meantime, he was giving Taylor and Simmons time to reshape the compromise, keeping faith with the coalition's priorities, but, at the same time, seeking language which might narrow the gap with Hyde. Neas continues:

It really got very, very brutal. It's the only time when I thought there was a very strong likelihood that everything could be lost—the bill, the coalition, the Leadership Conference. The hostility was unbelievable. I kept on insisting that everything that had been done had to have been done that way, that nothing had been done inconsistently with our agreed upon memorandum of understanding and the eight key points.

Then six people said, "We've had enough. You have not been truthful with us." And they walked out—just grabbed their briefcases and filed right past me out of the room. Everybody was stunned, including me, because as they walked by I could just see a lot of opportunities disappearing.

The dissidents stormed over to Edwards's office, confronted Bill Taylor, and demanded to see what they were drafting. They were hardly enthusiastic about the draft counter-offer but, as Taylor notes, "They at least realized that I hadn't given away the store while they were absent."

Throughout the late afternoon, Edwards shuttled back and

forth to Hyde's office, armed with Taylor's nonstop drafting and redrafting. Hyde began to give ground, and the gap between them began to close, and a compromise acceptable to most of the Leadership Conference was within reach.

Early in the evening Edwards and Rodino met with the members of the steering committee and put the ultimate question to them as a group:

> *"We're going in there [the committee meeting] at 10:00 A.M.," they said. "We've already screwed around for two or three days in a row. We need your advice. Do you want this bill or not? We're not going to go in there at mark-up, put something before the press and before 27 members of the committee, and then have you hold a press conference and lambast us for selling out the civil rights community!"*

Neas decided that the compromise was worth supporting, though it was not perfect. The calendar hung heavy on his mind. It was July 29; Congress would recess for a month on August 1. Without the compromise, there was a substantial risk that Hyde and his supporters on the committee could prevent any bill from being reported out before the recess, and that meant that the conference's grass-roots efforts during the recess could not be focused on a consensus bill reported out of committee and gathering momentum. And if they turned Hyde down, he would have gained the moral advantage as the rejected reasonable man.

Neas had consulted with the representatives of the major membership organizations within the conference. They had agreed to support the new compromise. And Neas, anticipating the meeting, had orchestrated the response to Edwards and Rodino:

> *I started to reply, when Rodino interrupted me and I said, "Please let me finish." I'll never forget that, telling Rodino that I had the floor. But I was petrified that, if I lost the floor, I would not get it again, and it would turn into a free-for-all. Prior to making this statement I had checked with all the major membership organizations—Althea Simmons of the NAACP, Sally Laird of the League of Women Voters, Jane O'Grady with AFL, Melanne Verveer of the Catholic Conference, and all the other ones. I knew that what I was about to say, they would cor-*

roborate. The scenario was, as soon as I stopped talking they would echo
my views, and we would isolate the people who would speak out against
me.

What I said was, "There is no official position, but I can assure you,
Mr. Chairman, that a substantial majority of the Leadership Conference
will support what you and Congressman Edwards do tomorrow, based
upon what we have before us right now."

Representatives of six or seven of the largest groups spoke out
in support of Neas, most importantly, Althea Simmons of the
NAACP, the largest black group. The dissidents grumbled, but
did not speak out.

Later that evening, Althea Simmons drove Neas home. Simmons marvelled at Neas's patience and perseverance, and they
sought to reassure each other that the next day would go well. But
they were uneasy; Neas had seen a group of the dissidents walking
together as they left the House office buildings, and that forecast
more trouble.

It came. At 1:45 A.M. Neas received a call from one of the litigators. She wanted him to know that the compromise was unacceptable and that her group would oppose it. The dissident group had
spent the evening calling civil rights leaders throughout the country, sounding the alarm that a rape of the Voting Rights Act was
about to take place, with the Leadership Conference as an accom-
plice. And they sought to blow the compromise up the next morning.

They had some success, though Clarence Mitchell himself,
whose support they eagerly sought, refused to return their phone
calls.

By early morning they had prepared a two-page, unsigned press
release, bearing no organizational name, but speaking in the apparent voice of the civil rights community, indicting the compromise that was to be offered to the Judiciary Committee.

[Neas] *We went to the mark-up, and someone gives me a copy of this
release, and I looked at it and showed it to Bill, without showing any*

facial expression, whatsoever. He looked at it, and said, "This is dis-honest. It's irresponsible. It's a piece of crap!"

At that moment, Henry Hyde stepped forward to save the Voting Rights Act, and the Leadership Conference, and Ralph Neas's day.

Not intentionally; Hyde simply overreached. He refused to remove a provision, obnoxious to the steering committee, which would allow state legislatures to "bail out" of the preclearance procedures even though there remained cities or counties within that state which were still covered. Hyde evidently considered his bargaining position so strong, the desire of the civil rights lobby for compromise so compelling, that he had decided to hang tough and resist Edwards's and Rodino's last, best offer.

[Neas] *He had, at that moment, within his grasp, a Hyde-Rodino-Edwards compromise and he blew it. I'm not sure whether he understood precisely how important these provisions were, but he blew it. And, within a 30 minute period, we have all reunited. There is a firm consensus: automatic rejection of whatever was to go before the Judiciary Committee.*

The committee met, locked in impasse, and adjourned. In the ensuing uproar and confusion, the press were distracted and even failed to report the damaging appearance of confusion and divisiveness within the Leadership Conference, a divisiveness which, with the heroic exception of Althea Simmons and the NAACP, broke painfully along racial lines, the most disaffected representing black and Hispanic groups.

For the next several hours, Edwards sought to reopen negotiations with Hyde, but to no avail. Then, at about 4:00 in the afternoon, Hyde issued a press release denouncing Edwards, Rodino, and the Leadership Conference as unrealistic and unreasonable, and declared his effort to reach a compromise at an end.

Edwards, normally the calmest of legislators, was furious. And Neas was ready with a plan. A week to ten days before the markup, Neas had asked a group of the litigators, just in case the compromise negotiations were to fail, "to draft up what they considered to be the perfect bailout provision—what we would like in the best of all possible situations." That draft had been prepared, and Neas proposed that the committee be reconvened the next morning, and that this ideal bailout provision be the basis for a new, substitute bill, to be offered to the full Judiciary Committee at 10:00 the next morning. They had to take on Hyde in an open fight. Neas argued to Edwards:

We are in a terrible position if we let tomorrow go by without the Judiciary Committee voting out a bill. We need something for the six weeks that the House will be in recess to lobby on behalf of. We have to have a positive theme for the next six weeks, and that is, "Vote for X!"

Hyde is out in force now. He has given the press the impression that he has made a good faith effort. He has seized the initiative, the momentum. Everything has broken down. If we leave here on Friday, without a bill voted out by the committee, we will be a dispirited group, with many tensions still evident, and nothing to unite around.

Alan Parker and the other committee staffers were dead set in opposition. "If you do this," they argued, "we will not have a Voting Rights Act extended. You will doom this entire effort to defeat, if not in the House, for sure in the Senate. Negotiations with Hyde are essential, and you should give us the time, during the August recess, to reach an accommodation with Hyde. If you don't, it's the end." Neas responded:

You might be right. If we pursue this course of action, we might not win. But if we pursue your course of action, we concede defeat. We will not get a good bill that our constituencies will accept. We might not get it by following our plan, but at least we've got a shot at it. We've got six weeks to work this country, and to work the press.

"Okay," said Edwards. "Now, what?"

And Neas replied:

We are willing to stay here all night. We have our plan B bill, and we have everything that Hyde agreed to up until yesterday. We'll incorporate that into the plan B bill and meet with you all the next morning.

"All right," said the subcommittee staff, "Use our office. Write
the bill. But we're going home." And they walked out. Neas asked
nine members of the steering committee to stay and draft. The
group included Taylor, as well as Armond Derfner, Lani Guinier,
and Frank Parker—all litigators whose expertise in the law was
widely respected. It also included Janet Kohn, a skilled lawyer
with the AFL-CIO, and veteran lobbyists Althea Simmons and
Jane O'Grady. The fever had passed, and the discussions were
productive, without animosity. And for the next eight or nine
hours, until 3:00 A.M., the group fine-tuned, provision by provision, a substitute bill which adhered to Neas's guiding rule: do
whatever can be done to adhere to the principles but appear to be
reasonable. The revamped bill was very similar to the draft
spurned by Hyde the day before. It contained a bailout provision
that was significantly tighter than that proposed by Hyde, but
which would still permit "angelic" jurisdictions to become exempt if they could demonstrate a record of compliance and good
behavior.

By 10:00 the next morning, the group had produced a bill so
carefully drafted and technically sound that it would remain essentially intact in its future passage through House and Senate.
They had also prepared a technical section-by-section analysis of
the bill and summaries for the press, a work product which, under
normal time pressures, would take three to four intensive weeks to
produce.

Between 7:30 and 10:00, Edwards had convinced two senior
and respected House Republicans to cosponsor the new bill:
Hamilton Fish, Jr., of New York, a long-time supporter of the act,
and James Sensenbrenner of Wisconsin, who ranked just behind
Hyde on the subcommittee. Edwards and Neas had calculated
correctly that these members would not want to see the Republicans now portrayed as the stumbling block to reasonable civil
rights legislation. They also banked upon Republican disaffection
with Hyde, whose arrogance and lack of deference to colleagues
who had led on civil rights issues in the past had become a grow-

ing irritant. Besides, the Republican congressmen were being handed, on a silver platter, the opportunity to become two main sponsors of an historic civil rights law—no mean incentive.

Other members of the steering committee had fanned out that morning, briefing key members and staffers. Taylor, on three hours' sleep, briefed Fish just fifteen minutes before the committee meeting. Fish, a quick study, quickly grasped the essential elements, and later deftly defended the bill in committee as if he had spent all night writing it! Neas recalls the moments before the committee met:

It's now about 9:45, and I'm walking over to the committee room with Jane O'Grady [of the AFL-CIO]. I have ten copies of the bill under my arm, and I can't believe we've done this in 15 hours. Every once in a while you get the feeling that somehow you'll turn the corner, and now the momentum and initiative is back to us and we're going to pull it off.

Jane, who in general has a more dour outlook on things than I have, looks at me and says,

"Why is this man smiling?"

And I said, "We're going to do it."

And she said, "Don't you realize, particularly in the last days, that not only the Voting Rights Act is at stake, not only is the Leadership Conference at stake, your job and my job, and our reputations in this city are riding on that folder you're carrying over to the Judiciary Committee?"

I said, "We're going to do it. We are going to blow them out of the water."

Neas expected to win by 4 or 5 votes in the committee, probably by 17–12. But he was wrong.

Hyde, of course, was not happy when he realized what was happening. But Edwards began by explaining what it was he proposed to do, paying elaborate credit to Hyde: "Henry, we've taken 95 percent of your bill and we give you great credit and we thank you."

There followed a vigorous one hour debate. Despite the brevity of their briefings, Fish and Sensenbrenner proved eloquent advocates, as did Edwards and Rodino.

At first, Hyde was simply furious that he had not received advance notice of the substitute bill. But when he realized he had been out-manuevered and did not have the votes, he chose not to make the fight. He thundered that a drastic mistake had been made, and that the proponents of the bill would rue the day that they had forced it through the Judiciary Committee:

"You might get it through the House of Representatives, but let me assure you, you will fail in the United States Senate!"

But he would not vote against it.

The vote was 25–1 in favor of the bill.

In less than 36 hours, Neas and the conference had gone from looming disaster to a 25–1 victory, on a bill which compromised not a single Leadership Conference objective!

The painful effort to seek a middle ground by accepting a modified bailout provision had been worth it: the combination of cosponsorship by Republicans Fish and Sensenbrenner and the lack of hard opposition from Hyde set in motion a bipartisan steamroller effect.

On October 5, 1981, the full House passed the bill by a vote of 389–24.

Wavering senators could not help but be influenced by the size of that vote. By December, 61 senators had cosponsored the House-passed bill—precisely the number needed to close off a filibuster. By the following spring, the number of cosponsors had risen to 65, almost enough to override a presidential veto.

And, yet, one more compromise was still forthcoming.

By late April, the Reagan administration had joined Hatch and other conservatives in full-throated opposition to the *effects* test. Hatch's subcommittee had voted favorably on a bill maintaining the *intent* standard, and the full Senate Judiciary Committee was deadlocked, with Chairman Thurmond controlling the timetable. The August 6 deadline—the date the Voting Rights Act was due to expire—was close on the horizon. A filibuster or a presidential veto was still a serious threat.

Again, the Leadership Conference's strategy was to cleave a wedge between moderate, mainstream Republicans and the radical right.

[Neas] *We were fortunate to have as our opposition, rigid ideologues: the Hatch-Helms-East-Brad Reynolds ilk of people. Very early on, all of us acknowledged that our best chance in the long run, not so much with respect to the House, but the Senate, was to isolate these people, make them appear to be extremists. They weren't Democrats and they weren't Republicans. They were just rigid ideologues. We were fortunate that the attorney general, over time, was to do so many foolish things. For example, his effort in the Bob Jones case to allow segregated schools tax-exempt status underscored our general theme: "These guys are wrong substantively, and politically, and they are out of touch with almost all Republicans in the country." We could therefore leave room for moderate, mainstream Republicans.*

The embodiment of mainstream Republicanism was Kansas Senator Robert Dole, now Senate Republican leader. Dole had remained "uncommitted" within the Judiciary Committee, holding the balance.

Once again, there was resistance to compromise. The *New York Times* quoted an anonymous member of the steering committee, plausibly, "We've got 65 votes. That's two-thirds of the Senate. What do we want to compromise for?"

But, with Neas, Taylor, Simmons, and Elaine Jones (of the NAACP Legal Defense Fund) in the lead, the Dole compromise emerged—a compromise that gained the support of 14 of the 18 Judiciary Committee members and, at the final hour, the reluctant acquiescence of the president.

What was compromised away? The Dole-Kennedy-Mathias amendment spelled out more clearly than the House version the intention of Congress that voting rights for minorities does not mandate proportional representation. (The Leadership Conference had never taken the position that voting rights require proportional representation.) Also, using language from earlier Supreme Court decisions which had been referenced in the House committee's report on the bill, the compromise spelled out in the bill the components of the *effects* test—and it provided that the supervisory provisions of the act would expire, unless again extended, in 25 years—three and a half times longer than any previous Voting Rights Act extension! The Dole compromise gave reassurance to legislators who had genuine reservations but believed in voting rights.

How much was given up? Perhaps the best judge was conservative columnist James J. Kilpatrick, who wrote, "Let me put the matter as bluntly as I can: The Dole 'Compromise' is not compromise at all. It is folly. In forty years of covering politics I cannot recall a more lamentable legislative error."

A few steering committee members protested to Taylor the 25 year extension—as opposed to a permanent law—one fearing that voting conditions would be no better in 25 years. "Look at the bright side," Taylor enjoined him. "We may have a nuclear holocaust in 25 years and there won't be any need for an extension."

In return, Dole acted as the Senate general in manuevering the bill around the procedural shoals of the Senate. On June 18, the Senate voted 85–5 to pass the bill, and on June 29, 1982, President Reagan, in a signing ceremony at the White House pronounced the right to vote "the crown jewel of American liberties," adding, "this legislation proves our unbending commitment to voting rights. It also proves that differences can be settled in the spirit of good will and good faith."

And good lobbying.

In the early spring, Neas and Taylor, and those, like Simmons, who supported them, had resisted the pleas of those who urged the conference to give up the effort to restore the *effects* test. Then, they pursued compromise with Hyde over the objections of the litigators. But they rejected the staff-wrought compromise with Hyde, despite the fears of the staff, and even members of the Black Caucus, that ultimate passage was in jeopardy. Then, they pursued their "plan B" substitute, a "compromise" that gave Hyde 95 percent of what he wanted, but gave away nothing they valued. They drew Dole to their side with a principled clarification, and thereby made certain that Hatch, Thurmond, and Reagan could do no mischief. And they had given us an obstacle course in the art of timely compromise.

Timely compromise (and resistance to untimely compromise) had produced an undiluted Voting Rights Act extension bill, and a bill which overturned, by affirmative legislation, the Supreme Court's adoption of the *intent* test.

When Ralph Neas walked into Congressman Don Edwards's office, following the 25–1 vote by the full House Judiciary Committee, most of the steering committee members had already gathered. Edwards stood up and applauded Neas; then everyone stood up and applauded. Neas muses:

To go in that short 36 hours from near and total disaster to applause! Then, to add to the irony, one of the first speakers had been one of the most troublesome steering committee members. And she said,

"I just want to thank you [Congressman Edwards] and the Leadership Conference for everything they've done, because I know we wouldn't have gotten this bill and wouldn't have a bilingual provision if you all hadn't done it."

And, no more than 27 or 28 hours earlier, she was complaining that we sold them out.

That night, Neas and many other members of the steering committee attended a funeral mass for Frank Pohlhaus, the NAACP's long-time legal counsel in Washington. Pohlhaus had actually attended the abortive mark-up session earlier that week, and gone home, lay down, and never got up.

[Neas] *You can imagine how moving it was, not only because of our love and long-time association with Frank, but because it brought to the surface so many issues that we had just combatted—whites trying to work with blacks, and the mistrust and divisiveness that can occur when things get really tense. And here you have the NAACP's white legal counsel in Washington, the long-time associate of Clarence Mitchell.*

I cried quite a bit that night at the funeral. It was a very, very beautiful funeral mass. In fact, Clarence gave one of the most eloquent eulogies I've ever heard. But it was a combination of relief from the last three days, and a reminder of all the issues, and of course everybody was thanking Frank Pohlhaus for sticking with it for so long and being such an exemplary model for everybody else.

Then we all went out for dinner afterwards.

THE STRAWBERRY DOUGHNUTS
THAT SWALLOWED A MISSILE

The battle against the MX had the capacity to go far beyond the issue itself, which is a basic ground rule in public interest lobbying: to find something that is not just winnable on its own terms, but has the capacity to have a rippling effect, since we have to choose our battles. . . .

The MX was an extraordinary turkey. It gave us the capacity, therefore, to defeat the Pentagon, the military-industrial complex. It was a centerpiece for this administration. It was very, very important to them. This was not simply a weapons system fight. It had much greater significance. And it became clear that the significance was for the whole nuclear priesthood—the bipartisan priesthood. . . .

I felt from the beginning that if we could win this fight, we could demonstrate what had never been demonstrated before, that the nuclear decision makers had to share decision-making power with citizens; not turn it over, but share it. So that we were potentially doing something quite extraordinary, which was changing the dynamics of nuclear arms decision making, and we were doing it through what appeared to be simply a battle over a single weapons system.

—Fred Wertheimer, president, Common Cause

AN EXTRAORDINARY TURKEY

The MX has been the love child of nuclear weapons; its legitimacy has been suspect from the start. Since the mid-sixties, various defense planners had yearned for a new intercontinental missile. But no one quite agreed precisely what this "Missile Experimental" was for. Some wanted a missile larger, more accurate, and with many more warheads than the existing Minuteman—a weapon that could destroy "hardened" Soviet missile silos and command centers—which the Minuteman could not. Others wanted a new missile invulnerable to Soviet missiles—which the Minuteman was not. There were others who wanted heavier missiles more or less because the Soviet Union was building heavier missiles.

It is not surprising that the MX soon became, for the arms control community, the line which must not be crossed. Somewhat more surprising was that their ranks swelled to include respectable members of the defense community, including three former secretaries of Defense, two former directors of the CIA, and a number of generals and admirals who had held leadership positions in nuclear defense. These critics argued that the MX was unnecessary—that our airborne and submarine-based nuclear missiles, coupled with our land-based missiles would remain an insurmountable deterrent to any Soviet adventurism. Worse, the production of a hundred or more MX missiles would create nuclear instability by placing us within reach of doing to the Soviets exactly what we were worried they would do to us: destroy our entire land-based missile force in a surprise attack. This would leave the Soviets no choice but to strengthen their offensive arsenal or quicken their nuclear trigger.

In the early years of its development, the MX also suffered from what might be described as faulty political design. Like many misbegotten progeny, the MX had trouble finding a home. To be invulnerable, the planners soon decided, the missiles could not remain in one place, but had to be shifted about like peas in a shell game to keep the Soviets guessing.

Ridicule is a deadly political weapon. And the MX invited ridicule not only through the oddness of the various basing mode plans, but the fits and starts with which each succeeding plan tumbled out over its predecessors.

There were no less than thirty-four plans soberly considered. Elizabeth Drew, in her enlightening *New Yorker* chronicle of the politics of the MX missile through the summer of 1983 (June 20, 1983)—upon which I have liberally drawn to set the stage for 1984—catalogued them: one plan, to keep the missiles constantly moving around within a cluster of holes, actually came to be nicknamed "The Shell Game." Another, to ferry the missiles around from place to place in cargo planes, was known as "Big Bird." There was a plan to hang the missiles under dirigibles, and another to bury the weapons deep underground and equip them with a corkscrew nose which could burrow up to the surface. The letter bore the unfortunate acronym D.U.M.B.

In October of his first year as president, Reagan announced that, for the time being, the MXs could be based in existing silos, though he couldn't exactly explain why, while the exploration of other basing modes would continue. By late November, a presidential commission came up with the curious theory that if the missile sites were packed tightly together ("Dense Pack"), incoming Soviet missiles attempting to target them would blow each other up (a process which was labelled "fratricide"), sparing the missile silos.

By December 1982, the coherence of the arms control lobby's campaign against the MX, coupled with budgetary pressures and the incoherence of the missile's supporters, led to a major embarrassment for the president and the missile.

In the just-concluded 1982 congressional elections, nuclear freeze proponents had played an aggressive role, which sobered a number of liberal to moderate congressmen who had been swept along, uncritically, in Reagan's arms build-up.

Unhappily for the proponents of "Dense Pack," they had also failed to notice the overtones this basing mode's nickname would have for a Congress in high political season. The election air that fall was filled with denunciations of the proliferating Political Action Committees—or "PACs." What with the doctor's "AMPAC," the right wing's "NCPAC," and such notorious entrants as the trucker's "SIXPAC," "DENSE PACK" proved a singularly inauspicious rallying cry.

In the lame-duck session which followed the elections, the House voted 245 to 176 to cut off procurement of production line MX missiles, pending the development of a rational basing mode. A compromise was reached with the Senate in which the president was to submit yet one more recommendation for a basing mode in the spring of 1983, at which time, the Congress would have 45 days to approve or disapprove further funding. If the MX was not dead, there were many observers who believed they were witnessing its death throes.

But the more the MX was scorned, the more the defense community rallied to it, blinded to its technical flaws by its symbolic significance. The challenge to the MX threatened the control over weapons decision making which had been exercised by the close, bipartisan community of specialists, known to its members as the "family," without challenge or interruption, through Democratic and Republican administrations alike, since World War II.

The administration very nearly solved the problems of the MX —not the technical problems, which proved insoluble—but the political problems. And the vehicle for solving them was a painstakingly constructed and orchestrated bipartisan commission, the Scowcroft Commission, formed by President Reagan in January 1983.

The formal assignment of the commission was to conduct a review of our nuclear strategy; its *sub rosa* mandate was to shape an MX proposal which would appeal to those Democrats in Congress who were unsteadily poised between the nuclear arms control movement and the defense "family," most especially Congressman Les Aspin of Wisconsin. Though the formal head of the commission was Brent Scowcroft, a retired Air Force lieutenant-general who had served as an arms control adviser to both Nixon and Carter, the key commission strategist, and the author of its report, was James Woolsey, who had last been Carter's under-secretary of the Navy. Woolsey worked in close tandem with Aspin—with whom he had served as Pentagon systems analyst in the Kennedy-Johnson era.

Aspin had risen to prominence in the House as the "thinking members' Pentagon critic." In acerbic press releases he had laid bare such Pentagon foibles as inflated military pensions and subsidized veterinary care for the pets of military families. But, as Drew observed in *The New Yorker,* Aspin was seen by some of his colleagues as aspiring overmuch to the approval of the community of defense intellectuals and, perhaps, to be secretary of Defense in the next Democratic administration.

Nonetheless, Aspin carried great weight with his moderate Democratic colleagues in the House, many of whom—including Aspin himself—had earlier voted against the MX.

Aspin had told Common Cause's Wertheimer, "Look, the MX is just one of those issues that's going to hang around forever. So the key to getting on with things is to reach agreement, and get the MX behind us." And, Wertheimer adds ruefully, "His way of getting the MX behind us was to build it!"

Together, Woolsey and Aspin shaped the commission's report to appeal to wavering Democrats. They cut the number of the proposed MX force from Carter's 200 to 100—still enough, in the minds of critics, to constitute a first-strike threat. The reduction appealed to Democrats who were looking for a politically safe middle ground. They found merit in the idea that the MX should only be considered a transitional weapon to the so-called "Midgetman," a single-warhead, smaller missile, which theoretically could be deployed in large enough numbers to provide relative invulnerability, but not constitute a first-strike threat—a weapons concept warmly espoused by Rep. Albert Gore of Tennessee, another respected young Democrat. And they stressed the importance of arms control negotiations, sweet reassurance to Democrats who doubted Reagan's commitment to arms control. (Later, Aspin and others would argue that the MX provided a positive impetus to arms control, the ubiquitous "bargaining chip" which would bring the Soviets back to the bargaining table, though proponents of the MX such as Defense Secretary Weinberger swore it would never be dealt away.)

And—oh yes, the solution to the basing mode dilemma: simply house the 100 MXs in precisely the same Minuteman silos whose vulnerability had spurred the development of the MX in the first place. It made little strategic sense, but it made political sense in alarming no community which was not already home to a missile.

Oregon Democratic Congressman Les AuCoin, a leader of the MX opposition, characterized the Scowcroft Commission report bitterly: "The president gets an MX missile and the country gets a statement of sincerity about arms control."

For all of its policy deficiencies, the Scowcroft report was politically targeted with precision at the vulnerability of the anti-MX campaign. It drew a group of the most respected Democrats in Congress into the position of leading the fight for the MX—including all the congressional Democratic leaders except Speaker Tip O'Neill.

Democrats had been pressured by the wave of popular support for the freeze resolution, but many remained uneasy with their pro-freeze votes, too close for comfort to what they feared might be tarred as the pacifist, "unilateralist" fringe. As Democratic Congressman Norman Dicks of Washington, who jumped aboard the Aspin campaign, put it with characteristic bluntness, "I'm getting identified as a freezie and I've got to get back."

New York Democratic Congressman Thomas Downey, another leader of the anti-MX group, understood well the source of the slippage: "Some of these people were for the freeze, and now they're for the MX. It's the same old game: everyone seeks the middle ground."

Aspin knew his colleagues. In May 1983 the House voted, 239 to 186, to release funds for the construction and deployment of 21 MXs, and the Senate followed, 59 to 39.

For many of those who had fought the MX, this vote seemed

the end of the road. Aspin and his allies had argued that if the administration went back on its commitment to arms control, Congress could halt the MX program. But, in the impassioned debate that led up to the vote, Congressman AuCoin warned his colleagues that this vote was irretrievable:

> [T]here is no strategic system that has ever been funded that has ever been permanently cancelled. The fallacy is that Al Gore and Norm Dicks and Les Aspin, despite their obvious skill, are not strong enough to turn off the system when a massive missile like that develops an industrial and political constituency. It can't be done.

But the campaign against the MX was not over. It was not over, in large part, because, while the administration, the Scowcroft Commission, and Les Aspin were building political momentum for the MX, the arms control lobby was also building, and by January 1984 had become one of the most effective citizen lobbies ever wrought. In a July House vote, authorization for the MX was again upheld, but by only 27 votes; and in November 1983, in the final House MX vote to release funds for MX construction, the margin of MX support had shrunk to 9 votes.

SOMETHING MISSING

Even as 1983 began, there was great strength and richness of human resources in the diverse groups and individuals who formed the arms control coalition.

There were those who had worked alone for more than a decade in arms control advocacy, such as the Council for a Livable World, and the Union of Concerned Scientists. There were 32 religious groups joined in the Coalition for a New Foreign and Military Policy. There were progressive labor unions. There was SANE (National Committee for a Sane Nuclear Policy and Peace), which had been active in the antiwar movements of the 1960s and had now revived as a strongly led mass membership lobby (90,000 members by 1982). And, late in 1982, they had been joined by Common Cause, with 250,000 dues paying members and a core of dedicated citizen activists.

The spontaneous, brush-fire freeze movement had drawn together with the more seasoned, though thinly-based, arms control lobbies. In the spring of 1982, an *ad hoc* freeze coalition—the Monday Group—began to gather each Monday in the Supreme Court cafeteria to coordinate strategy and lobbying on the freeze. By December 1982, most participants in this Monday Group coalition had turned their energies towards the MX.

In the spring of 1983, former Connecticut Democratic Congressman (and former public interest organizer) Toby Moffett organized members of Congress concerned about arms control into a "Members' Group," by all accounts a critical vehicle for coordinating the MX campaign—in conjunction with the lobbyists' Monday Group—among House members themselves.

But, as strong as the arms control coalition had become, in the winter and spring of 1983 it was not yet strong enough.

There remained an undercurrent of divisiveness, fueled by the mutual disdain of the veteran arms controllers and the "Freezeniks." The arms controllers had invested many years in Washington, mastering the intricacies of arms technology and the congressional decision-making process. They were prepared to challenge the MX on its promoters' own terms—as a poorly conceived and designed weapons system. They viewed the premises of the freeze campaign as simplistic and naive. In turn, the freeze advocates saw themselves as apostles of a movement, scorning what they perceived as the arms controllers' plodding incrementalism. A shared strategy was not easily come by; trust, even less so.

As in so many coalitions, potential energies were drained by the claims of vanity, and by the unacknowledged but real economic need for each group to differentiate itself from the pack, to justify its separate identity and distinctive claim on the limited universe of arms control contributors.

For many of the newly energized citizen advocates, the freeze campaign had been an expression of moral commitment. Among them, and among the scientists, physicians and others whose analytical powers led them to condemn the irrationality of the arms race, there lingered a contempt for the untidy politics of arms control. Even among those who had made their commitment to political action, there was a perceptible hanging back from the essential close encounters of lobbying.

David Cohen, the former president of Common Cause and unfrocked dean of public interest lobbyists, joined the MX battle early in 1983. By January 1984, he had agreed to coordinate the arms control lobbying activities of professional groups: Physicians for Social Responsibility, The Union of Concerned Scientists, and the Lawyers' Alliance. He was troubled by his first perceptions of the arms control coalition. "I thought the toughest moments were at the early stages when the energy level wasn't high enough. Some of the groups lacked the skill or the sense of how you negotiate and how you generate an issue. They wanted to spell out compromises at a very early stage, which is a mistake. There were fights over priorities."

In short, the coalition lacked cohesion; and, worse, confidence.

In November 1982, the working members of the lobbying coalition had gathered in retreat at Coolfont, a West Virginia resort modest enough to have become a public interest gathering place. They met to assess their political fortunes and plan for 1983.

Mike Mawby, then SANE's lobbyist on the MX, points out that this was the first time that "lobbying played an important enough part in their daily activities to justify getting together."

To enlighten—and inspire—them, they had invited Ralph Neas, still high from the voting rights triumph, to keynote the conference. Mawby vividly recalls the reaction to Neas's talk:

When he stood up after dinner and gave his presentation, he spent about forty, forty-five minutes running through the way they had pulled it off, and it just left people dumbfounded. None of them had the successes the civil rights groups could look back on. None of them had ever achieved their stature. We were a relatively inexperienced group of peo-

ple. If you look at the senior staff people of the groups involved, it was a young crowd. We hadn't had the chance yet to learn from mentors like David Cohen.

Jay Hedlund, the veteran Common Cause lobbyist who, fresh from the voting rights battles, had been assigned to arms control by Wertheimer the previous spring, had been scheduled to represent Common Cause at Coolfont. It was he who had urged the group to bring Ralph Neas to Coolfont, but a family illness led Kathleen Sheekey to stand in for him.

Sheekey was a veteran lobbyist, too—with a shelf-full of battle ribbons. It was she who, as chief lobbyist for the Federal Trade Commission while I was chairman, had the herculean task of shielding the commission from the lobby-inspired congressional onslaughts. Coolfont was Sheekey's first introduction to the arms control coalition. It left her troubled:

I was quite shocked by the lack of organization, by the lack of optimism. I remember sitting in on a strategy meeting on the MX. There was an anticipated House vote in a week or two. And one of the group discussion leaders said, "I think we should go right on to the Senate, because the Senate vote won't be for a month. We know we're going to lose in the House."

I came back to Common Cause, and I said to Jay, "Thank God this is your assignment and not mine, because I'd go nuts with this group!" And within three weeks, I'd been assigned the issue along with Jay, and our real work began.

It was not that the arms control community lacked able advocates. (Many of the most able and effective were citizen advocates who campaigned within their congressional districts and never strayed within a thousand miles of Washington). There were seasoned lobbyists, such as John Isaacs of the Council for a Livable World, Ed Snyder of the Friends Committee on National Legislation, and Gretchen Eick of the United Church of Christ. Then there were young lobbyists like Mike Mawby and Laurie Duker of SANE, who despite their limited campaign experience, were seen as "comers" by the veterans.

For Cohen and the Common Cause lobbyists, though, the MX campaign, however vital, was only the latest in a career of public interest campaigns, stretching over many years and many fields of public policy. They brought to the coalition the lesson-yielding scars of those campaigns. Their commitment to the MX campaign was not to be doubted, but they were not primarily arms control advocates but public interest lobbyists—and thus were better able to look with unsentimental clarity upon the coalition's political strengths, vulnerabilities, and needs.

To win, the lobbyists knew that the coalition had to be strengthened and focused. They had, first, to gain the trust and respect of the arms control community; then to help knit the coalition together so that all of its human resources were focused and directed at a common goal: the MX. The younger lobbyists and the newcomers had to learn those generic lobbying lessons and attitudes that had served the public interest community well in earlier battles. And, together, they must fan and nurture the intensity necessary to close the remaining gap.

THE VIRTUES OF THE "300 POUND GORILLA"

Hedlund recalls that Wertheimer was determined to have Common Cause play a leading role in the MX campaign:

Fred's an extremely aggressive political thinker and strategist. His view was that the MX was going to be the critical nuclear arms issue on which we could take on Reagan and defeat him—and to do that Common Cause had to take the lead in the Monday Group.

We had to figure out a way to accommodate Fred's interest in our playing a strong, visible role. Fred understood that one of the rules in coalition politics is that you don't throw your weight around. You try to accommodate and include people. . . . And, while we were the 300 pound gorilla—there were some terrific small gorillas.

Sheekey and Hedlund moved gingerly. As Sheekey recalls, "We took our time and we did a lot of listening. We volunteered.

We got our hands dirty; took assignments—more than we needed to."

In the fall of 1982, Common Cause sent fifteen staff members out from Washington for a month to hold fifty workshops for 5000 of its members around the country, to alert them to the issues and the scenario of the MX campaign. While most groups in the coalition had a handful of staffers, Common Cause had 80, and at least as many veteran volunteers working the Common Cause "Washington connection"—through which a designated volunteer maintains a close and continuing telephone liaison with Common Cause volunteer leaders in key congressional districts.

Skeptical as they might be, the other members of the coalition took notice of Common Cause's resources. Mawby, who had felt lonely and isolated often since he began working on the MX in 1979, concluded, "they had so much to bring to it that we couldn't afford not to have them involved."

By the spring of 1983, Hedlund and Sheekey had dispelled any residual distrust. Indeed, several members of the Monday Group had urged that Sheekey be made permanent chair of the Monday Group, which had grown from eight or nine lobbyists meeting informally early in 1982, to about 50, representing as many as thirty different groups. Though it would have gladdened Wertheimer's heart, Sheekey demurred: "I suggested that there be an alternating chair, month by month. So that's exactly what was done; and about six of us from the major groups alternated."

KNITTING

Once having gained the trust of their colleagues, Cohen, Sheekey, and Hedlund worked through the Monday Group to strengthen the coalition: "There's an important aspect of a lobbying campaign which could be called legislative socialization," observes Cohen. "It's a form of knitting together and cohesion building. . . ." He recalls:

I began to overhear a different kind of discussion among the lobbyists: "Who's going to chair the Monday meeting this month?" "What do you think should be on the agenda?" "How should we handle this?" Everything was geared to trying to reach consensus, not be divisive but to share information. Everybody was an intelligence gatherer. . . . So there was an application of the principle that everyone's needed. That's a very important form of coalitional culture.

In the winter of 1983, after Congress had recessed for the year, the Monday Group retreated again to the woods of Coolfont to survey the battlefield and plan for 1984.

Again, there were problems and hard choices to be made at Coolfont. But it was a different group that convened that year: more closely knit, more comfortable, more trusting, more sure of themselves and of each other. They plunged into arduous self-critical evaluation sessions, in which they reviewed and challenged past strategies and looked toward the future.

Hedlund describes the way in which they had come to work with each other—and play:

You get there; it's Sunday at six; you go until midnight and then you start the next morning at eight; go until ten. On Monday at 10 o'clock we finished our work and we all went back to a house at Coolfont; one group upstairs played poker until 4; there was a group playing ping-pong until 4. [Mawby recalled that "The poker pooped out a little earlier; nobody has a lot of money."] There were three people not there out of 50 people. I mean, everybody there just wanted to spend more time together.

These feelings were to continue throughout the fight. One night we had a pizza and bowling night where we all went out pizza and bowling in Washington. At another point, I think it was probably late spring, we said, "let's just arrange to have some fun." Then at the end of June or July, all of a sudden, Common Cause had a 1950s style prom. . . .

Mike Mawby cites the Coolfont meetings as milestones in the political maturation of the arms control lobby:

That second Coolfont meeting was important because it sparked the self-knowledge that we were becoming something more than what we

*had been. It gave people a sense of our potential. The first year, Ralph
Neas had laid out something for us to strive for. The second year we had
the feeling we might actually be getting there.*

*In my own mind, the spirit that existed within this coalition was as
important as anything we would do in the context of strategy or tactics.
I've heard of other campaigns—the egos and fights that develop, the
splits that occur. Somehow we were able to work together on the MX
and other issues and not be at each other's throats. And we retained a
real spirit.*

TEACHING

The way was now open for the senior lobbyists to share their
skills and attitudes with the younger and less experienced participants. Sheekey recalls one of the first lessons:

*One of the first fights we had within the Monday Lobby Group was
when someone in charge told us to divide up the House at random
among the groups, so that Common Cause would get 30 names, and
each other group 30 names. We said we wouldn't do that.*

*And that began kind of the first lesson. "Well, why not?" We ex-
plained that although we had no permanent friends and no permanent
enemies, there were some members of Congress who just couldn't stand
us, whom we could never approach, at least in the near term. Others
might be sympathetic but we could not ask them to be leaders on this
issue, because they were carrying our flag on another issue. At first, these
other groups did not have these kinds of relationships, though many of
them now do. So we began to divide assignments on the basis of compar-
ative relationship: Who has the best relationship with whom and who
wants to have a go at it.*

The lobbyists were similarly disturbed to discover that when
members of the Monday Group took assignments to "see" members of Congress they would rarely see the members themselves,
but diffidently settled for meetings with junior staff members.

Gently, the lobbyists made their point. When a coalition member would report back to the group on the results of an assigned
visit to a congressional office, he or she would be asked, "Is that

the word directly from the member, or just his staff person?"

More often than not, the answer would come back, "Well, we haven't been able to get an appointment with the member."

"Why don't you try catching him off the floor?"

Frequently, recalls Hedlund, a lobbyist who had spoken to a staff member would confidently report unwavering opposition, yet one of the older lobbyists would tell of catching the member off the floor, and hearing the congressman say directly, "Well, I'm rethinking it."

David Cohen teaches by anecdote and analogy, like the great Talmudic scholars, drawing upon his bottomless reservoir of campaign stories. "David makes what we do seem less foreign," says Mawby. "He makes us realize how the system works. And David's a master at pointing out why all the little things we do are so important."

The younger lobbyists could not be taught judgment, but they could learn from the example of the older, more experienced lobbyists. Mawby speaks of learning from watching Sheekey: "Kathleen's political judgment, her sense of what's happening on the Hill is so sharp—it's a guide for those who are still learning and trying to figure things out. She always has a way of crystalizing the situation for people."

Perhaps no lesson better illustrates the dictates of the lobbying culture than the virtues of "hanging out." The young lobbyists learned that even the most senior of public interest lobbyists still functioned as an information rag-picker, a collector of bits and pieces of intelligence, a strategic quilt-maker. Cohen, especially, is a great listener; a champion listener; a translator of grunts, mumbles, sighs, shrugs, and silences into vital data. "David," says Wertheimer, "can talk to a brick wall."

Hedlund recalls what Cohen told him one night as they were leaving the Senate after a long vigil on the MX:

Let's just walk over through the House just to see who we might bump into. Don't lose any opportunity. Find out what you can find out. Ask questions. You see a member: "How're things going?" or "What are you hearing?" That kind of seasoning brings you much better instincts for trouble. You hear one or two things that would otherwise take us a long time to catch up on.

Cohen knows the members not as statistics on a vote tally sheet, but as individuals. That is his bridge to them. So when he runs into Frank Horton, a Republican from upstate New York, he not only knows that Horton has a moderate voting record, but remembers that Horton, unlike most Republicans, supported the creation of a National Consumer Protection Agency. And before he talks MX, he talks baseball, because he also remembers that Horton had headed the Rochester franchise in baseball's International League. Hedlund illustrates the importance of direct contact:

Steve Neal (a North Carolina Democrat) was going to be a problem. David had a relationship with Neal and picked up early that Neal was going to have his own amendment. Then we were in a position to make sure that his amendment would not cut the legs out from under everything else, but could be shaped in a way that reinforced our effort. That's one example of David's antenna.

David Cohen had spent 20 years building relationships. The younger lobbyists found ways to compensate. Common Cause traditionally visits freshman members and attempts to develop relationships with them at the beginning of their careers.

Cohen estimates that he has some relationship with half the members of the Congress; Sheekey has somewhat fewer. Cohen calls about 100 members by their first names. Sheekey calls almost no members by their first names. They both attribute the difference to subtle, even unconscious distinctions of age and seniority, and, perhaps, sex.

Cohen notes that in any event, there evolved within the coalition a natural and useful generational allocation of relationships. Sheekey, for example, tended to know the newer members better; the youngest coalition lobbyists tended to have uniquely good relations with the generally younger congressional staff members.

A critical sub-species of "hanging out" is "standing off the floor"—not just wandering through the halls, but standing at the entrances to the chambers where the members must pass to go in and out. If there is any activity of the contemporary public interest lobbyist that echoes back in time to the genesis of the very term "lobbyist," standing off the floor is it.

Why is standing off the floor so important?

[Jay Hedlund] *I think the strongest impact standing off the floor has is on your own supporters, your leaders inside. They have a feeling of strength if you're there. It's reinforcement. I don't think you turn people around off the floor.*

We work off the floor a lot a week or two before a vote with packets, lists and stuff, but on the day of the vote I think the most important thing it does is that it shows that you care enough, that you're there supporting your people.

It's also the closest you can be to the pulse without getting in to vote. And if there's something that comes up, if there are absentees, your people can come out and say, "We've got to track down some of them." It's also the best place to hear and spread rumors and that kind of stuff.

Standing off the floor helps because the members on your side will come over earlier. They'll work the floor harder to talk to their colleagues because you're there, because you can see who's working the floor.

The sense of drama and excitement goes up. The congressman thinks, "It's an important vote; I'm being watched; I've got to be careful about this."

Early in 1982, shortly after Hedlund had been assigned to arms control issues, there was a key vote scheduled in the House on the freeze. Hedlund looked around and saw only one or two of the other arms control lobbyists. He discovered that the others were huddled around a TV monitor in a "boiler room" a sympathetic congressman had procured for them in the bowels of the Capitol, passively watching the speeches and votes on the House floor. "It just really struck me then," he remembers, "how the freeze movement advocates had gotten into Washington but hadn't become players. They still weren't engaging the system. They were still observers."

By contrast, as the hour approached for the first vote on the MX in 1984, *Congressional Quarterly*'s Pat Towell noted that "Twenty-two anti-MX lobbyists clogged the corridor leading to the House floor. Two Administration lobbyists stood among them, all but engulfed in a sea of bright red 'stop MX' lapel buttons."

To win in 1984, the lobbyists had to persuade the arms control community to keep the MX fight the central, overriding focus of the arms control movement for as long as it took to win. First, they had to convince other leaders of the coalition (and their grass roots), then those in Congress who would lead the fight (and, in the hardest moments, themselves), that the fight was winnable.

That done, the lobbyists had then to sustain the coalition's high energy level through setbacks, losses, defections, distractions, physical and emotional exhaustion—and then utilize every feasible lobbying skill and scheme to convey to the "swing votes" in the House and Senate the intense antipathy of their constituents toward the MX.

And, by the final votes, they had to create and sustain within the Congress a psychology of implacable momentum against the MX, countering Aspin's psychology of its inevitability.

That is what Cohen calls a "strategy of intensity." Hedlund spelled out the challenge:

> How can you keep going back to your grass roots and to ourselves? How can you keep telling them, "We've lost but we're closer"?
>
> How can you build the intensity amongst ourselves and convince ourselves that it's a new issue we can win? How can you build the intensity inside, make the members who oppose the MX but who've got so many issues—and so short an attention span—want to raise the stakes themselves?

For Wertheimer, Common Cause was the veteran infantry regiment, whose task was to show by example that, "You cannot win these fights without intensity, cannot win these fights without focus. You cannot win without persistence; you can't win without long term willingness to lose. You can't win a fundamental battle easily, or quickly."

By the end of 1983, the Monday Lobby Group, which dealt with the full range of arms control issues, had grown so large and unwieldy that the participants at Coolfont decided to establish a sub-group of the Monday Group (which drew together arms control lobbyists). The sub-group, which was to meet on Friday mornings became known, of course, as the "Friday Group." There was, in addition, a field organizers' coordinating group which also met on Fridays, just before the Friday (lobbyists') Group, whereupon they would report to the lobbyists on activities in the targeted districts. To add to the confusion, recall that the group of congressmen and women arms control advocates organized by former Connecticut Congressman Toby Moffett met each Wednesday, thereby becoming immortalized as—you guessed it—the Wednesday Group—and the senior lobbyists attended all three meetings each week. (I am assured that the proliferation of working groups was by no means as confusing to the players as it must be to the reader).

In any event, two weeks after Coolfont, lobbyists for the 20 odd organizations which made up the MX working sub-group convened on a Friday morning, at 8:30. The new Friday Group was not to miss a session until Congress adjourned in the fall. Kathleen Sheekey chaired the first meeting; after that, the chair rotated among Mike Mawby of SANE, Sheekey, and Hedlund. They met at Common Cause.

The organizers took responsibility for the formation and nurturing of broad "Stop the MX" coalitions in each key congressional district—identifying and supporting the strongest indigenous leadership in each district, regardless of organization.

The executive heads of the larger organizations which made up the coalition also began to meet periodically (but not frequently enough to be christened by a day of the week) in a Peace Leadership Caucus. Formally, these meetings were designed to attend to the setting of grand priorities for the arms control movement. Informally, the caucus kept the peace among the peace groups.

"Once the MX Working Group took off," says Sheekey, "It really took off!"

Hedlund remembers, "We had contact with over 90 other organizations, trying to get them involved; everybody taking assignments; doing things; working real hard; having the regular weekly meetings with the members that Toby Moffett arranged—where we found we were getting much better vote counts than the members were!"

Consistently, throughout 1984, the MX Working Group's vote counts proved more accurate—and more encouraging—than the Democratic leadership's counts. They were reinforced by a "two-source rule," by which the intelligence gathered by constituents in the districts, by the lobbyists, and by their own congressional leaders was brought together in the Friday meetings, compared, weighed and evaluated—and no conclusions were drawn that were not supported by at least two independent sources.

And Cohen recalls the spirit: "Even though there were always the overly analytical types, who had a static view of things and could tell you why you'd never get anywhere, the spirit took with enough people so we gained cohesion."

Even the literal "care and feeding" of the coalition took high precedence. Hedlund bought the doughnuts:

One of the things about intensity is getting people there. So we decided we'd give them doughnuts every Friday morning. It was a little bit of a Working Group joke, especially the variety of doughnuts. I'd pick up the doughnuts.

The question is, "Do we just have plain and chocolate-covered and glazed, or do I start getting strawberry and coconut and what have you." Well, as the year gets on you start to change the variety, so that people know that their doughnut is going to be interesting if they show up. It was just a way to keep it a little bit lighter and keep it a little more human.

William Greider had followed the fortunes of the MX as a journalist, recording its ups and downs. By the fall of 1983, he noted, in *Rolling Stone* magazine, the fruits of the organizing effort:

> *From across the country, cards, letters, phone calls, radio spots, and newspaper ads began to pummel those middle-minded Democrats who thought they had made a safe deal. Many congressional politicians, in truth, have always dismissed the freeze movement as mom-and-apple-pie sentimentality, lacking the political bite to do them harm. This summer they began to feel the bite.*

Probably no task before the coalition was more critical than to motivate and inspire those members of Congress who would be their leaders. Then the coalition had to inform, coordinate, counsel—sometimes press—and, when all else was done, follow and cheerlead.

"One of the hardest, hardest parts of winning a public interest lobbying battle," says Wertheimer, "is to convince the members that they can win the fight."

Of course, every lobbyist seeks to convince his potential flag bearers in Congress that they will be on the winning side. But a sensitively attuned lobby, like the MX Working Group, can have better intelligence than the members themselves, and in this case that intelligence helped convince the members that an all-out effort, again, could yield victory.

Beyond the informal cheerleading by the lobbyists, especially the veteran lobbyists, and the expression of intense constituent support and appreciation, the bridging of the MX Working Group's intensity to its congressional leaders relied heavily upon the Wednesday Members' Group. The lobbyists worked hard with Moffett to make certain that the members' meetings were focused and productive, and didn't waste the members' time. They successfully urged the Members' Group to implement a "buddy system," in which each congressman in the group took on the task of lobbying—from March through the final votes—at least one friend who was a swing vote.

The lobbyists constantly sought to expand the leadership group within the Congress. They had to work subtly, of course, sensitive to seniority and other congressional sensibilities.

"There's an interesting talent scouting that goes on," observes Cohen. "You're constantly looking for members who will talk to other members, who will play an effective role on the inside." Sheekey and Cohen, for example, discovered a freshman congressman from Indiana, Frank McCloskey, who had quietly sought out defense experts at MIT and elsewhere, first to understand and then to develop soundly based positions on defense issues. He had come out strongly against the MX, and working closely with the lobbyists became an effective leader within the Armed Services Committee. And he was to play a key role on the showdown MX vote.

Sheekey and Hedlund also found Congressman Charles Bennett of Florida, or to be more precise, Congressman Bennett found them, but they well appreciated, if others did not, his value.

Bennett had been a member of the House of Representatives for 35 years and a member of the Armed Services Committee for 30; he had never voted against a major weapons system. Bennett had grumbled about the MX in earlier debates, but kept his own counsel and did not work with the Wednesday Group and other House liberals.

Late one afternoon early in 1984, Bennett called Common Cause and asked to talk with someone working on the MX. Sheekey took the call. He said he wanted to lead the opposition to the MX in the Armed Services Committee, and would Common Cause help him work through the issues, and the arguments and the dynamics, and help him prepare statements.

Sheekey knew that Bennett, as a southern conservative, could speak to fellow conservatives with an authority which liberals could not match. But to be effective, his efforts had to be linked to the MX campaign. She jumped at his invitation, and, over the next several months, was to forge a solid working relationship with him. At one point, she asked him why he had called Common

Cause. He said, "I chose Common Cause because you're not crazy. . . ."

MEDIA STRATEGY

The MX campaign seized upon media opportunities, or created them, from the customary Capitol mass press conference parading representatives of 50 organizations opposed to the MX, to the steady stream of radio and TV interviews and newspaper op-ed pieces with one or another of the anti-MX defense experts.

But three aspects of the campaign's media strategy were particularly intriguing: (1) the effort to get *Congressional Quarterly,* the weekly which defines the agenda and the framing of issues for Congress, to take the campaign seriously; (2) the cultivation of editorial writers, especially in the swing districts; and (3) the limited, very selective use of targeted direct mail.

Mawby, for one, early recognized the influence of *CQ* in determining who and what Congress takes seriously. "Back in '79 when I was first starting, I said to myself, '*CQ's* read all over the Hill. How do these people get in *Congressional Quarterly?* That's where I want to be!' "

The lobbyists sought to impress Pat Towell, *CQ's* expert on defense issues, with the substantiality of their efforts, of which he was at first skeptical. They invited him to observe the second Coolfont meeting. Though there was resistance within the group to allowing a member of the press to attend Coolfont (although he had agreed to off-the-record confidentiality), the senior lobbyists believed it was important to convince Towell of the coalition's weight. After Coolfont, Towell paid closer attention to the coalition. As Mawby observes, "He helped make us a much more credible force up on the Hill. . . . His articles on the authorization and appropriations process all of a sudden began to include our assessment of what was going on!"

Common Cause, almost since its founding, has sent out to newspaper editorial writers across the country, periodic background editorial memos, carefully tempering advocacy with balanced factual presentation. They came to be trusted, appreciated, and used. So early in 1984, an editorial memorandum documenting the history and deficiences of the MX went out. Then, during the early congressional recesses, Wertheimer, Sheekey, and Hedlund fanned out to every editorial board in the swing districts who would see them.

Cohen observes, "Ordinarily, reporters do not share their sources of information with the editorial writers; they are competitive. A Common Cause visit from Washington is important, especially someone who is knowledgeable about what's going on on the Hill. Kathleen and others are able to exploit that competitive situation, to become a source—a credible source—especially if they're not coming in bonkers extremism with those editorial writers. And that's a very important tool in a long sustained campaign."

Editorial writers are demanding, says Sheekey. "I think it's one of the hardest things I've had to do as a lobbyist, to sit down with an entire editorial board. It's challenging because those people are well-prepared; they know the issue; they enjoy playing devil's advocate; and, sometimes, they're jaded."

But, more often than not, the editorial writers were convinced, and most of the visits resulted in editorials opposing the MX.

A strategy of intensity, to Fred Wertheimer, meant "to try every conceivable thing we could think of to make sure we had taken every step." So, in the months leading up to the May vote, Common Cause utilized a new technique: direct mail targeted in promising swing districts to lists of potential opponents of the MX. Wertheimer's idea was to reach people who might be sympathetic but who were not already members of organized arms control groups. (The mailing lists were purged of Common Cause members and the members of other arms control groups.)

Common Cause, with the help of the direct mail specialty firm, Craver Matthews, sent out a mailing of just 60,000 pieces—tiny by direct mail standards—to the constituents of wavering Democrats. 10,810 went to Congressman Vic Fazio's constituents in and around Sacramento. Five hundred and fifty-three of those who received them wrote letters to Fazio opposing the MX— and a card to Common Cause noting that the letter had been sent. In response to smaller mailings, Congressman Marty Frost got 174 letters from his Dallas, Texas, constituents; Congresswoman Lindy Boggs, 85 from New Orleans; and Congressman Tom Foley, 82 from Spokane, Washington. Fred Wertheimer is probably right when he notes that others no doubt sent letters to their congressperson, but skipped the card to Common Cause.

THE EXPERTS

The highest caliber weapons deployed by the anti-MX lobby were the experts, the military and foreign policy Brahmins of the past four administrations. The more hawkish they were, the more they had accumulated military brass and decoration, the more they belonged to the old-boy network, and the more they had been unrepentant apologists for the Vietnam War, the better.

This uneasy alliance provoked an undercurrent of black humor among some of the younger lobbyists about "War Criminals for Peace." But Hedlund points out that it was "political growth to recognize that we were in a political battle and had to use whatever legitimate tools we could find to help us in that battle." David Cohen spoke of the importance of the experts in legitimatizing and strengthening the challenge to the MX:

> There has been a radical change in the arms control environment in Congress. Congress has institutionalized its capacity to deal with defense policies, to develop alternative policies, to establish ground rules, set boundaries, contain the executive, place restraints. That's the longer legacy of the Vietnam War and Watergate.
>
> The administration no longer has a monopoly on defense experts; and the experts are challenging administration experts—op-ed pieces by a William Colby carry enormous credentials.

All through this fight, you have the Bundys and the MacNamaras and the Colbys going up, wholesaling visits with groups of House members and senators.

SANE and the Council for a Livable World, especially, had reached out to build relationships with former military men and defense policy leaders who had expressed qualms over the drift in defense policies. Gradually they were integrated into the targeted lobbying effort.

The Monday Group and, later, the MX Working Group, would target the available experts with precision, matching Republicans with Republicans, or former admirals with military-minded congressmen or women.

[Sheekey] *The lobbyists who were making the office visits would pick up that a particular member was very troubled on verification or the usefulness of the MX as a negotiating tool. So we would come back to our MX Working Group or the Monday Group and say, "Steny Hoyer needs a visit from an expert; he has a concern that can be addressed by an expert." And then we'd have a call placed, asking his legislative assistant, "Would Mr. Hoyer like to meet with William Colby?" Well a visit like that is almost never turned down. . . .*

Many of the experts themselves were at first hesitant about full-throated political advocacy. But, as David Cohen observed, they, too, were energized by the "socialization process":

I heard Pete Scoville [deputy C.I.A. director under Truman] talk about how he went out in the swing districts in North Carolina and Tennessee and campaigned against the MX: meeting with constituents, meeting with editorial writers, going on the radio. So you have this very elite community, which was never used to dealing with people but only dealt with ideas and fellow experts, getting into the midst of things and enjoying themselves enormously.

8

ONE BY ONE

THE EXPERIENCED LOBBYIST knows that a single tactic or event rarely claims a vote. The process that would determine any congressman's decision on the MX, as on any vote, could be approximated only by an elaborate natural history, a chronicle of thousands of events, impressions, and bits and pieces of information and relationships bombarding each member—who, in turn, harbors complex, often discordant understandings, ideologies, loyalties, jealousies, ambitions, and humours, through which these inputs are filtered.

Also, the prudent lobbyist (and prudence is the lobbyist's dry powder) rarely claims that anything he or she did or said influenced a particular member's vote, since pride and reputation require that each member preserve the appearance of autonomous decision making. Lobbyists may be seen and heard, but most appear impotent.

Yet all lobbyists cherish the memory of critical moments or events, of strategems which seemed to have turned a tide, or at least made a ripple. So as the lobbyists against the MX recall the events of 1984, they dwell on the high moments, but are quick to remind themselves and the listener that high moments occur only because of the layered groundwork—"inside," in the corridors of Congress, and "outside," in the districts—which has taken place day after day throughout the campaign.

The coalition's energies were *now* focused securing the votes of the "swings," the 16 Democrats and the 12 Republicans who would be the "prime focus" of MX efforts in 1984. There were lists of "secondary prospects" among MX supporters; there were lists of insecure opponents of the MX to "reinforce." But the central focus would remain the 28 swings. And within this group was a critical core: the members of the 1983 Aspin Group, including Democrats Tom Foley of Washington, Al Gore of Tennessee, and Vic Fazio of California. Their importance lay beyond their individual votes, for they were respected by their peers, and representative of a new generation of moderately liberal congressional Democrats. That was precisely why Aspin and the White House had so assiduously courted them. And it was why their shift to opposition could signal the sinking of the MX.

To the arms controllers, a number of the swings were seen as relatively pure of heart, but befogged of mind. Others came to be seen less charitably. Even Kathleen Sheekey expected high-mindedness on an issue of such cosmic import:

When I was first assigned the arms control issue, I thought this, at last, would be an issue we could fight on the substance—the arguments against the MX were so strong. This would be an issue that would transcend politics because it was so important. Even though I've lobbied for a long time, it was disappointing and shocking that, in fact, this turned out to be the most political of all issues. I remember one Republican congressman telling me bluntly that he was not going to vote against the MX simply because, if he did, the Republican party was going to put somebody up against him in the primary.

But there were uncommon advantages, too, to this campaign in the spring of 1984. David Cohen reflected on them:

The focus was going to be the Defense Authorization Bill—and everybody knew that. Everybody knew when it was going to come up. We could work backwards against the calendar so that we could escalate the pressure.

Among the ways that intensity was built up was the spreading out. Kathleen and the working lobbyists would spend time talking to staff people, talking to members, rechecking our soft votes, talking to some of

the swing votes, or their staffs, just to see what the lay of the land was.
Then we'd feed all the alerts to the district coalitions that would focus
on the target people.

VIC FAZIO—THE NOT SO TENDER GRASS ROOTS

Vic Fazio was a three-term liberal Democrat from Sacramento.
He was one of the nine key Democrats who co-signed an Aspin-
Gore-Dicks joint letter supporting the MX in 1983. Kathleen
Sheekey describes his district as "urban California, with quite a
sophisticated constituency that was into arms control issues." But
it also contained an Army base and an Air Force base.

Fazio was thus free to vote his conscience, since, either way, he
would gladden or infuriate roughly equal segments of his constituency.

There was a strong local coalition in Fazio's district, working
closely with a Common Cause "Washington connection," a volunteer organizer in the Common Cause national office, who was
constantly on the phone to political activists in Sacramento, seeking out those who had access to Fazio. The coalition had generated letters to the editor focusing attention on Fazio's role. And
different groups within the coalition sought meetings with Fazio
when he was home. So when representatives of women's groups,
knowing that Fazio had been responsive to women's issues, met
with him to discuss the broad agenda of women's issues, they
would take the occasion to express their strong opposition to the
MX.

Encouraged by the Washington lobbyists, the local coalition in
Fazio's district invited him to attend a panel discussion on arms
control during the Easter recess. To Fazio's surprise, he ended up
not as a member of the panel, but as the focal point of the panel's
concerns.

Fazio was grilled by the panel, and was hard put to defend his
position. But the panelists and the audience modulated their
disapproval. He had a good record on arms control issues other

than the MX. So they applauded when he spoke of his other votes on arms control, but sat on their hands as he sought to defend his support for the MX. They didn't threaten to throw him to the political wolves at the next election. But they expressed their sorrow and disappointment. David Cohen draws some generic lessons from the Fazio campaign:

> The Fazio set of visits illustrates the strategy—repeated in the other targeted districts—of lobbying based on highly informed laymen's knowledge of the issue, communicated through panel discussions and visits, rather than through confrontation.
>
> By contrast, some people out of control in the freeze movement in Portland, Oregon, kept hitting Les AuCoin over the head because he was not willing to go for every clause and semi-colon on a "Quick Freeze" resolution—even though he played a leadership role on the freeze, generally, and a leadership role on the MX and on every other arms control issue!

Far more typical in the MX campaign—and vastly more effective—was the light touch hit upon by the SANE coordinator in the suburban Maryland district of Steny Hoyer, another respected moderate Democrat. SANE launched a door-to-door canvass in Hoyer's district, which turned out nearly a hundred citizens at a town meeting held by Hoyer. The meeting was held shortly after Valentine's Day, and the coordinator arranged for Hoyer to be presented with a Valentine reading "Please don't break our hearts this year!"

BOEHLERT: A LOCAL MEDIA BLITZ

As the showdown votes drew close, the campaign's media strategies became increasingly custom tailored to the swing districts. Kathleen Sheekey, for example, spent a long afternoon priming the media in Utica, New York, the heart of Republican Sherwood Boehlert's district. Boehlert, a moderate Republican, tentatively supported the MX, but very quietly. Sheekey would help raise the costs of that decision, in what she describes as "a lobbyist's dream of an afternoon":

I arrived in Utica at 1:00, went directly to a meeting in Presbyterian church, to which the organizer—the convenor—had asked members of the press to come so that the activists and I could do a joint press conference on what was happening in the upcoming vote, and why Mr. Boehlert was important.

There were only two or three activists who showed up—the representative from the Physicians for Social Responsibility had to deliver a baby—but it didn't matter.

We had about six or eight members of the press there, who thought they had either just missed the meeting, or were too early. Instead, they taped interviews with me and with the local arms control coordinator. That was two TV stations, both networks, and four radio stations. I went on, then, to do a drive time radio call-in talk show on a popular local station.

I finished that up about 5:00 and decided to drop by Congressman Boehlert's office. He was home for the Easter recess. He had said to me off the House floor, the previous week when I told him I would be in Utica—I did not say why—"Stop by and have coffee with me."

So I ended the day by knocking on the door of his office and entering the office, as he swung around in his chair and said to two aides who were with him, "That's her, that's her! You have absolutely turned our afternoon on end!"

I had mentioned to every interviewer that Boehlert was in his local office that afternoon and each one of them, apparently, had gone from the interview with me directly to Bohlert.

So, either personally or on the phone, he had to respond. (The TV stations went there and the radio people taped it.)

He said, "Boy, you have been all over this city! I just heard you on the radio." I said, "I just heard you on the car radio, as I drove over here." (Because they were back-to-back interviews. The TV interviews ran on the 6:00 and the 11:00 news.)

He gave a healthy acknowledgement that we were both doing our jobs —my job was to apply pressure; his job to respond to it. And we had that cup of coffee and we talked about the vote and he told me the difficulties he was having in arriving at his position.

It was a lobbyist's dream of an afternoon in terms of seeing the direct evidence of your efforts, in a world where you never know what piece of the puzzle will fit, or if anything that you do makes a difference. I knew that there was a cause and effect that afternoon. That's the best kind of a day you can have.

TOM FOLEY: DIGGING FOR A PERLE

Tom Foley, congressman from Spokane, Washington—an historically conservative district—was a key figure in the MX struggle. He had been elected by his Democratic peers as their Whip, the third ranking member of the House Democratic leadership. He was to become the overwhelming favorite to be elected Democratic Majority leader after the 1986 elections. By convincing Foley that the Scowcroft Commission's plan, with a commitment to the single-warhead Midgetman, was a genuine compromise, Aspin hoped, according to Elizabeth Drew, "that Foley would be the key to getting the support of, or at least neutralizing, other members of the Democratic leadership." And, in 1983, Aspin had been right.

Foley was David Cohen's responsibility. They were old friends, and Cohen holds Foley in great respect:

Since he was first a congressman, I remember having conversations with him no different from the kind that I have now. We would talk over a problem and agree that the extreme remedy was unworkable—that the fanatics on an issue generally get in the way of its being solved—why sometimes members have to take risks, standing against pressures, not jumping through the hoop. He doesn't ever want to be seen as an extremist. So how the issue is cast becomes important.

Tom likes to talk to people, and I had three or four long conversations with him [before the May 1984 MX vote] usually in the evening when the House was in session late. We'd run into each other, and we stop and talk, and he'll tell me things that were just useful to know.

I would generally open up the conversation with an open-ended question, such as, "What are you hearing?" It was oblique; I never asked for a commitment; never asked where he stood, but would try and deduce it *from the conversation; and then I'd say to him where I thought he was heading—but then he would always pull back a little bit, so his options were always open.*

From Foley, you'd get a sense of the mood of the House, the concerns that might motivate members, what they were hearing from each other. That was extraordinarily valuable.

The most important thing for Foley was that he had to have an appropriate rationale. Foley believes what he believes. He's an arms controller, but he's skeptical. So the key was getting Foley on the merits and Foley himself provided the clue.

The clue was Richard Perle. Perle was assistant secretary of Defense, and so relentless a foe of arms control that he became known in the arms control community as "The Prince of Darkness." Worse, he was known to enjoy the trust of Defense Secretary Weinberger. So long as Perle remained a powerful force at Defense, the administration's commitments to the pursuit of arms control agreements were suspect.

In one of his conversations with Cohen, Foley had stressed his desire to avoid association with either the "unilateralists," or the extremists, whom he saw embodied in the person of Richard Perle.

"That's when the light went on," recalls Cohen. "Richard Perle is the guy to beat up on when you talk to people like Foley!"

As Jay Hedlund points out, the great appeal to moderates of the Aspin/Scowcroft package was that: "they could get a commitment on arms control in exchange for the MX. But that appeal rested on Aspin trusting the administration—and the weak point there was Richard Perle." Perle was doubly distasteful to Democrats as a renegade Democrat himself, now serving the Reagan administration.

So, whenever Foley or one of the other wavering Democrats would echo the administration's arguments for the MX, such as, "We won't get the Soviets back to the bargaining table unless we have the MX!," Cohen or Sheekey would respond, "Richard Perle couldn't have said it better, himself!"

"I think the Richard Perle factor helped us a great deal in this fight," says Sheekey. "David had found a way of polarizing the administration's position."

At the same time as he was carefully feeling his way toward persuading Foley, Cohen restrained and channeled the efforts of impatient MX opponents, both in Foley's district and among his colleagues in the House. He encouraged constituents to write Foley, expressing, as strongly as they felt, their distaste for the MX. It was important for Foley to know that there would be support in his district for a decision to oppose the MX. But the letters had to avoid crude threats of political retaliation.

Because Foley was an unannounced, but certain, future candidate for party leader, a number of the restive anti-MX Democrats in the House were ready to send Foley a letter threatening to oppose his bid for Majority leader.

Both Cohen and Wertheimer pleaded with them not to send the letter. They were convinced that Foley would so resent the threat that the letter would serve only to reinforce his support for the MX.

Instead, they encouraged AuCoin, as a representative of the group, to talk directly to Foley. He did, and came away encouraged.

The letter was never sent. But, it didn't hurt that Foley learned —indirectly—that his colleagues had seriously considered sending the letter (because that fact was an index of the depth of their feeling), nor that Cohen and Wertheimer had convinced them not to send it. The lobbyists had thereby averted an act that would only have antagonized Foley, and earned his gratitude in the process. "It worked out wonderfully for everyone," Wertheimer chortled, "including the right result!"

LINDY BOGGS

Sometimes, though not nearly so often as lobbyists would like, the chemistry of a meeting will have a detectable impact upon a vote. One such meeting took place, in the last days of the campaign, with Democratic Congresswoman Lindy Boggs of New Orleans.

Mike Mawby, who arranged the meeting, carefully drew together a customized delegation. Fred Wertheimer came, not only as the chief executive of the major membership organization campaigning against the MX, but because he and Boggs like and respect each other. Mawby and Wertheimer were joined by Nancy Sylvester and former CIA Director William Colby.

Sylvester was a nun, the executive director of Network, a social justice lobby. Mawby had included Sylvester in part because New Orleans has a large Catholic population—Boggs, herself is Catholic—and in part because Network had taken the lead in New Orleans in coordinating the campaign for Boggs's vote. Mawby also knew that Boggs was supportive of Network and had spoken often at national Network meetings.

As Mawby and Wertheimer recall the meeting, its "chemistry" proved exactly right, beyond the words spoken. In fact, Mawby and Sylvester said little. Wertheimer, in low key, raised questions about the genuineness of the president's new-found commitment to arms control. Then, he recalls, Colby spoke:

Colby made a strong case on the national security arguments. He had something that was essential. It was essential for him to be at that meeting because she had to feel comfortable on the national security issue. We couldn't do that.

And Lindy was listening. I know Lindy and I respect her very much and this was a tough vote for her and she was listening.

That was one of those rare meetings—maybe twenty times in twenty years—where you feel you made a special difference.

WHEN LESS IS MORE: ERODING THE INTENSITY OF THE OTHER SIDE

Of course, a vote switched from support to opposition is the lobbyist's pot of gold. But something less than an overt switch could prove almost as helpful: for example, as we shall see, an "unavoidable" absence at the crucial vote, a "walk" in congressional parlance.

There are even more subtle gradations of change that the lobbyist looks for. Jay Hedlund pointed out that the most that lobbying can be expected to do is "move [members] incrementally, but it's the incremental change that can make the difference."

For example, even where a member remains formally committed to the other side, and where the final printed record yields no sign of remorse, significant change can lie in the lessened vigor with which a position is pursued. Does the member, like Aspin, lobby his colleagues strenuously? Or does he just say his piece in support, and sit down?

[Hedlund] *We had a little project for election day. In Aspin's, Gore's, and Dicks's districts, we were trying to get people to stand at the polls in their home precincts, so that when they went to vote they'd see a "NO MX" sign. Some people in the Monday Group said, "Well, you're not going to turn around Aspin and Gore on this. Why are you doing it?"*

The answer is you've got to make them respond to you, even if you make them back off just a little bit. It's not always turning their vote, but it's just keeping them quiet when they could have said something.

Al Gore and Norm Dicks stood as close to Aspin on the MX as any members of the House. Yet the arms controllers did not give up on them. Their silence would mean almost as much as a switched vote.

THE RACE FOR THE STRATEGIC MIDDLE

Long before the first MX votes in 1984 were cast, a strategic minuet was taking place just below the surface of public debate. Aspin and the arms controllers both understood that victory lay in claiming possession of the high middle ground. They knew that the overriding concern of the swing congressmen was the search for that vote, or series of votes, which would best allow them to claim simultaneously to their local arms control coalition that they had taken a stand against the MX, and to their local defense contractors and unions that they had voted to preserve at least part of the MX program, thus staving off its total destruction.

How much to compromise? When to compromise? These questions again proved painful. In 1983 Congress had authorized construction of 21 MX missiles. For the MX Working Group in 1984, the goal was not only to deny Reagan's request for 40 more MXs, but to roll back the authorization for the first 21, which had not yet actually been built.

The first bars of this strategic minuet took place within the arms control coalition itself. It was the one significant issue on which even the professional lobbyists were split. Fred Wertheimer and Kathleen Sheekey were convinced that the coalition should aggressively seek to roll back funding for all the missiles (including the 21 authorized to be constructed in 1983) at least until the very last moment, at which time a vote opposing only the 1984 request for 40 additional missiles would be seen as a genuine middle ground. Wertheimer argued that holding out for no missiles gave the coalition room to compromise: "It gave us a hard edge."

Cohen, among others, disagreed, fearing that taking on both Reagan's 1984 request and seeking to roll back Congress's 1983 vote was simply not realistic. It was, he argued, "not credible." If forced to a vote, this strategy ran the risk of resulting in a lower supporting vote than the year before, a debilitating signal of lost momentum.

Characteristically, the coalition struggled with these conflicting strategies without tearing the fabric of their working relationships. They fudged, both to avoid divisiveness and to remain flexible. The coalition adopted the slogan, "No New Missiles," and since the first 21 authorized in 1983 had not yet actually been built, the slogan was sufficiently ambiguous to contain both strategies. It retained the essential requirement of simplicity and directness. Yet it left the coalition free to move to one or the other strategy as the vote drew near.

From January to May the coalition's lobbyists were unambigu-

ous in pressing for a rollback—leaving room for a possible future
compromise halting only authorization of the 40 additional missiles. For five months, the line held. But by May, the congressional leaders of the anti-MX forces had grown increasingly insecure
at the prospects of prevailing on a rollback vote, and publicly embraced the "no additional MXs" compromise. Common Cause
was torn between two of its lobbying maxims: (1) maintaining the
"hard edge," against future compromise; (2) and "going with your
leaders in Congress." They went with the leaders, but the Common Cause lobbyists remained convinced, in Wertheimer's
words, that they "gave it away too early."

Aspin's allies, not only Richard Perle in the Defense department but the president himself, were even less inclined to compromise. As Cohen observes, "They may have thought, theoretically, that they were in trouble, but they didn't really believe it. So
they were late focusing and they were inflexible, almost to the
very end. So we were able to argue that these White House guys
were really, as we say in Yiddish, "Farbrenter"—super-duper, red-
hot ideologues."

The Armed Services Committee, dominated by supporters of
the president, nevertheless understood the need for compromise.
They therefore voted to reduce the authorization from the 40 additional missiles requested to 30 (though, in the midst of the committee mark-up, one of the president's supporters received a call
from Reagan insisting that all 40 missiles be approved).

But Aspin sensed gains by the arms control coalition, though
they were gains made partly at the expense of giving up the "hard
edge" of a rollback to zero missiles. So six days before the scheduled vote, Aspin offered a new compromise, seizing the new middle ground. The Aspin compromise would have authorized not
40, or even the 30 additional MX missiles approved by the House
Armed Services Committee, but 15, at a total cost of $1.8 billion.
Aspin further came up with a set of enticing conditions: none of
this new money would be spent until April 1st of the following
year, and then only if the Russians were not indicating a willingness to negotiate in good faith on missile limits. Though the judg-

ment as to Russian good faith was to be left to the determination of the president, a suspect arbiter of such matters, Aspin had plainly taken the middle ground. The White House lobbyists reluctantly supported the Aspin compromise, because they finally realized that without it they would get nothing.

The first votes on the MX in 1984 took place May 16. Just before the vote, Fred Wertheimer was, naturally, standing off the floor. Bill Greider of *Rolling Stone* magazine described him:

Wertheimer wagged his open palm up and down: too close to call. "People are going to hurt like hell if we lose this one. But this is an issue we lost three times last year, and when we went back to the citizens' groups again, they leapt in. No loss of heart. People saw us go from a losing margin of fifty-three votes in May to only nine votes in November, and they saw that this could be won."

There was no "boiler room" from which the lobbyists would monitor the floor debates on the House TV cable. About thirty arms control lobbyists stood and worked off the floor throughout the long debate and the votes, well into the night.

They lost. The Aspin compromise was adopted—by six votes. But Tom Foley parted company with the Aspin group, as did Democrats Lindy Boggs and Steven Neal of North Carolina, Budget Committee Chairman James R. Jones of Oklahoma, and Republican Larry Coughlin of Pennsylvania. In all, seven Democrats and three Republicans switched to oppose production.

But several others who had last voted against the MX, lobbied heavily by defense contractors and the White House, many fearful of election challenges in conservative districts, switched to a vote for the Aspin compromise.

It was a bittersweet loss. Hedlund earned the Pollyanna award hands down when he told *Congressional Quarterly*'s Pat Towell, for the record: "The way I look at it, in all that time we picked up three votes and they only picked up one. That means we were three times more effective than they were, right?"

Yet, it was too painful a loss for the lobbyists simply to disperse and go home. They milled about, and then, in a group, walked over to the office of Congressman Nicholas Mavroules of Massachusetts, the senior Democrat on the House Armed Services Committee who had led the fight against Aspin on the floor, to thank him. Then, still together, they walked up Pennsylvania Avenue, near the Capitol to a local bar, ironically named the Hawk and Dove. Gradually, their mood lightened. Kathleen Sheekey was there:

> You have to remember that this was a losing vote at which 40 or so people gathered. It became almost celebratory. The mood was fine. The mood was upbeat. One of the comments that was often made was, "Well, what a hell of a party this would be if we had won!"

They were not finished. "It's tough. This thing is hanging by a thin reed," Wertheimer said. "We were very close to winning. We just have to pick up and keep going after it."

They may have lost the vote, but they succeeded in convincing one person who had not been convinced before that the fight was winnable—that was the Speaker of the House, Tip O'Neill. O'Neill, as the leader of the Democrats and the man who controlled the agenda for the House, had the power to schedule another vote quickly, within a week or two, and that's what he had in mind. As David Cohen saw it, "I don't think Tip O'Neill ever believed this vote was winnable until we lost by just six votes. And then I think he said to himself, 'Goddamn it, this thing could have been won!' "

But neither the "outside" lobby, nor their "inside" congressional leaders jumped at the chance for a quick revote. If they tried, yet lost again, the defeat would have taken on the aura of finality. For several days after the vote, the decision to schedule a revote was held in abeyance as both members and lobbyists took the temperature of the House. The lobbyists placed no pressure on the House leadership, but shared intelligence openly in a common effort that reflected the maturing of mutual trust and respect.

The spirit of the coalition held firm. As Wertheimer observed, "It was the kind of loss that gets you angry. Anger, as opposed to depression, is wonderful. It's the key to winning."

That anger was fueled by the words of the president's chief arms control negotiator, General Edward Rowney, who appeared on the McNeil-Lehrer TV news show on the night of the first votes. To a question on the administration's arms control policy, Rowney had responded by acknowledging, in effect, that the administration had no arms control strategy and had no faith in arms control.

"It was a very good quote, a very damaging quote," recalls Cohen. "There was an arrogance to it. We picked up that quote and flooded it throughout the House; it was pound, pound, pound! We said to the swing votes who went with Aspin, 'He was saying this at the same moment you were voting.' That made it even more dramatic!"

And an appealing strategy began to emerge out of the very fabric of the Aspin compromise. The lobbyists began to pick up signs of discomfort among some of those who had voted for the Aspin compromise. Under its terms, either the Soviets or the president would control the decision to build the MX: if the Soviets stayed away from Geneva, the MXs would automatically be built. If they returned to Geneva, then a president who didn't believe in arms control would decide whether the Russians were bargaining in good faith. In either event, the decision was out of the House's hands.

The arms controllers, most notably Fred Wertheimer, began to craft a new compromise—a compromise which could be portrayed as a technical variation of the Aspin compromise. As in the Aspin proposal, funds for building the MX would be suspended for six months. But instead of the Soviets, Congress would decide for itself whether to release the money. Wertheimer understood well that Congress, especially House members, regardless of party or philosophy, are reluctant to delegate power to the executive branch, much less to the Soviet Union. The new compromise would achieve what the coalition sought, at least for six months: the denial of funds to build any more MXs.

The arms control coalition could not wait for the final decision to be made on whether or not to chance another vote. "We really had no choice," recalls Sheekey, "even given uncertainties as to whether there would be another vote. We had to get the word out to the grass roots in preparation for more votes, if they were to come."

So the next Sunday after the May 16 vote, the first clear and sunny spring weekend in months, the Common Cause volunteers were at their phones, making phone calls to activists in ten or so of the districts of swing members whose votes had been lost. The callers asked constituents to call or telegraph their congressmen and express their disappointment with the MX vote. That day, 500 people agreed to do just that.

At that point in the conflict, could just 50 calls in a district have an impact? They could, says Cohen: "It has to do with timing and the visibility of the issue. Suddenly, a congressional office gets 50 plus calls. The member senses that something's stirring out there. Suddenly, the people out in El Paso know what Ron Coleman's doing. That worries any politician."

"We did some more calling after that Sunday," says Wertheimer. "And we thanked the people who switched the first time with us. But that Sunday was a crucial day. That was a crucial day."

The decision was made, by consensus, to schedule another vote. Mavroulis would offer what had come to be known as the "Common Cause compromise."

The critical House votes took place on the evening of May 31. Before the first vote, Majority Leader Jim Wright, who had earlier seemed a reluctant dragon in the fight against the MX, rose to speak:

For 40 years we have been leapfrogging each other, the Soviet Union and the United States, each building weapons of greater and more awesome destructive capacity.

For 40 years we have gotten no closer to peace. . . .

What are we going to do next? We are going to put in these MX missiles. They build up; we build up; they build up; we build up.

Are those steps toward peace? No, they are not. They are steps in the escalation of more and more terror, more and more uncertainty, and more and more tenuous balance of fear in the world.

Somebody has to take a step at some point in the other direction. If we ever were in a position where we could afford to take that step, now is the time.

David Cohen reflected upon how well the new amendment strategy was working:

Throughout the debate, the buzz was getting around. It was very clear that what people were really voting on was the same as the Aspin amendment, except that Congress accepted the responsibility to cast out the MX, rather than the Soviets or the president. And so the issue was drawn very sharply. It clearly gave room for the pro-Aspin people to shift with us. Even Aspin, in debate, acknowledged it came a long way— though he wouldn't go along with it, of course.

[Kathleen Sheekey] We were praying. We were talking to people. That last night there actually was more work to do than there usually is because we won the first vote by two votes, and then the second vote, which took place immediately, by only one vote.

The next vote, the final vote was not going to take place for 2½ or 3 hours. We went over to the Methodist building, to the various church offices, and called everyone who had been with us on the first and second votes to make sure they were sticking around.

We found out who missed the vote, and called their offices to find out where they were—and, in fact, a couple of members were around. They were in Washington and we got two of them back; nailed them down. And we called the offices of every good vote and made sure they stayed around for the three hours.

[David Cohen] Normally, the members go through the corridors, to the Democrat or Republican side of the House floor, and don't say any-

thing. They see you. They know why you're there. If a member talks to you, obviously you answer any question that he or she asks. But there's none of this how to vote thing. And there's certainly none of the stuff that some labor lobbyists used to do many years ago, which was up or down with their thumbs.

But this night, Kathleen and I and others went to the Republican side, where the White House lobbyists were mostly standing. There was a lot of shouting. It was the one time I can remember that people were saying, "Vote Yes!" or "Vote no!" It was all legitimate. It was grandstand talk; but it wasn't grandstanding. In its drama and intensity, it was the only time I'd ever seen it like that.

Two swing members remained faithful to commitments not to vote against the Aspin compromise, yet helped to defeat it. One, Martin Frost (the Dallas Democrat), did this by entering into what is called a "live pair": one of the members who was committed to voting against the MX, Democrat John Bryant, his fellow Texan, was absent, and therefore could not be recorded. Frost withheld his vote, announcing that, had he voted, he would have voted for the MX, and, had Bryant voted, he would have voted against the MX, thereby letting the would-be votes cancel each other out. But Frost could have voted, had he chosen to, and Bryant's vote would not have counted. That is precisely what happened with another pair of votes: Congressman Mickey Leland, a liberal Democrat from Houston, who was against the MX; and Congressman Wilson, a conservative Democrat from East Texas, who was for it. Leland was present; Wilson was not. On the first vote, Leland withheld his vote and announced a live pair with Wilson. But on the next two votes, Leland voted, and Wilson's vote was lost. Congressman Fazio, on the other hand, voted for the Aspin compromise twice, then simply missed the last vote. Wertheimer describes this arcane process:

We won the first vote 199–197, by two; the second vote, by one, 198–197; and the third vote, by three, 199–196.

After the first vote, Marty Frost comes out and says to me, "Well, you owe me for that one. I gave you half a vote." And I say, "What are you talking about, Marty?" And he just repeats. "Oh, I gave you half a vote."

I didn't understand what he meant, except I knew that two members had voted "present" [not voting].

Then Mike Synar comes out after the second vote and tells me what happened. On the first vote, Marty Frost pairs with John Bryant. Bryant is our vote, Frost is against us. Leland pairs with Charlie Wilson. Leland's our vote; Charlie Wilson's against us. So that accounts for the two people voting "present"—we win by two votes; Marty is paired.

On the second vote, Marty keeps true with his pair. But Mickey Leland says, "I've met my commitment to Charlie Wilson on the first vote, and now I'm voting!"

He votes. Marty doesn't; he sticks with his pair. . . . I don't even know whether he knows about Leland or not.

That was the fulcrum point of this battle. Going back, we did everything we conceivably could. I remember all the work that had been done with Marty Frost; he was intensely lobbied by the Members' Group, by AuCoin, Gephardt, by me, by everyone, over and over. He didn't change his vote, but he let us win.

In the course of this process, most of the original members or signers of the Aspin group were weaned away. When it came down to the end, even Dicks and Gore were quiet. While they were still voting for the MX, I don't think they worked those last votes. Only Aspin was still talking.

[Kathleen Sheekey] Ron Coleman had been with us on the MX in 1983, but we lost him on the May 16 vote. The volunteers who worked the phones that Sunday reported that the constituents in Ron Coleman's district were the angriest. So we knew that a lot of calls and mail had gone to Ron Coleman in those two weeks.

Meanwhile, Frank McCloskey, who had been working his colleagues on the Armed Services Committee, had apparently done some good work on Ron Coleman.

After the first vote, out comes Frank McCloskey, and I say, "Thank you. Wasn't that good?" He has his hand on the shoulder of another member, whom I don't know, and he says, "Kathleen, I want you to meet Mr. Ron Coleman. Mr. Coleman was with us this vote."

I thank Mr. Coleman.

The second vote, we win by one, and Frank McCloskey comes off the floor with Mr. Coleman again. The same thing in the third vote. He had taken Mr. Coleman for the night.

Final passage, and overwhelming vote. He still has Ron Coleman by the shoulder and walks through with Ron Coleman.

It was close to 11:00 P.M. when the final vote came.

Kathleen Sheekey recounts the final moments:

The final passage was thrilling. It was like seeing your team come into the locker room, because a lot of us had done so much cheerleading, we'd lost our voices and could barely whisper.

They'd been cliffhangers all night. On this vote, we were behind, then ahead, and for the longest time, tied, 182–182, 190–190. Off the House floor, there's an electronic board. And you see those big red numbers, and you stand there and see the clock running out.

We'd stood there for so many weeks and months, that we got to know all the doorkeepers. One of them, a rather serious, even stern fellow, in the weeks before the votes, gradually became more and more generous in sharing information: when the House would vote on something, or adjourn, that sort of thing. He was standing at the door. Actually, he was standing on the step going into the door so he could see Rostenkowski [the senior Democrat, presiding] in the chair.

And we were tied 197–197, and there was no time left on the clock. It was a tie vote and we would have lost with a tie.

And we were standing there, waiting, waiting and praying.

It was a beautiful night. The doors were swung open to the outside.

Fascell [Democratic Congressman Dante Fascell from Florida] had been standing in the back of the chamber, talking. He suddenly realized that he had never voted, and he rushed down and put his card in, and the vote was 198–197.

But the gavel wasn't coming down yet. And this doorkeeper who had been standing on the steps had his hand in the air high over his head, as if representing Rostenkowski with the gavel.

All of us were holding our breath; we couldn't see the chair. And when Rostenkowski brought the gavel down, the doorkeeper's arm came down. And we cheered.

And he came out to us, the doorkeeper, and he said, "This cheering is against every rule in the House, but I want to tell you people, you deserve that win. You have worked very, very hard."

I'll always remember that.

There were to be more votes on the MX in 1984 and in 1985. There may yet be still more. Though Congress did proceed to halt funding in 1984, the pressures of summitry and "bargaining chip" psychology swung the swings back in the spring of 1985, and Congress authorized the construction of up to a total of 50 MX missiles, setting a statutory ceiling at that limit. It was not, of course, a clear victory. But Wertheimer and others believe that the difference between the 200 MX missiles initially sought, or even the 100 recommended by the Scowcroft Commission, and the 50, is not just a difference of degree. Kept at 50, argues Wertheimer, the MX is no longer a vulnerable first-strike weapon: fifty MXs cannot pose a realistic threat of knocking out all Soviet land-based missiles. And that is a victory worth celebrating.

But the significance of the 1984 MX campaign does not rest there. The vote of the House was the first time that either chamber had voted to halt production of a major nuclear weapons system. It was the first time that citizens working upon and through their elected representatives had challenged the wisdom and control over nuclear decision making of the tight "family" of nuclear defense experts. It was a true citizen revolt, but its instrument was not an armed uprising but a formidable, professionally guided, citizens' lobby.

Looking back, Wertheimer exults, "The MX was one of the best grass-roots lobbying campaigns I've ever seen. It really helped convince members that people cared about the MX. Without that, the congressional leaders would not have taken on the Pentagon, would not have taken on the issue of national security. They would not have taken on the administration; it simply wouldn't have been worth it."

Wertheimer insists that, "The true story, the real MX story, is not what was done on the Hill. Take away what was done out in the country and there's no story. We did something, and led others to do something that was almost unheard of: we went out to grass-roots people seven or eight times in a two-year period on the same issue. And, each time, they responded."

Still Wertheimer acknowledges that without the MX Working Group, without the work of the professional lobbyists, there would also have been no story: "You need both; you need both."

9

WHO WAS THAT MASKED
MAN/WOMAN?

What is more fluid, more yielding than water?
Yet back it comes again, wearing down the rigid strength
Which cannot yield to withstand it.
So it is that the strong are overcome by the weak,
The haughty by the humble.
This we know
but never learn.

—*The Way of Life According to Lao Tzu*, translated by
  Witter Bynner

THE HEROS AND HEROINES of these stories have been mostly
unsung. Even David Cohen, the dean of public interest lobbyists,
has never been enshrined in *People* magazine as a certified celebrity. So, when tobacco company executive officers or missile makers or AMA officials come together to survey the wreckage of their
schemes, they may well ask themselves, "Where did these people
come from?"

And they will be tempted with some unkind answers. Neo-con-
servatives will tell them that they have been assaulted by members
of the new class, the children of privilege, sons and daughters of
well-to-do eastern businessmen and professionals, graduates of
elite universities, turning on the business and conservative institutions which fed them. In an earlier day, they would be scorned as
"parlor pinks."

Well, who are they? Nobody here but quintessential Americans.

We've highlighted ten lobbyists in the five campaigns, with no pretense to scientific selectivity. As a group, they may at least offer some clues: a startling proportion, it turns out, come from New Jersey—but that's probably not the foundation for a new cultural anthropology of public interest lobbying. What is striking is that almost all the lobbyists come from working class, largely apolitical families. Few went to elite colleges—though the lawyers (about half of the lobbyists) went on to leading law schools.

Kathleen Sheekey's grandfather was a trusted member of Jersey City Boss Hague's awesome political machine, rewarded by appointment as deputy warden of the Hudson County jail. Her father, who she says "has no taste for politics," served as a civil servant in Jersey City for 46 years. Jay Hedlund's mother, an independent widow of modest means and a staunch Republican, was elected and served for many years as town clerk in Braintree, Mass. She did not lightly receive the news that her son was contemplating running for the state assembly as a Democrat. That about sums up the group's activist political heritage. Small businessmen, workers and union members, civil servants: not a Brahmin or a Bolshevik in the lot.

As the lobbyists talk about the evolution of their careers, common themes emerge. There's generational cleavage, with David Cohen, Bill Taylor (and, alas, myself) representing an older generation, raised in families in which Roosevelt was still venerated, and drawn to public life by the excitement of Kennedy and the moral appeal of the civil rights movement.

Cohen is the dean and, many would argue, the archetype of the public interest lobbyist. He arrived in John F. Kennedy's Washington in 1963, as the 26-year-old apprentice lobbyist for Americans For Democratic Action (ADA). His only relevant experience was two years as a contracts administrator and negotiator for the Upholsterers' Union in his home town, Philadelphia. His first taste of the possibilities of citizen lobbying was in the campaign for the Civil Rights Act of 1964—an act that emerged stronger, less compromised than any sober observer had predicted. For Cohen, that campaign remains a cherished memory—and a seminal experience.

He lobbied for civil rights; he lobbied against cigarette advertising; he lobbied against efforts to weaken minimum wage laws and for housing for the poor. After ADA, he lobbied for the Industrial Union Department of the AFL-CIO, and the Center for Community Change. Then he lobbied against the building of anti-ballistic missiles, and against the confirmation of Nixon's Supreme Court nominee, Harold Carswell, and for antipoverty measures.

So when John Gardner formed Common Cause, in 1971, in the image of a citizens' lobby that was both participatory and professional, he asked Cohen to develop the new organization's lobbying strategies and style. So he did—along with Wertheimer— and became Common Cause president in 1975.

In 1981 he stepped down because, "I have never believed that officer positions in Common Cause are lifetime peerages."

But he did not change course. "I want to continue working on issue politics, public interest matters, and help strengthen the independent sector," he said at the time. "I know what I'm not going to do. I am not going to be a hired gun and represent special interests."

And that is what he has done—and what he has not done. And his organizing and leading the Professionals' Coalition is typical of the role he has hammered out for himself.

The younger lobbyists were politicized—but not radicalized— by the Vietnam War. They weren't among those who took to the streets, or trashed the dean's office; nor were they prominent among campus leaders; but they were moved and activated by the antiwar movement.

The other common influence on their public lives was Ralph Nader. Ralph Neas had never met Nader until a few months ago. Neas told Nader he'd been waiting to tell him for fifteen years that Nader had cost him his first job. It seems that in 1969, merit (and his uncle's position as deputy general counsel) had presented

Neas with the opportunity for a coveted summer's internship with the law department of General Motors. His interview with G.M.'s general counsel went well for almost an hour—up to that moment when the general counsel asked Neas who among all Americans he most admired. Without flinching, Neas declared his admiration for Ralph Nader. Today he says he might not have given the same answer—but he still would have believed it.

Jay Angoff insists that he had yearned to work for Nader since he was thirteen. The others may not have had so dramatic a public interest epiphany, but Nader served each as hero and exemplar.

These ten are not so different from millions of others of their generation, including, no doubt, many who ended up lobbying for the other side.

How, then, do public interest lobbyists differ from other lobbyists? This is probably as good a place as any to clear the air about this term, "public interest lobbying." Some wise advocates simply abandon it, preferring the less freighted term "citizen group lobbying." But we use it all the time, despite our misgivings, so we ought to face up to it.

How are public interest lobbies different from all other lobbies? I'm not sure.

It is certainly possible that George Koch and the Grocery Manufacturers of America were not wrong on all of the issues on which we clashed over the years; that a godly calculus might have concluded that the sum of public interests might have benefited more, and lost less, from George's advocacy than from mine. Certainly, I've never met a private interest lobbyist who didn't argue with some passion that what was good for General Motors, *et al.*, was good for America. That's what these Mobil ads have been preaching to us for almost a decade.

For all that, no one, including George, would call him a public interest lobbyist.

I certainly won't argue that Kathleen Sheekey or David Cohen are morally superior to George Koch. I know George to be a man of great personal integrity and courage.

I also know too many public interest lobbyists to nominate

them collectively for sainthood. Pettiness, personal ambition, vanity, envy, and power-hunger are as common among them as nobility of spirit. Ask any long-term colleague of most public interest lobbyists for a candid portrait, and you will get a chastening portrait of human strength and frailty.

Burton Weisbrod, the economist, has defined a "public interest organization" group as "(1) a voluntary sector organization, and (2) the activities of which bestow significant external efficiency or equity benefits"—benefits that are not reaped by the organization or its members. That takes care of George, since his members are certainly the prime beneficiaries of his efforts.

My own pet formula includes as public interest lobbyists all those for whom the psychic rewards of lobbying substantially outweigh their salaries.

That also excludes George, since his advocacy for the GMA (unlike his advocacy for the Congressional Country Club workers) does not entail financial sacrifice.

Unfortunately, both definitions lump public interest groups in with a lot of discomforting causes, like the heartfelt but benighted Moral Majority, as well as the KKK and the American Nazi Party. And all sides of the abortion rights controversy.

Political scientist Andrew McFarland gets a little closer. In looking at groups such as Nader's Congress Watch and Common Cause, who view themselves as public interest lobbies, he sees as a common theme the devotion to what he calls a "civic-balance" system of values: the belief that "special interests tend to control particular areas of policy unless public interests are organized. The role of public interest groups, in this view, is to intervene in politics to redress the balance of power to the benefit of the public."

So the public interest lobbyist is the champion of the underdog. That's not bad; I could go with that. There's no way General Foods—or its new parent Phillip Morris—comes up as the underdog (though they may come to feel like underdogs). Byron Kennard, a veteran environmental organizer and lobbyist, celebrates the rewards of representing the underrepresented: "Playing the game of life with a weak hand makes winning ever so delicious."

But there's a difference between those who speak for the underdog, and those who help the underdog speak. And there's a strong strain of faith and commitment to democratic participation in much public interest lobbying. There is also a sense of community, and of traditional shared values—of what philosopher William Sullivan calls the "civic republican tradition," in which citizen activists are "motivated by a combination of self-interest and a great deal of disinterested civic concern."

You won't find them talking about it, but the observable fact is that a great strength of the public interest lobbyist lies in simple moral suasion. I was struck by Kathleen Sheekey's observations on the attitudes of some of those members who did not switch but continued to vote for the MX to the end: "The fact of the matter is that they knew they shouldn't have voted the way they did. There is an uneasiness we've planted in the minds of some of these representatives. They have a hard time looking us in the eye."

Which is not to suggest that public interest lobbies have a monopoly on values, just that values run deep in them.

That's not exactly an objective definition, but it is as close as we're going to get.

THE ART OF PUBLIC INTEREST LOBBYING

If public interest lobbies and lobbyists are, indeed, different, are their lobbying strategies and art also different from private interest lobbying?

Much isn't different. All lobbyists need to understand the social psychology of Congress, and to keep book on the political and behavioral profiles of its members. Basic advocacy skills, parliamentary finesse, intelligence gathering, comfortable and trusting relationships with legislators and staffs—even the possession of a lovable, if not seductive, personality—are all common needs for competent lobbyists. David Cohen describes his role as "diagnosis and prescription . . . maybe because our mothers wanted us to be doctors." All lobbyists need to do that well.

Legislative campaigns are forms of combat, so it is not surprising that martial arts manuals, from Clausewitz to the Samurai *Book of Five Rings,* can yield insights into lobbying strategies and tactics. And where they are concerned with the ability of a small or weak opponent to defeat a large army, or a giant, they can shed light on the lessons to be drawn from the campaigns we've followed.

Of particular relevance are the central concepts relating to the marshalling, transforming, and focusing of energy (T'ai Chi), and the importance of moderation and balance, the avoidance of excessive agressiveness (Yang), or yielding (Yin).

The public interest lobbyist's raw material is the unfocused energy of the public will. To succeed, the lobbyist must focus and unleash that energy so that it will move legislative mountains. As we have seen, in providing support and encouragement for their congressional leaders they nurture energy. In coalition building, they harness energy. In shaping legislative strategies, they focus energy. In directing the focus of organized grass-roots constituencies toward the appropriate target legislators at the right time and in the right way, they unleash energy. In the face of frustration and defeat, they sustain energy. So Common Cause founder John Gardner's evocation of Common Cause's "operating philosophy" is framed in terms of the focusing of energy:

In Common Cause, we guard against aimless dissipation of energy by a simple operating philosophy: with rare exceptions we do nothing but fight specific battles—legal or legislative. We enter each battle seeking a specific outcome. And we stay with it until we win or lose.

We do not engage in educational campaigns for their own sake, nor research for its own sake (though we use the research of others). Nor do we make pronouncements or engage in debate on any issue unless we intend to fight that issue through to a conclusion.

That operating philosophy has forced us to focus our energies and resources on specific targets. It has spared us the vague and intangible efforts to "do good" that absorb so much of the energies of well-intentioned organizations.

The transformation of energy can serve as an apt metaphor for the public interest lobbyist's engagement with powerful adversaries. Even the novice martial arts student learns that the essence of combat is to turn the aggressive energy of the charging adversary to advantage, through yielding, deflecting and redirecting that energy. Those who lack experience in lobbying campaigns are easily intimidated by the apparent power and resources of their adversaries. The mature lobbyist sees both power and vulnerability. So he or she takes advantage of the musclebound giantism of the adversaries to transform and redirect excessive aggression—a flood of PAC dollars, a host of arrogant lobbyists—back upon its source.

Finally, the martial arts practitioner himself avoids both excessive aggressiveness or excessive yielding, seeking balance, rootedness, flexibility. In each of the case studies, the lobbyists manifest balance in two common—and critical—strategic principles: (1) the seizing of the middle ground, the perceived moderate center, and (2) timely compromise.

"The General knows when to march and when to halt," says the *Book of Five Rings.* Nothing is more taxing to a coalition than confronting the need for compromise. Nothing challenges the leadership—and character—of the lobbyist more than resisting the rush to compromise born of despair or frustration, or, worse, risking the scorn or denunciation of purists by counseling that the time to compromise has come.

It is always tempting to shelter one's reputation for uncompromising purity, rather than risk shunning as a "sell out." For if compromise should prove successful, and the legislation passes, no one will ever know for certain whether it really was necessary. It was in the art of timely compromise that the lobbyists we have examined most showed their balance and flexibility—and courage.

Sustained, "focused energy" and balance not only characterize the campaigns led by the lobbyists, but their own individual behavior as well. So looking back, Cohen believes that the 1984 anti-MX campaign was successful in part because they wore out their adversaries: "They weren't used to as hard a fight as they had; they weren't quite equipped to take it on. While our kind of lobbying is for the long-winded."

Recently, Patricia R. Powers at the University of Maryland studied what she has called "the culture of advocacy." On the basis of interviews with fifty current and former public interest advocates, most of whom had worked with Ralph Nader, she concluded:

Advocates combine a high energy level and a high degree of task focus with sustained moral purpose. But "energy" and "focus" are more than aspects of personality. In the advocacy culture, these concepts help explain role, identity, and themes. Certain themes run through the written and oral statements of the advocates: voice, focus, energy. From the perspective of the advocates, they pit their . . . time, energy and skill against the organizational and monetary resources and political influence of "industry" representatives . . . viewing energy as the capacity to catalyze and to surmount, and focus as the capacity to concentrate and to render.

I found that the advocates I studied had a belief in personal energy . . . The responses reveal that [they] learned the necessity of pacing themselves for long distance running.

Among their universal "themes": drive, stamina, hope, push, grit, commitment, excitement, adrenelin, workaholic, will, determination, resolve.

For most private interest lobbyists, lobbying is a job, and the causes they plead are determined more by the external chance of the job marketplace and client fortune or misfortune than deliberate choice. For the public interest lobbyist, lobbying is a calling; commitment and belief in the justness of the cause are bound to be a source of sustained energy.

But not the only source. Quite aside from moral virtue, almost every one of the key lobbyists is a fierce competitor. Half of them, as adolescents—and beyond—would have sacrificed the "calling" for a chance to play shortstop for the Boston Red Sox, or win at Wimbleton. Even Fred Wertheimer, who confesses to modest athletic prowess, devoted heroic effort coaching twenty-five intramural teams and playing on one, for his college fraternity, in order to win the intra-campus laurels. In relatively advanced years, Cohen, Taylor and Sheekey, though not exactly picturesque players, are wicked competitors on the tennis court. They may have warm and giving personalities, but they do not like to lose.

Of course, the effort needs to be rewarded by at least modest success from time to time, or even the most energized advocate will begin to droop. But it is also clear that the effort itself sustains energy through its integral rewards. As Powers notes, the advocates "tell us they got as much as they gave out of the experience."

"Balance," like "energy," is a term which depicts an essential quality of the successful public interest lobbyist, as well as a quality of the successful campaign: balanced judgment; balanced emotions; balance between aggressive pursuit of the goal and unproductive rigidity; balance in the vision of a just society; balance in perceptions of the possible.

THE POLITICS OF HOPE

Erich Fromm, in *The Revolution of Hope*, cites "hope" as "a decisive element in any attempt to bring about social change." But in so doing, he first distinguishes active from both passive and millenarian hope:

> While passive waiting is a disguised form of hopelessness and impotence, there is another form of hopelessness and despair which takes exactly the opposite disguise—the disguise of phrase making and adventurism, of disregard for reality, and of forcing what cannot be forced.

From his two decades of hands-on lobbying experience, David Cohen draws up a taxonomy of public interest lobbyists, strikingly parallel to Fromm's categories of hope. Three types of lobbyist are amply represented within the public interest community, Cohen notes: the "apocalyptic, "the "bureaucratic," and "the movement."

The apocalyptic lobbyist, who most resembles Fromm's adventurist, lacks neither energy nor the fires of conviction. But he or she proves a poor—and unwilling—lobbyist. In the extreme, as Byron Kennard has observed, "People are attracted to social movements for a variety of reasons. . . . Some people turn out to be motivated by deep wells of anger and bitterness. They wallow in disappointment and defeat. To these people, winning is unthinkable, even distasteful. They set up a self-fulfilling prophecy: to win is to sell out, that is, to lose."

Bureaucratic lobbyists are most often found in the larger, well-established (and better funded) institutions. Though the lobbyist himself may have been drawn to the organization by concern for its cause, the organizational culture soon wears down the edge of aggressive pursuit. The bureaucratic lobby is unwilling to risk, unwilling to challenge, unwilling to press its friends or tangle with its adversaries in the public arena. It is the most addicted to the illusionary compromise. In Fromm's terms, the bureaucratic lobby is mired in "passive waiting."

"Hope," writes Fromm, "is neither passive waiting nor is it unrealistic forcing of circumstances that cannot occur. It is like the crouched tiger, which will jump only when the moment for jumping has come." Which is why its chairman, Archibold Cox, proudly calls Common Cause "opportunistic". The "movement" lobbyist, observes David Cohen, is hopeful both as to issues and people:

Movement lobbyists believe it is possible to push and make demands and bend the legislative/policy system. They are also optimistic about participation, because they believe in the good sense of people to be able to do things well. This contrasts with the bureaucratic style of lobbying which rarely shares its tasks with its members or volunteers.

The quality of hopefulness stands out among the "cultural themes" drawn by Powers from her study of Nader's group activists. They embrace (ironically as much as Ronald Reagan would surely embrace) the "belief that with enough effort, anyone can do anything in this country."

Indeed, they believe that their "high energy" can overcome: "Apathy (own, initial), burn-out (own, later), despair, hopelessness (own, mental); organizational inertia (own and adversaries), organizational resource superiority (adversaries), cynicism (potential allies), and distraction (potential allies, pulled in many directions)."

That's hope.

CONCLUSION: THE LOBBYIST AS LEADER

We end with some paradoxes.

Most of us think of lobbying, when we think of it at all, as corrupt, or at least unsavory. After all, the first recorded use of the term lobbyist derived from the sleazy favor seekers who lurked in the corridors of the New York State Capitol in Albany, in 1928.

In the 1980s, we find that the sleazier favor seekers, having discovered the PAC campaign contribution as the surefire congressional door opener, no longer have to lurk in the halls, but are welcomed into congressional inner sanctums. By contrast, public interest lobbyists, who lack PACs, still lurk shamelessly (only they call it "hanging out").

As we have seen, public interest lobbyists perform prodigious feats: as coalition builders—builders of mutual trust, confidence, sustained intensity—as social psychologists of victory. They are strategists, parliamentary wizards, rag-pickers of intelligence, networkers of knowledge, accurate head counters, deployers of experts, media mavens, modulators of intemperance.

To faint-hearted or wavering congressional supporters, they are the physical embodiment of watchful constituencies. To their congressional leaders, they are resourceful guides and steadfast followers. To their younger colleagues, they are teachers. And they teach not only the needs and the skills, but the joys of political engagement.

But they do not, themselves, change very many votes.

David Cohen has actually kept track since 1963 of the number of times he can fairly claim single-handedly to have altered a congressman's or senator's "course of action—less even than changing a vote." He calls such modest achievements, "belt notchers," and he counts a total of 22 notches—less than one for each year he has been lobbying. Wertheimer claims "about 20" in twenty years, roughly the same level of vote productivity. That's not exactly a record to be known by.

How, then, should we know the public interest lobbyist, if not as "artful persuader"?

I suggest, "leader."

John Gardner, who, not entirely by coincidence, hired both David Cohen and Fred Wertheimer, who, in turn, hired Jay Hedlund and Kathleen Sheekey, has written of the essence of leadership:

Leaders don't invent motivation in their followers, they unlock it. They work with what is there. Of course, "what is there" is generally a great tangle of motives. Leaders tap those that serve the purposes of group action in pursuit of shared goals.

. . . They release energy rather than smother it, motivate rather than deaden, invite individual initiative rather than apathy. . . . And it's the task of the leader to keep hope alive. It is the ultimate fuel.

Such leaders . . . understand the wants and purposes and values of their people, and they must know how to overcome the inertia that afflicts most of the people most of the time.

I once asked David Cohen to write a short paper differentiating the role of the public interest lobbyist in our democratic society.

"Priestly and prophetic," he had written.

Wait a minute, I thought, isn't that a little grandiose?

Then I thought of these campaigns, especially the MX campaign; perhaps David was right. I retrieved that paper. Here is what he had written:

America's political experience welcomes change. Our democratic political system responds to those who participate. It will bend its power relationships so that those excluded are included. Those who pursue the politics and constituencies of public interest happen to be citizens so engaged and energized that "outside" efforts will be orchestrated with the efforts of elected officials to correct the imbalances of power and access. It will unhesitatingly de-mystify the tribal rites of the legislative process by enabling people, who are coming at their politics from a basis of values and beliefs, to participate in sustained and effective ways.

Such an outlook rejects the fantasy of leader-rescuers. But rather, its strength comes from organizational skills, stamina and persistence reinforced by a leadership that challenges the experts with their technical fixes, by involving and informing people beyond Washington's Beltway.

Citizens who petition their elected officials with their grievances and tell their story publicly, reinforce their values and experience, making a difference through their participation. This condition goes far beyond exercising self-interest or keeping something harmful from happening. People recognize [that] they and their organization cannot accomplish change alone. Change requires the politics of issues.

To move ideas and experiences into operating institutions and practices requires our ability to be prophetic and priestly. Prophetic so that we draw on ideas and themes and so we get past ourselves. Priestly so that our mind and senses focus on the group's mission and so that it has the ability to organize and involve others and be psychically independent. The challenge is to blend the visionary with the mundane. One must not drive out the other; each is needed.

Index